the
beatles .
again?

For
Julia Podrazik

pierian
press
1977

the beatles again?

by harry castleman
& walter j. podrazik

ISBN 0-87650-089-0
LC 77-92320

Copyright ©1977

by Walter J. Podrazik
and
Harry Castleman

THE PIERIAN PRESS
5000 Washtenaw Ave.
Ann Arbor, MI. 48104

contents

illustrations

introduction

In late 1975, we wrote *All Together Now, The First Complete Beatles Discography, 1961-1975*, designed as a complete guide to the recorded works of the Beatles, both as a group and as individuals. By necessity we left many facets of their career out, and assumed in the public a fairly high general knowledge of the Beatles' history. In the time since the publication of *All Together Now* many people have urged us to do a follow-up, bringing the information presented in the book "up to date." For this reason we began work on *The Beatles Again*, a follow-up which, at the same time, also incorporates other features.

The Beatles Again is actually two books in one. Part of it, particularly the sections dealing with releases and events of 1976 and 1977, is meant as a supplement to *All Together Now*. The bulk of the book is intended to stand on its own as both a concise overview of the Beatles' career, and an in-depth look at topics only lightly covered in *All Together Now* (other Apple artists, for example). Hence, in a way, this book is slightly schizophrenic (which actually is appropriate, since many find that an apt description of the authors).

Purchasing a copy of *All Together Now* is not a necessity for appreciating *The Beatles Again*, but it helps.

* * * * * *

The Beatles Again is layed out in much the same style as *All Together Now* and a little time might be well spent explaining its organization.

The book is divided into four sections. The first of these, *It's Like You Never Left*, chronicles the Beatles' careers from their prehistory to the present. Each annual survey includes important dates, recommended recordings, and a perspective on the group's own development as well as the public's perception of it. The records released in 1976 and 1977 with which the Beatles were associated as producers, writers or performers are presented in great detail, including backing musician credits and the original performers of the songs the Beatles played but didn't write. For information on pre-1976 releases, consult *All Together Now*.

Section Two, *Pandemonium Aerial Ballet*, provides a perspective on performers less directly associated with the Beatles, and also acts as a sort of "consumer's guide" in sorting out myths, legends, facts and fiction. "Bootlegs" covers Beatle performances in 1976 and 1977 not commercially released. "No, You're Wrong," a very popular section in *All Together Now*, sets straight a few more misconceptions. "Friends, Relatives and Total Strangers" covers such divergent characters as Mike McGear and the Chipmunks. And "Was Paul, In Fact, Dead . . . And More Reasonable Questions" answers some of the most frequently asked questions about the Beatles and Beatle recordings, including a step-by-step purchase plan for acquiring a complete Beatles' collection for only $160!

Section Three, *Gumbo Soup And Vinyl Wafers*, looks at the Beatles' association with other artists on their own labels: Apple, Dark Horse and Ring O' records. Special promotional material is also covered in this section.

Section Four, *Live And In Color*, presents the most complete Beatle touring schedule ever assembled in one place, tracing the band's road show from the Silver Beatles in Scotland down to Wings over America. Additionally, British chart movements, gold and platinum records and special awards are listed.

Finally, a very unique Index covers both *The Beatles Again* and *All Together Now*--making it possible to find information easily in both volumes.

Ultimately, that's what *The Beatles Again* offers: information. In *All Together Now* we presented well-researched documentation on the records the Beatles released in America and Britain. In *The Beatles Again* we supplement and update that information, while adding a clearer perspective to their overall careers as reflected in their recordings. All of this for the purpose of appreciating the group's contributions to music. Whether you view them as an historical artifact or as four current, active musicians, the Beatles are a topic which will be discussed to a greater, not lesser, degree as time wears on. Even the youngest person reading these words will be hearing Beatle songs, via whatever form of communication then extant, up till the day they die.

Acknowledgements

We would like to thank the following for their help in researching and preparing this book.

Businesses and Institutions:

Arista Records
Atlantic Records
Capitol Records
Columbia Records
EMI (London)
Specialty Records
Warner Brothers Records

The Library of Congress
New York Public Library--Rodgers and Hammerstein Collection
Melody Maker
  Mr. Ray Coleman
R.I.A.A.

Friends

Peter Gibbon
Mark Guncheon
Flawn Williams
Joe Rufer
Arno Guzek

Special Thanks To

Skip Groff, our eyes and ears
Ed Mann, for surveillance in Chicago
Tom Schultheiss, who's still waiting for the Russian album

                                        Wally Podrazik
                                        Harry Castleman
                                        July 1, 1977

Nuts and Bolts

Throughout *The Beatles Again* there appear detailed accounts of particular records (albums, EPs and singles). The chronological disc history begun in *All Together Now* and continued in *The Beatles Again*, for instance, presents the complete history of the Beatles on record. Other sections focus on special listings (e.g., The Apple, Dark Horse and Ring O' records discographies). All the record listings employ a visual code which conveys a great deal of information in a very compact space. Using these samples as reference, the following line-by-line guide should clearly explain just what the code means.

241.   MAR 6, 1970 (UK) Apple R 5833
           MAR 11, 1970 (US) Apple 2764
           A side recorded: Late January 1969
           B side recorded: Early 1967
           by The Beatles Prod: George Martin
           A: Let It Be---3:50
          B: You Know My Name (Look Up My Number)---4:20

449.   JUN 2, 1975 (US) RCA JB 10320
           JUL 18, 1975 (UK) RCA 2579
           by David Bowie Prod: David Bowie and Harry Maslin
           A: FAME---Lennon--David Bowie--Luther Andross---3:30
           B: (right)

516.   JUL 25, 1976 (UK) Parlophone R 6016
           by The Beatles Prod: George Martin
           A: BACK IN THE U.S.S.R.---2:45
           B: TWIST AND SHOUT---Bert Russell--Phil Medley---2:32

520.　AUG　2, 1976 (US)　Shelter SRL 52003 (LP)
　　　by Larry Hosford
　　　CROSSWORDS　Prod: Dino Airali and Larry Hosford
　　　side one
　　　　cut three: *Direct Me*---Larry Hosford---*3:30*
　　　　　George: Slide Guitar
　　　　cut five: *Wishing I Could*---Larry Hosford---*3:14*
　　　　　George: Harmony Vocals

526.　OCT　1, 1976 (US)　Shelter SRL 52007 (LP)
　　　DEC　3, 1976 (UK)　Shelter ISA 5013 (LP)
　　　by Leon Russell
　　　Ringo: Drums
　　　BEST OF LEON　Prod: Denny Cordell and Leon Russell
　　　side one
　　　　cut two: *DELTA LADY*--Leon Russell---*4:00*
　　　　cut five: *SHOOT OUT ON THE PLANTATION*--Leon
　　　　Russell---*3:10*

528.　OCT 15, 1976 (UK)　EMI 2546
　　　by Billy J. Kramer with The Dakotas　Prod: George Martin
　　　B:　BAD TO ME--L-McC--*2:18*
　　　A:　(little children)

554.　MAY　5, 1977 (US)　Dark Horse DH 3021 (LP)
　　　JUN　3, 1977 (UK)　Dark Horse K 56385 (LP)
　　　by Attitudes
　　　GOOD NEWS　Prod: Jay Lewis and Attitudes
　　　side two
　　　　cut five: *Good News*--Paul Stallworth--*3:45*
　　　　　Ringo: Drums

first line

A number beginning an entry is its index reference number.

After the number, the release date is given, followed by the country of release, the record label and record number. If the disc is either an "extended play" (EP) or an album (LP), those letters follow the record number; the record is otherwise understood to be a 45 rpm.

All releases in both Britain and the United States are listed.

When both countries release exactly the same disc with exactly the same cuts in exactly the same order, the release dates are stacked one over the other. If there are any differences, the releases are listed as separate entries.

Records issued in other countries are listed only if they affected

the British or American markets, or if the material was released only in those foreign markets.
on the next line
The recording date is listed if known.
on the next line
The name of the performer is listed.
on the next line
The name of the album or EP is listed; the contents are then listed side after side.

Or, the two sides of the single are listed.

General Assumptions:

1. Writing credits, titles and timings of particular songs listed on various records are sometimes unclear, conflicting or even totally inaccurate. The information presented in any entry reflects, to the best of our knowledge, what is actually on the record (as opposed to what the record says it is).

2. A number appearing before an entry indicates the disc is part of the continuing chronological listing of all the discs with which the Beatles have been associated as producers, writers or performers, since 1961. These entry numbers are used in the Indexes to refer to each particular disc. Numbers above 500 refer to entries appearing in *The Beatles Again*; 500 and below refer to entries in *All Together Now* (241, 449, etc.). If no number appears, the entry is part of a special record listing (for instance, Dark Horse, Apple or Ring O' records), and is indexed by page number or artist.

3. All songs performed by the Beatles are written by Lennon and McCartney unless otherwise stated. (241,516)

In all other cases, the song authorship is spelled out in full. The only abbreviations used are the last names of the Beatles (i.e. Lennon, McCartney, Harrison, Starkey), or a special code L-McC. (449, 528) The L-McC code refers specifically to that body of songs authored by the Lennon/McCartney team while they were members of the Beatles, and then subsequently "given" to different performers for their own use. Lennon/McCartney songs performed by artists like Billy J. Kramer are included in this category, of course; so are Lennon/McCartney songs performed by solo Beatles (Plastic Ono Band, Wings).

4. If a Beatle-authored song performed by another artist is included and no Beatle is listed as a backing musician or producer, it has been included because it was specifically "given" to that performer by a Beatle. (528)

5. Producer (Prod) credits are always given and they appear:

After the performer's name if they apply just to the cuts listed from an album or EP; or if they apply to a single. (449)

After the album or EP title if they apply to the entire disc. (520,526,554)

6. Any Beatle who appears as a backing musician on another performer's recording is listed here only if his presence is the sole reason for the disc being included in the chronological listing (520, 526,554).   Otherwise, all such information should be sought in the musician credits immediately following the entries. In the cases of songs originally issued before 1976, musician credits in the "Linear Notes" section of *All Together Now* should be consulted.

The Beatle-as-backing-musician credits which are listed follow the name of the performer (526) if they apply to all cuts listed. If they apply differently to particular cuts, they are listed under the individual cuts (520).

Pseudonyms used by the Beatle as a backing musician are listed only for the first entry of a song, not on each reissue.

7. The date listed for a record's release reflects more when the record was first commercially available to the general public than the record company's "official" release date (which occasionally was quite different from when the disc was first available to the public).

8. A song appearing in ALL CAPITAL LETTERS is a reissue (a song which has appeared previously on an album or single). We took into consideration the common record company practice of issuing "lead" singles to promote a forthcoming album. In the early and mid 60's, this lead time was usually two weeks or less; by the end of the decade, it had expanded to four to six weeks. We have used our own judgment in the cases where a single was released technically after an album, but was still generally meant to accompany the album's release. Note: The general rules used to determine a reissue are as follows: cuts released at about the same time in the US and the UK are not reissues; singles which are released at about the same time as the album they are from are also not reissues; but singles released after the album are reissues.

9. A song in parentheses and in all lower case italics is completely unrelated to any of the Beatles; it is listed merely to show what was on the other side of a Beatle-related song on the single. (449, 528)

10. An asterisk (*) indicates that the song appeared only on a single and was never subsequently issued in any other form in either the US or the UK as of September 1977. (241)

Note: Several songs marked with an asterisk in *All Together Now* can now be found on albums listed in this book. These songs include: *Misery* (8), *I'm Down* (121), *Bangla Desh* (290), *Rock And Roller* (370), and *Lucy In The Sky With Diamonds* (416).

11.   Finally, lest it cause unnecessary confusion, we should point out the reason that *The Beatles Again* picks up the listing of

Beatle-related records at entry 501, even though *All Together Now* ended at record entry 469. Since *All Together Now* was first layed out, numbered and indexed, we've come across a number of additional discs which should have appeared in the original chronological listing. Some included Beatle appearances we missed the first time around, while others included additional reissues of songs we'd already noted. We managed to include some of these in *All Together Now* either directly in the chronological listing (as entry 372a, for instance), or in the "Oh, Really?" addenda section. Others are noted in the question and answer section of *The Beatles Again*. Thus, if *All Together Now* were retyped and renumbered, with all these records placed in the proper chronological order, the total number of Beatle-related discs released before January of 1976 would reach 500.

Specifically, six records were placed directly into the chronological order of *All Together Now* as follows: the **My Bonnie** LP in Germany, by Tony Sheridan and The Beatles (4a); the **Ya-Ya** EP in Germany, by Tony Sheridan and The Beatles (5a); the American release of *Liberation Special* backed with *Power Boogie*, by Elephant's Memory (340a); the American release of **More Hot Rocks** featuring *We Love You*, by The Rolling Stones (341a); the American and British release of the *So Sad* single, by Alvin Lee and Mylon Le Fevre (372a); and the British release of *Dark Horse* backed with *Hari's On Tour (Express)*, by George Harrison (436a).

The remaining discs are listed here, with entry numbers assigned to help place them properly in the chronological listing of *All Together Now*.

170a.   SEP 12, 1967 (US) Fontana SRF 67570 (LP)
         by Various Artists
         ENGLAND'S GREATEST HITS
         side two
            cut five: *YOU'VE GOT TO HIDE YOUR LOVE AWAY*---
            L-McC---*2:20*
               by Silkie Prod: John Lennon and Paul McCartney

170b.   SEP 18, 1967 (US) Brother ST 9001 (LP)
         NOV 20, 1967 (UK) Brother ST 9001 (LP)
         Recorded: April 11, 1967
         by The Beach Boys Prod: The Beach Boys and Paul
          McCartney
         SMILEY SMILE
         side one
            cut two: *Vegetables*---Brian Wilson—Van Dyke Parks---*2:05*

186a.   OCT 25, 1968 (SPAIN) Apple 3
         by Mary Hopkin Prod: Paul McCartney
         *A: En Aquellos Dias—Gene Raskin—*5:06*
         *B: Turn! Turn! Turn! (To Everything There Is A Season)—
            Pete Seeger—*2:48*

186b.   OCT 25, 1968 (FRANCE) Odeon FO-131
by Mary Hopkin Prod: Paul McCartney
*A: *Le Temps des Fleurs*—Gene Raskin—*5:06*
*B: *Turn! Turn! Turn! (To Everything There Is A Season)*—
Pete Seeger—*2:48*

186c.   OCT 25, 1968 (GERMANY) Odeon O-23910
by Mary Hopkin Prod: Paul McCartney
*A: *An Jenem Tag*—Gene Raskin—*5:06*
*B: *Turn! Turn! Turn! (To Everything There Is A Season)*—
Pete Seeger—*2:48*

190a.   NOV 22, 1968 (UK) Pye 7N 17660
Recorded: November 1968
by Donovan Prod: Mickie Most
A: *Atlantis*—Donovan Leitch—*4:58*
Paul: Tambourine and Backing Vocal
B: *(i love my shirt)*

193a.   JAN 20, 1969 (US) Epic 5-10434
by Donovan Prod: Mickie Most
B: *Atlantis*—Donovan Leitch—*4:58*
Paul: Tambourine and Backing Vocal
A: *(to susan on the west coast waiting)*

197a.   MAR   3, 1969 (ITALY) Apple 7
by Mary Hopkin Prod: Paul McCartney
A: *Lontano Dagli Occhi*—Sergio Endrigo—Sergio Bardotti
—*3:22*
B: *THE GAME*—George Martin—*2:37*

216a.   JUL 18, 1969 (PORTUGAL) Parlophone QMSP 16459
by Carlos Mendes
*A: *Penina*—McCartney—*2:34*
B: *(wings of revenge)*

217a.   AUG 11, 1969 (US) Epic BN 26481 (LP)
by Donovan Prod: Mickie Most
BARABAJAGAL
side two
cut three: *ATLANTIS*—Donovan Leitch—*4:58*
Paul: Tambourine and Backing Vocal

233a.   JAN 16, 1970 (UK) Apple 22
JAN 29, 1970 (US) Apple 1816
by Mary Hopkin Prod: Paul McCartney
B: *LONTANO DAGLI OCCHI*—Sergio Endrigo—Sergio
Bardotti—*3:22*
A: *(temma harbour)*

245a.   APR   7, 1970 (US) Atco 33-326 (LP)
JUN 19, 1970 (UK) Atlantic 2400 013 (LP)
*Recorded Live: December 7, 1969 at Croydon's Fairfield
Hall, Britain*
by Delaney and Bonnie Bramlett

DELANEY AND BONNIE ON TOUR Prod: Jimmy Miller
and Delaney Bramlett
George: Guitar
side one
Things Get Better---Steve Cropper—Eddie Floyd—Wayne
   Jackson---*4:20*
medley: 5:00
   Poor Elijah---Delaney Bramlett—Jim Ford
   Tribute To Johnson---Delaney Bramlett—Leon Russell
Only You Know And I Know---Dave Mason---*4:10*
I Don't Want To Discuss It---Beth Beatty—Dick Cooper—
   Ernie Shelby---*4:55*
side two
That's What My Man Is For---Griffin---*4:30*
Where There's A Will, There's A Way---Bonnie Bramlett—
   Bobby Whitlock---*4:57*
Comin' Home---Bonnie Bramlett—Eric Clapton---*5:30*
medley: 5:45
   Long Tall Sally---Robert Blackwell—Enotris Johnson—
   Richard Penniman
   Jenny, Jenny---Enotris Johnson—Richard Penniman
   The Girl Can't Help It---Bobby Troup
   Tutti Frutti---Dorthy LaBostrie—Richard Penniman

276a.   MAR 5, 1971 (UK) Music For Pleasure MFP 5175 (LP)
by Various Artists
   (By Billy J. Kramer with The Dakotas Prod: George Martin;
    † Peter and Gordon; % Fourmost; $ Cilla Black; + Kenny
    Lynch)
THE STARS SING LENNON AND MCCARTNEY
side one:
   cut one: *BAD TO ME*---L-McC---*2:18*
†cut two: *A WORLD WITHOUT LOVE*---L-McC---*2:38*
%cut three: *HELLO LITTLE GIRL*---L-McC---*1:50*
   cut five: *I'LL BE ON MY WAY*---L-McC---*1:38*
side two
$*LOVE OF THE LOVED*---L-McC---*2:00*
†*NOBODY I KNOW*---L-McC---*2:27*
   I'LL KEEP YOU SATISFIED---L-McC---*2:04*
+*MISERY*---L-McC---*2:04*
†*I DON'T WANT TO SEE YOU AGAIN*---L-McC---*1:59*
%*I'M IN LOVE*---L-McC---*2:07*

302a.   NOV 30, 1971 (US) A&M 1319
by Gary Wright Prod: Gary Wright
George: Guitar
A: FASCINATING THINGS---Gary Wright---*2:55*
B: LOVE TO SURVIVE---Gary Wright---*4:48*

315a.   MAR 1, 1972 (US) Warner Brothers WB 7566
MAR 10, 1972 (UK) Elektra K 16163
Recorded: January 1972
by Bobby Hatfield Prod: Richard Perry
*A: Oo Wee Baby, I Love You---Richard Parker---*3:35*
   Ringo: Drums
B: (rock 'n' roll woman)

319a. APR 10, 1972 (US) Atco 45-6883
by Delaney and Bonnie Bramlett Prod: Jimmy Miller and
Delaney Bramlett George: Guitar
A: *WHERE THERE'S A WILL, THERE'S A WAY*---Bonnie
   Bramlett—Bobby Whitlock---*2:28*
B: *(lonesome and a long way from home)*

327a. MID AUGUST 1972 (US-TV OFFER) A Columbia Musical
Treasury P2S 5760 DS 951/952 (2 LPs)
by Various Artists
20 MONSTER HITS
record two
side one
   cut two: *ATLANTIS*---Donovan Leitch---*4:58*
   Paul: Tambourine and Backing Vocal

334a. OCT 16, 1972 (US) Atco SD 7014 (LP)
NOV 17, 1972 (UK) Atlantic K 40429 (LP)
by Delaney and Bonnie Bramlett Prod: Jimmy Miller and
Delaney Bramlett
George: Guitar
BEST OF DELANEY AND BONNIE
side one
   cut three: *ONLY YOU KNOW AND I KNOW*—Dave
   Mason---*4:10*
   cut five: *WHERE THERE'S A WILL, THERE'S A WAY*---
   Bonnie Bramlett—Bobby Whitlock---*4:57*
side two
   cut one: *COMIN' HOME*---Bonnie Bramlett—Eric Clapton
   ---*5:30*

336a. NOV 6, 1972 (US) Tumbleweed TWS 108 (LP)
DEC 1, 1972 (UK) Tumbleweed TWS 3504 (LP)
by Rudy Romero
George: Guitar except † Backing Vocal
TO THE WORLD Prod: Lee Kiefer
side one
†cut one: *If I Find The Time*---Rudy Romero---*3:24*
   cut two: *Lovely Lady*---Rudy Romero---*2:43*
   cut three: *Nothin' Gonna Get You Down*---Rudy Romero
   ---*4:01*
side two
   cut one: *Doing The Right Thing*---Rudy Romero---*4:14*

353a. JUNE 1973 (US MAIL ORDER) K-Tel TU 229 (4 LPs)
by Various Artists
ORIGINAL HITS—ORIGINAL STARS
record one
side two
   cut three: *A WORLD WITHOUT LOVE*---L-McC---*2:38*
   by Peter and Gordon
record two
side one
   cut two: *MY BONNIE*---Charles Pratt---*2:06*
   by Tony Sheridan and The Beatles Prod: Bert Kaempfert

362a.   OCT 26, 1973 (UK) Sounds Superb: EMI Music For
        Pleasure Series SPR 90019 (LP)
        by Cilla Black
        STEP INSIDE LOVE Prod: George Martin
        side two
            cut three: *STEP INSIDE LOVE*—L-McC—*2:20*

364a.   OCT 29, 1973 (UK) RCA SF 8395 (LP)
        by Billy Lawrie
        SHIP IMAGINATION Prod: Billy Lawrie and Gary Osborne
        side one
            cut two: *Rock And Roller*—Starkey—Billy Lawrie—*3:35*

382a.   MAY 9, 1974 (US MAIL ORDER) Warner Brothers PRO
        583 (2 LPs)
        by Various Artists
        HARD GOODS
        side four
            cut five: *VEGETABLES*—Brian Wilson—Van Dyke Parks—*2:05*
                by The Beach Boys Prod: The Beach Boys and Paul
                McCartney

412a.   OCT 28, 1974 (US) Reprise 2MS 2167 (2 LPs)
        by The Beach Boys Prod: The Beach Boys and Paul
        McCartney
        FRIENDS/SMILEY SMILE
        record two: Smiley Smile
        side one
            cut two: *VEGETABLES*—Brian Wilson—Van Dyke Parks—*2:05*

417a.   NOV 19, 1974 (US MAIL ORDER) Warner Brothers
        PRO 591 (2 LPs)
        by Various Artists
        DEEP EAR
        side one
            cut two: *ROCK 'N' ROLL IS MUSIC NOW*—James
                Taylor—*3:25*
                by James Taylor Prod: Dave Spinozza
                Paul: Backing Vocal

449a.   JUN 17, 1975 (US) Columbia PC 33575 (LP)
        JUL 4, 1975 (UK) CBS 69146 (LP)
        Recorded: 1971
        by Stephen Stills
        STILLS
        side two
            cut three: *As I Come Of Age*—Steve Stills—*2:36*
                Ringo (as English Ritchie): Drums

454a.   SEP 19, 1975 (US) Epic BG 33731 (2 LPs)
        by Donovan Prod: Mickie Most
        BARABAJAGAL/HURDY GURDY MAN
        record one: Barabajagal
        side two
            cut three: *ATLANTIS*—Donovan Leitch—*4:58*
                Paul: Tambourine and Backing Vocal

Apple Records.

IT'S LIKE YOU NEVER LEFT

doo wop   **Specialty SPS 2114**

July 7, 1940. Richard Starkey born.
October 9, 1940. John Lennon born.
June 18, 1942. James Paul McCartney born.
February 25, 1943. George Harrison born.
June 15, 1956. Ivan Vaughan introduces Paul to John. They per–
form together for the first time that same night at a church hall in
Woolton, Liverpool in John's group, the Quarrymen.
July 15, 1958. John's Mother killed in a car accident.
August 1958. Liverpool's Casbah Club opens. George, John and
Paul perform together.
1959. John, Paul and George perform together on and off all year,
backed by various other members. For an appearance on the Carroll
Levis TV talent show *Discoveries* they dub themselves Johnny and
the Moondogs. They perform a couple of old Buddy Holly tunes
It's So Easy and *Think it Over.*
April 1960. John, Paul, George and Stu Sutcliffe audition for
Larry Parnes. Johnny Hutch sits in on drums.
Spring 1960. Short tour of Scotland as a backing group (the Silver
Beatles) for Johnny Gentle. Tommy Moore on drums.
August 1960. First trip to Hamburg. The Beatles take on Pete
Best as their drummer. Over the next few months they perform at
Hamburg's Indra, Kaiserkeller and Top Ten clubs.
Fall 1960. John, Paul, George, Stu and Ringo cut *Fever* backing a
singer from Rory Storme's group. The group meets Astrid Kichener
and Klaus Voorman.
December 1960. Beatles asked to leave Hamburg.
December 27, 1960 Welcome Home concert at Litherland Town
Hall.

The Magical Mystery Tour

To most people who were growing up in the early 1950's, all of rock'n'roll's pre–history went on with hardly any public notice at all. Nineteen–fifty–four saw the first white cover versions of black rhythm and blues/rock'n'roll songs *(Sh–boom, Shake, Rattle & Roll)* hitting the top of the charts. Disc jockey Alan Freed came to WINS in New York City from Cleveland, and made rock'n'roll a household word. In early 1955, Freed began holding public rock 'n' roll concerts which elicited both wild teenage reaction and shocked adult response. In the spring, the movie *Blackboard Jungle* brought the style, feel and sound of rock 'n' roll to every movie house in the country; it also caused a sensation when shown in Britain. Bill Haley and the Comets' *Rock Around The Clock*, performed in *Blackboard Jungle,* became the first non--cover rock'n' roll song to hit number one, doing so in June of 1955. The next month, Chuck Berry released his first record, *Maybelline.* By this time, other black artists, both individuals (Little Richard, Ray Charles, Fats Domino) and groups (the Coasters, the Drifters, the Platters) were finally beginning to make a dent on the pop charts on their own, not just through cover versions by "safer" artists like Pat Boone. By the end of 1955, rock 'n' roll was firmly established as the latest fad, but there was one more step needed before it could dominate pop music: a single identifiable, preferable white, superstar.

In November 1955, RCA bought Elvis Presley, then considered a hillbilly singer, from Sun records, where he had had moderate success for a year and a half. His second RCA disc, *Heartbreak Hotel*, released in February 1956, hit number one in April. Suddenly, rock 'n' roll covered the charts. Carl Perkins' *Blue Suede Shoes* topped the Pop, Rhythm & Blues and Country charts at the same time. Perkins himself, on the verge of stardom, was nearly killed in a car crash in March on the way to his TV debut on the *Perry Como Show.* It had taken television a few months to accept rock 'n' roll's popularity and to begin inviting its stars to appear.

3

Elvis appeared on the *Milton Berle* show in early June, and was all at once thrust in front of all the parents in America. He was even the rage among English youth. It was at exactly this point (early June) that the young John Lennon first met the younger Paul McCartney, who was said to vaguely resemble Elvis Presley.

On September 9, Presley made his first appearance on the *Ed Sullivan* show. Elvis was, by this time, a national institution, idoliz-- ed by most teenagers and ridiculed or damned by most adults. He was topping the charts with a double sided hit, *Hound Dog/Don't Be Cruel*. The widely discussed question of Presley's pelvic gyrations forced CBS to limit Presley's appearance to waist--up.

Teenagers and rock'n'rollers had taken over the music industry, Elvis was King, and many others wanted the same. The rest of 1956 and all of 1957 saw many new faces pop up. Some of real lasting quality (the Everly Brothers, Buddy Holly and the Crickets, Gene Vincent, Sam Cooke) and others who were either plastic imitations or just dolled--up singers (Tommy Sands, Ricky Nelson, Paul Anka and Tom & Jerry, later known as Simon & Garfunkel). Now secure at the top, Elvis, under the direction of Colonel Tom Parker, began turning out simplistic formula movies which put more stock in ballads (*Love Me Tender*), although when he wanted to (*Jailhouse Rock*) Presley could still send a crowd into a frenzy. For stars still on the way up, the best place for national exposure soon became Dick Clark's *American Bandstand*, on for years in Philadelphia but joining the ABC network in the summer of 1957. November brought Eddie Cochran, first seen as yet another Elvis imitator, with his catchy and tricky guitar piece *Twenty Flight Rock*. It was Paul McCartney's nimble proficiency on this tune which had first earned him entrance to John's group, the Quarrymen (then a struggling teen-age band in Liverpool) back in 1956. And within two years, George Harrison's fancy picking on the Bill Justis hit *Raunchy* had gained him a spot with the group as well.

In early 1958, rock'n'roll had become big business. Alan Freed's traveling rock'n'roll shows were pulling in enormous box office re-- turns. Dick Clark got a Saturday evening show in addition to his daily *Bandstand* chores. Elvis, the leader of the pack, kept hitting number one over and over. But would it last? Every six months, people in the music industry would convince each other that the rock'n'roll craze was fading (*really*, this time). They were jealous of the new--found power of the new entrepreneurs (Freed, Clark, etc.) who were elbowing their way into a previously restricted and much more sedate club. Traditionalists in general were genuinely outraged at what they considered the moral degeneration being brought about by rock'n'roll. All that was needed was a good event with which to nail rock'n'roll to the cross.

4

The first decline of rock'n'roll began on March 24, 1958, when Elvis Presley sailed for Germany to begin a two–year stint in the army. With the King gone, the lesser lights would vie for his title, and the overall quality of rock'n'roll would slip. The moralists finally got their long hoped–for incident on May 3, 1958, when a "riot" broke out at one of Alan Freed's shows in Boston. A few people were roughed up, and a number actually stabbed. The whole mess got plenty of newspaper build–up and the always assumed link–up of rock'n'roll and juvenile delinquency seemed confirmed. Freed was actually indicted by the city of Boston for inciting a riot, and his traveling road show ground to a halt, severely damaging the market for similar shows. Freed was squeezed out of WINS, but soon re–turned to the airwaves on WABC, and even got his own local TV record hop.

The fall of 1958 and all of 1959 were bad days all around for the broadcasting industry. The TV Quiz Show scandal flared up in August of 1958, but for a year was kept under wraps in judicial pro–ceedings. Blatant Elvis imitators e.g., Fabian and Ed "Kookie" Byrnes somehow got to be big stars via horrendously mediocre re–cordings. Novelty records *(The Chipmunk Song, The Purple People Eater)* kept topping the charts. On the night of February 3, 1959, three of the brightest hopes of rock'n'roll, Buddy Holly, J.P. "Big Bopper" Richardson and Ritchie Valens, were all killed in a single plane crash in the midwest. Even Little Richard quit rock'n'roll, temporarily, to join the ministry.

British rock'n'roll, if there was such a thing, was virtually un–known in the United States. Cliff Richard, the first real home–grown British rock star, was totally ignored in the U.S. when his first British smash, *Move It*, was released in late 1958. Britain's premiere rock TV show, Jack Good's *Oh Boy*, made a disasterous summer run on ABC in 1959. Around the same time, a local Man–chester England talent show, Carroll Levis' *Discoveries*, featured the television debut of Johnny and the Moondogs, as John, Paul and George now called themselves. (John and Paul had, in fact, already begun writing their own songs, such as *Love Me Do* and *One After 909*.)

Back in America, November 1959 brought two body blows to the world of radio and TV. Charles Van Doren, America's favorite egghead, admitted in public that he had been given the answers to the questions during his triumphant quiz show run. The admissions of Van Doren and many others gave not only the quiz shows but the entire television industry a black mark. Out of fear of offending *anybody*, the three networks then steered clear of any sort of in–novative (possibly controversial) programming.

Literally on the heels of Van Doren's confession came the first charges in radio's payola scandal. All radio DJs came under sus--picion, but payola centered on rock'n'roll DJs. After all, it made sense; those DJs were playing those awful records because they were getting kickbacks. The big ones, like Freed and Clark, even had business connections with record companies and talent promoters. Clark, after divesting himself of outside record interests, and a heavy grilling by a Congressional investigative committee, survived on his *Bandstand* program. Freed, however, was not as lucky. He was fired from WABC on November 20, and made his last appearance on WNEW--TV eight days later. The payola scandal resulted in a sharp move away from the smaller independent labels, the home of most of the best rock'n'roll, and a general tightening of radio play--lists, resulting in a move toward more pop--sounding material.

Elvis finally got out of the army in mid--March 1960, and im--mediately began recording again at RCA. The face of rock'n'roll, however, had changed radically since Presley sailed for Europe. To keep pace, Presley stuck to "gentler, less raucous material" like *Are You Lonesome Tonight?* His first post--army TV appearance, on the *Frank Sinatra* show in May 1960, featured a tame duet with Frankie on *Love Me Tender* and *Witchcraft*. Such demonstrations did not auger well for the vibrancy of rock'n'roll. While hitting the top of the charts regularly, Presley no longer dominated the music world, and spent more and more time churning out cheap movies like *It Happened At The World's Fair.*

Mainstream white rock'n'roll was in the midst of a miasma. "Death" and "Suicide" songs (*Teen Angel, Tell Laura I Love Her*) held an uncanny attraction for record buyers. At the same time, Chubby Checker's *The Twist* began two years of constantly chang--ing dance fad songs. The only real progress being made in rock'n'--roll was in the new black "Motown Sound" coming out of Detroit, beginning with Barret Strong's *Money* released in the last days of 1959. Such artists as Smokey Robinson & the Miracles, Mary Wells, the Shirelles, Marvin Gaye and others rapidly became black super--stars, but only slowly caught the attention of white teenagers.

One of the last bright lights of the late 50's rock'n'roll era, Eddie Cochran, whose *Summertime Blues* had become a classic, was, like so many others of equal talent, killed accidentally. In his case, it was a car crash in England on April 17, 1960. Cochran and Gene Vincent, who was badly injured in the car crash, had been in England to head up one of the first Alan Freed--type package tours to bring top American stars to the North of England. Allan Williams, one of the tour's local promoters, was forced to throw to--gether a show made of lesser known local talents. One of the groups who tried out for a slot, but were rejected, were the Silver Beatles, formerly Johnny & the Moondogs, with Stu Sutcliffe added on bass.

Although they failed this try-out, the Silver Beatles were soon pick-ed by big-time British promoter Larry Parnes after extensive lobby-ing by Allan Williams, who had by now begun managing the group's affairs, to back up home-grown Elvis imitator Johnny Gentle on a short tour of Scotland. It was the first time the Silver Beatles had ventured any distance from their Liverpool homes. Although their quality was nowhere near star status, they were better than your run–of–the–mill bar band. Due to this, and Allan Williams' vigorous promotion, the group, now known simply as "The Beatles," was soon signed to appear at the newly–opened (and soon to close) Indra Club in Hamburg, West Germany. The Germans seemed to take to raucous rock music, and Britain was a cheap source of talent. Williams, who had sent a few other groups over, already had contacts with club owners in Hamburg, one of the looser, raunchier of German port cities, heavily populated by American GIs.

The Beatles needed a more permanent drummer as they pre-pared for their first foreign venture (they had gone through many while playing in England). Long–time friend Pete Best was signed up at the last minute. However, the Indra Club folded soon after the Beatles arrived, so they moved to the Kaiserkeller. There they shared billing with fellow Liverpudlians Rory Storme and the Hurri-canes, whose drummer was none other than Ringo Starr. During this time, in the fall of 1960, the Beatles made their first known re-cording. They backed up a singer named Wally, from Rory Storme's group, in a rendition of the Peggy Lee hit, *Fever*. This "momentous" recording took place in a simple "Record–A–Message–For–Your–Mum" studio, the sort you might find at an amusement park. Rory's drummer, Ringo, sat in for Pete Best. By December, the Beatles had built a small local reputation and were talked into "defecting" to the arch–rival Top Ten Club, which featured English singer Tony Sheridan. They had also attracted the attention of a few members of Hamburg's arty/beatnik colony, and had befriended two such fans, Klaus Voorman and Astrid Kichener. By December, Stu and Astrid had fallen in love and were talking of marriage. Soon there-after, the German authorities suddenly noticed George was under age (he was seventeen) and deported him. A few days later, a minor fire incident in their "apartment" got the rest of the group evicted and they followed George home.

The Beatles almost disbanded at this point, figuring they had botched their one big chance at success. Fortunately, they were talked into playing at a post–Christmas show at the Litherland Town Hall. The four months of continuous lengthly performing in Ger-many had tightened the group enormously, and added the new ele-ments of power and magnetism to their performance. The English crowd, to whom this was all new, were knocked out.

English rock, like American rock at the time, was mostly bland and formalized. Everything was safe and choreographed. In America it was Bobby Vinton and Bobby Vee, while in Britain it was Adam Faith and the competent, but bland, Shadows. The Beatles seemed like a whirlwind amidst this breeze. Early 1961 had the Beatles ensconced as one of the top beat groups in the Liverpool area. It was at this time that they regularly played at the Casbah, run by Pete Best's mother, and on March 21, they made their first appearance at Liverpool's Cavern Club, then mostly all--jazz. By April of 1961, George had turned eighteen and was eligible for a foreign work per-- mit, and Allan Williams had cleared up the Beatles' legal problems with the Germans, so they returned to Hamburg's Top Ten Club. Stu immediately took up again with Astrid and ceased being a regular member of the band. Stu and Astrid got married in June and he re-- sumed his earlier work in the field of art.

The Beatles spent two months at the Top Ten Club. During this stay they entered a new phase of their career, by becoming re-- cording artists.

Sentimental Journey   **Apple SW 3365 (LP)**

Rock 'n' Roll   Apple SK-3419 (LP)

March 21. Beatles make their debut at the Cavern Club.
April. Second trip to Hamburg. Perform at the Top Ten Club.
May. Recording sessions backing Tony Sheridan. Stu Sutcliffe attends but doesn't play.
June. Stu Sutcliffe leaves the Beatles and stays in Hamburg to attend art school and marry Astrid Kichener.
July 6. First issue of *Mersey Beat* published. It includes a humorous fictitious article by John Lennon on "How the Beatles Were Formed."
October 28. (3 PM) Raymond Jones walks into Brian Epstein's record store in Whitechapel, Liverpool and asks for *My Bonnie*.
November 9. Brian Epstein sees the Beatles at a Cavern Club lunch show.
December 3. The Beatles' first meeting with Brian Epstein, at his Whitechapel store. They agree to let him manage their affairs.
December 13. Beatles sign contract with Brian Epstein at the Casbah Club.

1961

1961

The Beatles first record didn't even get their name on it. The word "Beatles" was too close to a German obscenity to allow it on disc, so the session–men catch name "the Beat Brothers" was substituted. Top listing west to English singer Tony Sheridan. Bert Kaempfert, German band leader, produced the session for Polydor records. The Beatles were quickly put under contract and, serving as Sheridan's back–up, recorded eight cuts (two were Beatle solos). *My Bonnie* and *The Saints* were put out immediately as a single. Three other cuts were released within the next year, with the remainder not issued until the Beatles had become stars in their own right. The first Sheridan single flopped and the Beatles promptly forgot about the recordings. In July, the Beatles, billed as "Polydor Recording Artists," returned home to Liverpool, which had become quite a center for rock (or *beat*) music. A bi–weekly newspaper dealing exclusively with the Liverpool music scene, *Mersey Beat*, appeared in July, with an article by John Lennon. By August, the group had begun regular performances at the Cavern Wednesday nights, and were generally considered Liverpool's top group. On October 28, 1961, Raymond Jones walked into Brian Epstein's Music Store and asked for the Beatles' *My Bonnie* single. It being an obscure import, Epstein didn't have the disc. After some nosing around, Epstein was shocked to discover that the Beatles were not only English but from his very town. He finally got the single, which eventually came out in Britain the next January, and went to see the Beatles at the Cavern. He took an instant liking to both their sound and personalities. Slightly bored with the normal business world anyway, he talked the group into allowing him to be their manager. He began searching for a recording contract while slowly sharpening the group's rough edges, and turned a sloppy punk band into the finished product the world was about to discover.

Recommended Recordings (1961/62): The Lennon/Harrison instrumental *Cry For A Shadow*; the Beatles first version of *Love Me Do*.

Love Me Do/P.S. I Love You   EMI R 4949 (45)

January 1. Decca Audition session, with A&R man Mike Smith.
January. Beatles win *Mersey Beat* poll.
March. Decca rejects the Beatles, noting that "groups are on the way out."
April. Stu Sutcliffe dies of a brain hemorrhage while in Hamburg.
April–June. Third trip to Hamburg. The Beatles open the new Star Club.
May 9. Telegram arrives from Brian Epstein: CONGRATULA-TIONS BOYS. EMI REQUEST RECORDING SESSION. PLEASE REHEARSE NEW MATERIAL.
June 6. Beatles audition for George Martin at EMI studios in St. John's Woods.
June 9. Welcome Home Concert at the Cavern Club.
June 11. First BBC radio broadcast from studios in Manchester.
August. Beatles sign contract with EMI.
August 16. Sack Pete Best and take on drummer Ringo Starr.
August 23. John Lennon marries Cynthia Powell.
September 11. First recording session at London's EMI studios. Record their first single *Love Me Do/P.S. I Love You*. Andy White plays drums on *P.S. I Love You* and some of the takes of *Love Me Do*.
October 1. Reconstituted Beatles sign new five year contract with Brian Epstein.
October 5. *Love Me Do* released. Gets its first spin on Radio Luxembourg.
November. Dick James agrees to be the Beatles' publisher and to arrange some promotion and tours.
November 1–14. Fourth trip to Hamburg. Beatles perform at the Star Club.
November 26. Record second single at EMI, *Please Please Me/Ask Me Why*.
December 17. Appear on Granada TV's *People And Places*.
December 18–January 1. Final trip to Hamburg. Again at the Star Club. Ted "Kingsize" Taylor records their stage act.

1962

IT'S LIKE YOU
NEVER LEFT

1962

1962 began, literally, with the Beatles' first big recording audi--tion. Held in London for Decca records, they played about fifteen songs, but were turned down. Groups were thought to be on the way out. In April they returned again to Hamburg where the owners of the Star Club had insisted that the Beatles, and no one else, open their club. Upon arrival, they learned of the death of former mem--ber Stu Sutcliffe, who had died of a brain hemorrhage. Now a familiar element to the Hamburg music scene, the Beatles were quickly signed up for a Christmas show. They were already bored with their position, however, and longed to start making their own records. Brian Epstein remained in Britain working toward exactly that goal, and in May finally convinced Parlophone producer George Martin to grant the Beatles a try-out. Held in June, the audition went better than the Decca session. Martin figured they had poten-tial, but wasn't sure about the drummer, Pete Best. The Beatles re--turned to the Cavern Club in Liverpool while waiting for word that they had passed the audition. Few, if any, Liverpool or Northern bands had cracked the impenetrable walls of the major London re--cord companies. So when the word came in August to report for a recording session, it was felt not only as a victory for the Beatles, but for the whole Merseyside. At this last moment, it was decided to replace Best with Ringo Starr, a drummer they had long admired in Hamburg. Pete's fans (fairly numerous) considered this treason. Nonetheless, the newly--constituted "Fab--Four--To--Be" recorded *Love Me Do* and *P.S. I Love You*, which came out in October. The single got a fair amount of notice, but nobody outside of Liverpool felt that a transcendental moment had arrived in music. It was in the charts for awhile, then dropped from sight. One thing about the Beatles that did garner attention was that they wrote both sides of their own single, quite an uncommon feat at that time. They return--ed to Hamburg in November for the lucrative Christmas season. In the midst of it, they made a quick return to London at the end of November to record their second single. By this time, they had signed with the Dick James publishing company, which began ar--ranging more extensive English touring dates. Back in Hamburg for the final time, they were captured on tape by King--Size Taylor, and then returned to England around New Year's.

February 11. In 12 hours the Beatles lay down the tracks for their first LP, **Please Please Me.**

February--March. Beatles appear on several package tours of Britain, backing Helen Shapiro, then Chris Montez and Tommy Roe.

March 2. *Please Please Me* becomes their first number one single.

May--June. Beatles head their own package tour of Britain.

Summer. Malcolm Evans joins Neil Aspinall as the Beatles' road manager.

July 15. Beatles record the tracks of their second album, **With The Beatles.**

July 21. A huge crowd outside the Blackpool Queens theatre. The Beatles have to climb in through the roof to perform.

July 22. Vee Jay LP **Introducing The Beatles** fails to register any interest in America.

August 3. Last appearance at the Cavern Club.

October 13. Beatles top the bill at the London Palladium. A near riot of fans trying to get in alerts the national press to Beatlemania.

November 4. Appear in the Royal Variety Show. Lennon utters his famous quip: "Those of you in the cheaper seats -- clap your hands; and those of you in the more expensive seats -- just rattle your jewelry."

December. The Beatles have seven hits at one time in the British LP, EP and singles charts.

December 24. The Beatles Christmas show opens.

December 26. The Beatles' first Capitol single is rush--released to meet the unprecedented demand in America.

1963

PLEASE PLEASE ME · THE BEATLES

Please Please Me   Parlophone PCS 3042 (LP)

Recommended Recordings: Although Lennon and Mc-Cartney gave songs to many artists in those early days, Billy J. Kramer (who received a half a dozen) produced the most consistent string of top-notch interpretations. In 1963 these included: *Bad To Me, Do You Want To Know A Secret, I Call Your Name, I'll Be On My Way* and *I'll Keep You Satisfied.* Also, The Rolling Stones: *I Wanna Be Your Man* ('cause it's the Stones); The Beatles own: *From Me To You, Money* and *You Really Got A Hold On Me.*

1963

The Beatles second single, *Please Please Me/Ask Me Why*, came out in January and immediately took off. An American contract was signed with Vee Jay records, but their records made no impact in the U.S. till the year's end. By March, the Beatles had Britain's number one record and were in the midst of continuous, unending tours of Britain. At first, they were near the middle of the bill, but were soon getting as much attention as the headliners. A quickly recorded LP, **Please Please Me**, took only five weeks to hit number one, and then spent an amazing seven months at the top, replaced only by their second album. Each new single took less and less time to become number one. *From Me To You*, in April, took only three weeks. Suddenly, the whole country was experiencing a rock'n'roll revival. Not a revival in the sense that it was nostalgia, but revival in its literal sense. Rock'n'roll, an art form nearly moribund, was having creative life breathed into it. Other groups from the Liverpool area (Gerry and the Pacemakers, Billy J. Kramer) became national stars. A whole generation of rhythm-and-blues-based English kids (Eric Clapton, Mick Jagger and Keith Richard, Jack Bruce, Ray Davies, Manfred Mann) came out of the woodwork and began securing recording contracts. By July, the Rolling Stones, with their first record, had begun to chase after the Beatles' runaway success. By October, after the Beatles quick but enthusiastic Swedish tour, the English press coined the phrase *Beatlemania* to describe the by-now nearly hysterical reaction the group was receiving.

The Beatles reached a pinnacle of sorts in November when they appeared on the Royal Variety Show, the height of the British musical stage. News agencies and record companies in America were now beginning to sit up and take notice. A week after President Kennedy was assassinated in Dallas, the Beatles released their fifth single, *I Want To Hold Your Hand*. It entered the British charts at number one. Top American talent hunter Ed Sullivan agreed to showcase them on his TV show in February. Capitol Records, which had purchased American rights to the Beatles, planned to release *I Want To Hold Your Hand* on January 13, but was forced to rush-release it on December 26, due to the amazing surge of American interest in the Beatles. It was the first time in memory any English singer or group had made any sort of impression on American youth.

Recommended Recordings: The **Long Tall Sally** EP showcases the R&B and C&W roots of the Beatles in four great songs. Billy J. Kramer: *From A Window*; The Strangers with Mike Shannon: *One And One Is Two*. Don't buy **The Beatles Story** (it's a terrible album).

February 1. *I Want To Hold Your Hand* tops the American Hot 100.

February 7. Beatles land at Kennedy Airport, welcomed by 3000 cheering fans.

February 9. First *Ed Sullivan* appearance.

February 11. First Beatle concert in America, at the Washington DC Coliseum. Filmed and shown in a closed circuit theatre broadcast on March 14 and 15.

March--April. Filming *A Hard Day's Night*. George meets Patti Boyd during the filming.

April 11. The Beatles have 14 of *Billboard's* Hot 100, including 5 of the top 10.

April 27. *In His Own Write* published in the U.S.

June--November. Almost continuous touring by the Beatles, all a--round the world.

June 3--13. Ringo taken ill and replaced by drummer Jimmy Nicol on the tour.

June 15. Biggest crowd ever (over 250,000) greets the Beatles (with Ringo) along the streets of Melbourne, Australia.

July 6. World premiere of *A Hard Day's Night* (London).

November 15. *Around The Beatles* TV show broadcast in America on ABC (originally broadcast in Britain on May 6). Program features an exciting version of the song *Shout*, with John, Paul, George and Ringo sharing the vocals.

December 24. Another Beatles' Christmas Show opens in London.

1964

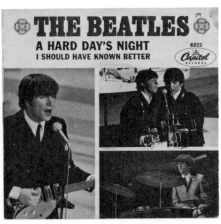

A Hard Day's Night/   Capitol 5222 **(45)**
I Should Have Known Better

IT'S LIKE YOU NEVER LEFT

1964

By the time the Beatles hit American living rooms on the *Ed Sullivan* show, their first Capitol single was already number one. With the unprecedented reaction to the two *Sullivan* appearances, the Beatles became the hottest, fastest rising rock'n'rollers since Elvis Presley eight years earlier. Everything they touched turned to gold. In one week in April, they had fifteen songs and four albums on the American charts. It is hard now, in retrospect, to comprehend the swiftness, depth and importance of the Beatles' superstardom explosion in the first few months of 1964. They revolutionized and revitalized the American music scene by bringing the essence of American rhythm and blues back to its home. They changed forever the hair (and later dress) styles of a whole generation. Almost instantly, they were number one all over the world, and would be for years. Like all superstars, they then began making a movie. The real shocker was that it was good! Using the *cinema verite* (spiced with zany imagery) touch of filmmaker Dick Lester, the Beatles were presented in their supposed natural habitat in *A Hard Day's Night*. For good or for ill, but for all time, the four Beatles were established as separate, distinct identities; John – the leader, the writer, and sort of a glib smart--ass; Paul -- the cute, baby--faced singer, just naughty enough to excite; George – quiet, musically oriented, and somewhat mysterious; and Ringo – the good--old--boy in the back, who pounds them skins and exudes the wisdom of The Common Man. Perpetually barraged by public attention, the Beatles took refuge in these stereotypes as their lives became public property. From June to November, they endured their first world tour, breaking all records as they went, and performing before crowds who could hardly hear them due to their own screaming.

Rubber Soul   Parlophone PCS 3075 (LP)

Recommended Recordings: The Beatles: *I'm Down, Bad Boy,* and the **Rubber Soul** LP; Silke: *You've Got To Hide Your Love Away* (produced by John & Paul).

February 11. Ringo marries Maureen Cox.
February--May. Shooting sessions for *Help!*
June 12. Beatles awarded the MBE.
June. A number of MBE holders return their medals in protest against the award to the Beatles.
June. Lennon's *A Spaniard In The Works* published.
June--August. Beatles conduct another world concert tour.
July 29. World Premiere of *Help!* in London.
August 15. Shea Stadium concert before 56,000 fans, filmed for a television documentary.
October 9. Paul, backed only by a string quartet, hits number 1 on the Hot 100 with *Yesterday.*
October 22. Beatles decline an invitation to appear on another Royal Variety Show.
October 26. Beatles invested with MBEs at Buckingham Palace.
December 3. **Rubber Soul** released.
December 17. Beatles' commence last tour of Britain.

1965

1965

1965 was 1964 again, only more so. They appeared on *Sullivan*. They made a movie. They did a world tour, and spent most of the year at the top of the charts. The film, *Help!*, was in color this time, and wasn't as good as the first. (It resembled some of the B–grade movies that Hollywood had been famous for two decades earlier. You take an established star, and churn out a few films. The plot is unimportant; people will come to see the stars anyway). A full six months, June to December, was spent on the road, highlighted by the Shea Stadium concert in New York City, which had the largest crowd ever (at that time) to see a concert performance. The only thing that really changed in 1965 was the most important thing, their music. They were now recording only their own material, and they were getting better. Most suddenly successful musicians don't last for one of two reasons: either success somehow destroys their ability to create at the level they did before, or they fall into a characteristic sound or style which soon may pass from public favor. The most amazing thing the Beatles accomplished was an avoidance of both these pitfalls. Their songwriting, musicianship and produc-- tion improved steadily, after a slight rut around the time of *A Hard Day's Night*. Paul's song *Yesterday* finally garnered the group some-- what reluctant praise from the older generations. More importantly, the Beatles' album **Rubber Soul** was a definite progression toward a more mature form of rock'n'roll. After urging from Bob Dylan, John and Paul were putting more work into their lyrics. *Norwegian Wood* is both lyrically and musically head and shoulders above *I'm Happy Just To Dance With You*. George's use of a sitar on this song, along with the Byrds' early use, were the vanguard of a whole- sale introduction of Eastern temper and ideals to the youth culture. The concept and implications of mild drug use permeated **Rubber Soul**. The Beatles, also with this album, began to transcend their re-- cord company. Having already given the LP, formerly the trash can of rock, a new dignity, they were now sliding towards thematic LPs which would not be cut up for use as singles. If for nothing else, this grant of new independence to the artist would be a well--remembered contribution.

Recommended Recordings: Peter and Gordon: *Woman* (written by Paul under the pseudonym Bernard Webb); The Escourts: *From Head To Toe* (produced by Paul); and The Beatles' **Revolver** LP.

Revolver   **Parlophone PCS 7009 (LP)**

January 21. George Harrison marries Patti Boyd.

May 1. Beatles appear in concert for a final time in Britain, at the *New Musical Express* Pollwinner's show.

June. Capitol withdraws the "Butcher" cover version of the American LP **Yesterday And Today** (featuring the four Beatles dressed in butchers' smocks and holding pieces of meat and the legs, arms, heads and torsos of some dolls). It is replaced with a more innocuous photo.

June 3. At the same time, the "Butcher" photo is used as part of an ad in *New Musical Express* for the *Paperback Writer* single, without complaint.

June 24. Beatles begin final world tour in Munich, Germany.

July 4. Largest concert audience ever for a Beatle show: some 100,000 fans jam the Araneta Coliseum in Manila. The group fails to appear at the President's palace, however, and are jeered as they leave the country.

July 31. A DJ bonfire of Beatle discs begins the American reaction to John Lennon's statement that the Beatles are more popular than Christ. Radio stations across the country ban Beatle records.

August 12. Lennon "apologizes" for his remark at a press conference in Chicago.

August 29. The Beatles' final concert appearance; they perform at Candlestick Park in San Francisco, California.

October. George Harrison in Bombay on holiday.

November. John meets Yoko Ono at the preview of her art exhibition at the Indica Gallery in London.

December 18. The London premiere of *The Family Way*, featuring a musical score written by Paul alone.

December. Ringo on holiday in Spain.

1966

1966

1966 began looking much the same as before. Talk of a new movie and plans for the inevitable world tour. The only problem was, the Beatles didn't want to do another movie and were getting very tired of touring. The music they were turning out was get--ting harder and harder to reproduce on stage, and what was the point if no one could hear? The movie was indefinitely postponed, but the tour went on. By this time, the Beatles had been undisputed kings for three/four years. People in general, and the press in particular, began searching for chinks in their armor. When John's observation that the Beatles were more popular than Jesus Christ got front page attention, all those who wanted (for any reason) to take pot shots at the Beatles now had something to throw. People burned their records, denounced them as heretics, but no one rebutted the charge. It was partly to be expected. They were violating one of the cardinal laws of entertainment: don't get involved in public controversies regarding politics, religion or sex. The Beatles were to be involved in all three soon enough.

After the somewhat less hectic but equally, if not more, ex--hausting tour (they were almost beat up in Manila after a supposed insult to that country's president), the Beatles decided, without telling anyone, that they would never perform in public again. Caught within the straight--jacket of the group identity long enough, all four began pursuing individual projects. Consequently, there was nothing really left for Brian Epstein to do, and he began coming apart. Musically, it was a slow year, with one major standout: the **Revolver** LP, perhaps the strongest, most revolutionary, and longest lasting album they ever made. The Beatles also began considering whether they could by--pass the bureaucracy of established compan--ies altogether. An independent consortium was envisaged, which would be run by and for artists of all sorts. Unfortunately, nobody quite knew how to accomplish this.

1967

January--April. **Sgt. Pepper** recording sessions.
February 6. Beatles sign 9--year contract with EMI.
May 20. BBC bans *A Day In The Life*.
June 1. **Sgt. Pepper** released.
June. In answer to questions from the news media, Paul McCartney reveals that he has taken LSD.
June 25. World--wide TV hook--up, featuring the Beatles singing *All You Need Is Love*.
August 27. Brian Epstein dies.
September--October. Filming *Magical Mystery Tour.*
October 7. Beatles turn down Bernstein offer of $1 million for a concert appearance.
October 18. World premiere in London of *How I Won The War*, featuring John as Musketeer Gripweed.
December 4. Apple Botique opens on Baker Street.
December 25. Paul and Jane Asher announce their engagement.
December 26. Premiere of *Magical Mystery Tour* on BBC-1 TV.

Recommended Recordings: Musketeer Gripweed (John) and The Third Troop: *How I Won The War* (an extremely rare record, though it only contains some of John's dialogue from the movie plus instrumental music); The Beatles: *I Am The Walrus.*

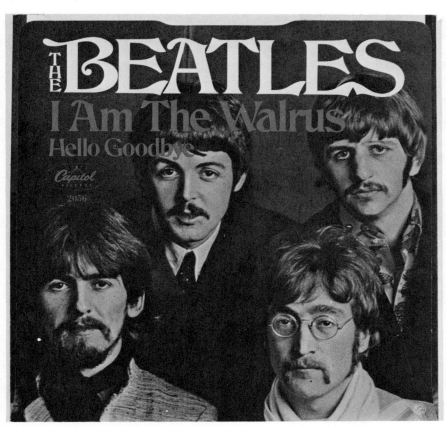

I Am The Walrus/Hello Goodbye   **Capitol 2056 (45)**

1967

It seems as if kids in general finally caught up with the "new" Beatles in 1967. Drug experimentation became wide--spread and everybody jumped at the chance to find drug references in **Sgt. Pepper**, often not really there, though many *had* been ignored on **Revolver**. **Sgt. Pepper** *was* 1967. The record industry was finally forced to accept the fact that albums might be something more than a collection of singles and could, in fact, be accepted as a unifi-- ed artistic statement. While important chunks of **Sgt. Pepper** now seem very dated, it quickly grabbed the attention of most people listening to music, and the era of Acid--Rock albums, still living on in your bargain basement cutout bins, began. Groups nobody had heard of, or wanted to hear from, began amassing cult follow-- ings. (The two extremes, one of deliberate outrageousness and the other of deliberate craftsmanship, could be exemplified by the Mothers of Invention and Cream.) The Beatles themselves talked openly of taking LSD, and took an interest in a funny little man who called himself a guru. In the midst of all this, Brian Epstein died. With him gone, the Beatles lost the most important thing they had: someone who could say "no" while also serving as a buffer from the voracious business world. His loss was immediately felt as the group launched upon two ill--fated ventures: the nice but sloppy and probably unnecessary *Magical Mystery Tour*, and the too--all--encompassing theory of Apple. The *Mystery Tour* was a quick flop, but Apple hung on like a leech. The original subsidiaries (clothing stores, inventions, films, publishing and art) swiftly dis-- integrated into chaos. The only marginally successful venture, re-- cording, wouldn't come until 1968. As the year ended, the Beatles finally seemed to get too far out in front of the public. People didn't like, and DJs actually didn't play, *I Am The Walrus*.

1968

February–April. All four Beatles, their wives and Jane Asher visit India for instruction by the Maharishi.

May 15. John and Paul on the *Tonight* Show talk about their new project, Apple, with substitute host Joe Garagiola.

June 15. John and Yoko's Acorn Event.

June 29. Paul attends the Capitol records convention in Los Angeles to promote Apple.

July 17. World premiere (London) of *Yellow Submarine*. All four Beatles attend.

July 31. Apple Botique closes, with its remaining stock simply given away.

September 8. Beatles appear on the David Frost show singing *Hey Jude*.

October 18. John and Yoko arrested on a drugs charge.

November 1. George releases his first solo album, the *Wonderwall* soundtrack.

November 8. Cynthia Lennon granted a divorce.

November 21. Yoko suffers a miscarriage.

November 22. The Beatels release a two–record set containing 30 new songs. It's immediately dubbed the *White Album*.

November 28. John found guilty and fined for his possession of cannabis resin.

November. John & Yoko release the **Two Virgins** album.

December 17. New York premiere of *Candy*, featuring Ringo as Emmanuel the Gardener.

Recommended Recordings: Apple's first four singles: *Thingumybob* (Black Dyke Mills Band), *Those Were The Days* (Mary Hopkin), *Sour Milk Sea* (Jackie Lomax), and *Hey Jude* (of course); One of the great lost Beatle B-sides, *The Inner Light*; James Taylor's Apple LP; and two discs produced by Paul: The Bonzo Dog Band's *I'm The Urban Spaceman* and Roger McGough and Mike McGear's LP **McGough And McGear**.

Unfinished Music No. 1: Two Virgins   **Apple T-5001 (LP)**

1968

1968 brought tremendous changes throughout the world, and the Beatles were no exception. It was the year of Apple, the Beatles' own record company. They began signing up artists (Mary Hopkin, Jackie Lomax, James Taylor, Modern Jazz Quartet) who could and should have been stars. The start, while not spectacular, was still pretty respectable. The Beatles, of course (also on Apple), were top sellers. Mary Hopkin also hit number one, but the others couldn't seem to get started, probably lost amid the attention the Beatles received. Additionally, a brand new weapon was given to Beatle detractors in the form of Yoko Ono, recipient of some of the vilest scuttlebutt since Jerry Lee Lewis married his thirteen year old cousin. John's affair with Yoko, combined with nude album covers and dadaist political espousals, added a literal *foreign* feel to the Beatles' activities. They were so far from the lovable mop--tops of just a few years earlier. John got arrested for marijuana possession which complicated his life for the next eight years, adding a criminal taint to his slightly crackpot public image. Paul had become engag--ed, broken it off, and taken up with an American photographer. George had become an Indian mystic, and Ringo was making movies. Musically, they were playing havoc with their records. *Hey Jude*, their first Apple single, was over seven minutes long. Nonetheless, it was number one for nine weeks, and is regularly among the songs voted Top Rock Song of All Time. The flip side was called (wait for it!) *Revolution*. The double--album released in November, with a totally blank cover as opposed to the elaborate cover of 1967's **Sgt. Pepper**, presented a complete guide to the Beatles' musical styles. Attracting great attention was the seemingly incomprehen--sible eight--minute track called *Revolution No. 9*. Attracting less attention was the fact that the *White Album* was more a collection of individuals, that is, John, Paul, George and Ringo accompanied by a back--up band. Even the outward appearances of group unity were beginning to deteriorate.

Abbey Road   **Parlophone PCS 7088 (LP)**

Recommended Recordings:
The Beatles' denouement: *Get Back, Ballad Of John & Yoko* and **Abbey Road**; John's **Live Peace In Toronto** and *Cold Turkey*; Jackie Lomax: **Is This What You Want?**; Paul's track with Steve Miller; *My Dark Hour*; George's track with Cream: *Badge*; and the one-and-only issuing of the first version of *Across The Universe* on the **No One's Gonna Change Our World** LP.

1969

January. Filming for *Let It Be*.

January 30. Rooftop concert sequence for *Let It Be*.

February 3. Allen Klein asked to be business manager for the Beatles.

February 3. Paul and Steve Miller record *My Dark Hour*.

March 12. Paul marries Linda Eastman.

March 20. John and Yoko get married in Gibralter near Spain.

March 26. John and Yoko Bed--In at the Amsterdam Hilton.

May 30. *Ballad Of John & Yoko* is released, featuring just John and Paul.

June 1. John and Yoko record *Give Peace A Chance*.

July. George records the *Hare Krishna Mantra* with the London Radha Krishna Temple group.

September 5. Allen Klein negotiates new deal for Beatle LPs, sub--stantially increasing royalities.

September 13. John Lennon and his Plastic Ono Band appear at the Toronto Peace Festival, performing live.

September 26. **Abbey Road** released.

October. John to Paul: It's Over! I Want A Divorce!

October. "Paul is Dead" rumors flourish.

October 20. John releases *Cold Turkey*.

November 26. John returns his MBE with a note explaining: "I am returning this MBE in protest against Britain's involvement in the Nigeria--Biafra thing, against our support of America in Vietnam and against *Cold Turkey* slipping down the charts."

December. Harrison tours with Delaney and Bonnie and Friends.

December. The Beatles reject two offers of 1 million pounds for a 13--show tour.

December. Lennon, in an interview with *New Musical Express*, says: "It's Over."

1969

The Beatles broke up for real in 1969, but nobody outside their circle knew it. It almost happened in January during the filming of what would become known as *Let It Be*. As seen in the movie, re--leased the next year, all four were either ignoring or being very snappy with each other. They weren't exactly redefining the word *music* either. After a few months apart, working on projects with other friends, or, in John and Paul's cases, getting married, they reunited for a few months and turned out some of the best music of the late 60's. First came a pair of nearly perfect singles, *Get Back* and *The Ballad Of John & Yoko*, followed by the finely-crafted **Abbey Road** LP, one of the best epitaphs a musical group could ever hope for. John immediately began releasing records on his own, under the catch name Plastic Ono Band. His first release, *Give Peace A Chance*, coming at the start of a new wave of anti--Vietnam War demonstrations, became a virtual anthem. John then put together one of the best pick--up bands in history, flew to Toronto literally on a whim, and staged a live concert for his new obsession, Peace, making him one of the first enemies of the new Nixon administra--tion. Accompanying these activities was more (**Two Virgins** had been the start) of the recorded self--indulgence John & Yoko were going in for. On one level, Apple had a successful year in 1969. Mary Hopkin was doing all right. Billy Preston joined the label, and a new group, Badfinger, was actually a success. Underneath this, however, was the growing realization that Apple was becoming the target for every con artist and freeloader on the face of the earth. Money, as they say, was disappearing like water through a hole in a bucket. Notorious tough guy Allen Klein was brought in at John's request to get Apple's finances in shape. Paul strenuously objected, preferring relatives of his new wife, Linda Eastman. This more than anything else brought the group's split out into the open a few months later.

1970

January 26. John Lennon writes, records and remixes *Instant Karma!* all in one day. It's released the next week.

March 6. *Let It Be/You Know My Name (Look Up The Number)* released.

March 15. Ringo films a TV clip to promote his new **Sentimental Journey** album. He sings the title track.

April 10. Paul McCartney announces he's left the Beatles and, by the way, his first solo album will be in the shops next week.

April 17. McCartney LP released.

April--August. John and Yoko undergo primal therapy treatment.

May 8. The final Beatles LP, **Let It Be**, released.

May 20. London premiere of the *Let It Be* film. No Beatle attends.

June 30--July 1. Ringo's whirlwind recording sessions in Nashville.

June. George works on albums with Billy Preston and Doris Troy, as well as on his own solo disc.

September 25. Ringo's **Beaucoups of Blues** released.

November 27. George's **All Things Must Pass** released.

December 11. John's **John Lennon/Plastic Ono Band** released.

December 30. Paul McCartney starts High Court proceedings to end the Beatles' partnership.

Recommended Recordings: Badfinger: **Magic Christian Music** (including the McCartney hit *Come & Get It*); Doris Troy's superstar LP: **Doris Troy**; George with Derek and The Dominoes on *Tell The Truth*; Ringo on Steve Stills' first solo LP; and the best of the first Beatle solo releases: John's *Instant Karma!* and **John Lennon/Plastic Ono Band**; George's **All Things Must Pass** and Paul's *Maybe I'm Amazed*.

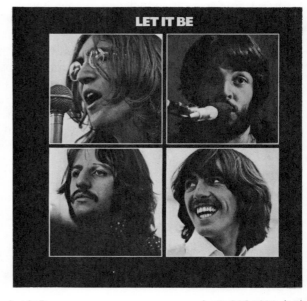

Let It Be   Apple PCS 7096 (LP)

IT'S LIKE YOU
NEVER LEFT

1970

1970 provided an unwanted postscript to the Beatles' career. After a successful single, *Let It Be*, the souped–up, year--old LP of the same name, was released along with the film in May. It was a pretty lousy album all the way around. Just before its release, McCartney finally told the world what John, Paul, George and Ringo had known for sometime: The Beatles were no more. It was a fact hard to accept for some people, as the group was the corner--stone, in feeling if not in fact, to a whole generation. It was this desire to keep them forever, like a child's teddy bear, which no doubt prompted the absurd "Paul Is Dead" reports of the previous year. While many people might have wished the group to remain intact forever, they had been playing together for almost fifteen years, which is a long time for anybody to stick together. Then, all four ex–Beatles released individual albums, to varying degrees of crit-ical acclaim. The least was first. Ringo's **Sentimental Journey** is best forgotten by all concerned. His second LP, **Beaucoups Of Blues**, recorded that summer in Nashville, is at least in the "listenable on a rainy day" category. Next came McCartney's *truly* solo (he played all instruments) LP, **McCartney**. Considered lightweight at the time, it seems more than adequate in retrospect, though no album could have met the high expectations of the public one month after it had learned the Beatles had split. Surprise of the year was George's triple album **All Things Must Pass**. Previously given only passing grades in singing and song writing, at least until **Abbey Road's** *Something* and *Here Comes The Sun*, George's super--star album came as a pleasant surprise. Many of the songs were, no doubt, left over from the days when only one or two Harrison songs got out per year. Once again, though, it was John who captured the most attention. His deeply personal "primal" album, **John Lennon/Plastic Ono Band**, still considered by many to be the best post--Beatle album, took all of John's inner psyches and transformed them into deeply moving lyrics and arresting musicianship. By this time, John had formed a solid partnership with long--time producer, Phil Spector. Already, the never--ending question: "Will the Beatles get back together again?" was becoming a cliche. John soon had a standard reply: "If it hadn't been for the breakup, the world would not have been able to hear all the good music the Beatles have been turning out as individuals."

1971

Recommended Recordings: Ringo's *It Don't Come Easy*; Paul's never-on-an-LP *Oh Woman Oh Why/Another Day*; John's **Imagine** and *Happy Christmas*; and George's **Concert For Bangla Desh**; plus Badfinger's **Straight Up** LP (with tracks produced by George) and the **London Howlin' Wolf Sessions** (with Ringo sittin' in).

Ram   Apple SMAS 3375 (LP)

IT'S LIKE YOU
NEVER LEFT

1971

On the last day of 1970, a proceeding occurred in a London courtroom which would have seemed unthinkable a few years earlier. Paul McCartney sued the Beatles. Ever since the Eastman/Klein split (regarding financial control of Apple) in 1969, the already confusing money situation of John, Paul, George and Ringo as individuals, the Beatles as a group, and the Apple Corps as a business, became incredibly complicated. When the group broke up, it would seem that the easiest thing would be to say: "OK, you take your money, I'll take mine, and we'll call it a day." Naturally, anyone who's familiar with lawyers realizes this is impossible. The only way Paul could get out from under the umbrella of Allen Klein and the Beatle partnership was to sue his three ex--mates. Needless to say, this did nothing to help their already strained relations. Vague, and some not--so--vague, references to the split began turning up in the Beatles' own songs. Ringo pleaded for *rapprochement* in *Early 1970*. Paul got in some digs at John in *Uncle Albert*, while John laid it on the line to Paul in *How Do You Sleep?* This public airing of dirty linen began to resemble the long--running Crosby--Hope feuds of the 30's ("Stay tuned for the next exciting chapter . . . . "). George seemed a bit more removed from all of it, but he did pen perhaps the best comment on it all, the *Sue Me Sue You Blues*, which he gave to Jesse Ed Davis that summer while working on the year's biggest event: The Concert for Bangla Desh.

John was in the depths of his political catch--phrase era, high--lighted (?) by the best forgotten *Power To The People*. His album **Imagine**, however, was much better, and the title cut became one of his most popular songs. Paul, perhaps subconsciously mimicking John, started making records with *his* wife, with only slightly less vicious critical reaction. During the summer he formed his own group, Wings, and announced his intention to soon return to live performing. Surprise of the year was unquestionably Ringo. With the breakup of the Beatles, Ringo, never known for his musical prowess, was expected perhaps to take up his long standing chal--lenge to run a hair--dressing shop. Fooling everybody after two flop LPs, he turned out, with George's help, a hit 45, *It Don't Come Easy*. The legal squabbling over the Beatles' monies dragged out all year. The court appointed a receiver, who froze all Apple assets. All that money they had made was now out of their reach.

Little Woman Love
1851

Little Woman Love/   Apple 1851 (45)
Mary Had A Little Lamb

Recommended Recordings: Paul's *Little Woman Love* (a *great* tune); **David Bromberg** (featuring a co-composition with George, *The Holdup*); Jesse "Ed" Davis' recording of George's *Sue Me Sue You Blues* and Bobby Keys' solo album **Bobby Keys**.

February. Wings' *Give Ireland Back To The Irish* banned on BBC.
February 8. Beatles Fan Club officially closed.
February 9. Wings first live appearance, a concert at the University at Nottingham.
February 14--18. John and Yoko co--host the *Mike Douglas* show for a week. One of John's guests is Chuck Berry, and the two per--form several numbers together.
February 29. John's non--immigrant U.S. visa expires.
March 23. Film of *The Concert For Bangla Desh* opens in New York.
March 25. Ringo is hardly noticed by screaming fans while he films their latest idol, Marc Bolan.
March. Mary Hopkin quits Apple.
April 29. New York mayor John Lindsay asks federal authorities to let John and Yoko stay in the U.S. permanently.
August 30. The "One--To--One" benefit concert by John Lennon, Yoko Ono, the Elephant's Memory Band, and guests.
September 6. John and Yoko on Jerry Lewis Muscular Dystrophy Telethon.
October. Ringo filming *That'll Be The Day*.
December. Wings' *Hi Hi Hi* banned on the BBC.

1972

1972

In many ways 1972 was like a long, bad late–night movie. Aside from such diversionary activities as Richard Nixon's re-election and the Watergate break-in, the four ex-Beatles hit an all-time low in both quantity and quality of their activities. Ringo turned out his oblig-- atory one single a year. George seemed to have vanished from the face of the earth. John, the only ex-Beatle to release an album that year, wasted his and our time with a totally unnecessary LP (double LP yet) **Sometime In New York City**. Oddly enough, the one cut that got him in the most trouble, *Woman Is The Nigger Of The World*, was perhaps the best thing he did all year. More importantly, John had passed the stage of being a political gadfly and was now viewed by the Nixon administration as an actual threat to the coun-- try. Having taken up residence in New York, originating in a search for Yoko's child from a previous marriage, John suddenly found himself in political trouble of the highest caliber when his non-- immigrant visa expired. Using his 1968 British drug arrest as an excuse, John Mitchell and his Justice Department began serious deportation proceedings against Lennon almost the same month as the plumbers were first breaking into the Watergate. In Britain, Paul and Wings suddenly found themselves embroiled in a political brouhaha (of a British nature) when McCartney's mild *Give Ireland Back To The Irish* was deemed unacceptable by the BBC. *Hi Hi Hi*, out in December, was also banned by the BBC, in this case for sup-- posed drug and explicit sex references. McCartney, though, seemed the only one of the four who had a clear idea of what he wanted to do and the best way to do it. Having assembled a back–up band, Paul resisted the temptation to immediately launch a world tour to "prove" his independence. He knew the band wasn't ready and would look sloppy to those expecting the Second Coming. Instead, McCartney took the slow and steady course of beginning at the bot-- tom and working his way up. In this case, the "bottom" was the English university circuit. Appearing suddenly and unannounced, and without expectant trade critics in the audience, the two weeks spent before real live human beings was an invaluable base on which to get Wings ready to really go public. Next came a six--week tour of the European continent. A regular schedule this time, but still no great fan fare.

March. John ordered to leave the U.S. by immigration authorities.

March. Heavily advertised unauthorized Beatle anthology sold over TV and radio, prompting the release of the "official" *Greatest Hits* packages by Apple. George helped in choosing the tracks.

March--July. Ringo records a new LP, including appearances by John, Paul and George.

April 12. London premiere of *That'll Be The Day,* featuring Ringo as Teddy--boy Mike.

April 16. *James Paul McCartney* TV special on ABC TV.

May. Wings embarks on its first scheduled tour of Britain.

June. Allen Klein sues John Lennon for $200,000.

June 29. New York premiere of *Live And Let Die*, featuring title track written by McCartney and performed by Wings.

August 25. Henry McCullough leaves Wings.

August 30. Denny Seiwell leaves Wings.

September 1. Paul, Denny Laine and Linda journey to Lagos to re--cord **Band On The Run.**

October. John and Yoko separate.

October. John's sessions in Los Angeles with Phil Spector for his Oldies LP.

November. Three Beatles sue Allen Klein.

1973

Recommended Recordings: Paul's *The Mess* and *Country Dreamer* (two more excellent McCartney B-sides); Ringo's co-composition for Billy Lawrie, *Rock and Roller*; George's composition *So Sad* (recorded by Alvin Lee and Mylon Le-Fevre); plus Ringo's star-studded **"Ringo"** album and Paul's against-all-odds **Band On The Run** LP.

Mind Games   **Apple SW 3414 (LP)**

1973

George finally released his own version of *Sue Me Sue You Blues* in 1973, but by this time most of the real antagonism among the four had passed. John, George and Ringo finally had a falling out with Allen Klein. Klein sued them, and they sued him. An un-authorized four record *Best of The Beatles* set prompted Apple to put out a different, but equally long *Best Of* set. Later, the closest thing yet to a Beatle reunion occurred in Los Angeles. Ringo, re-turning to making albums, called in almost every friend he knew in the industry. His *Early 1970* hope came true: all three (John, Paul and George) came by to play. Not all at one time, mind you, but almost. The result, the **"Ringo"** LP, was a genuine accomplish-ment, as Ringo overcame what everyone felt were his weaknesses. If he couldn't write great tunes or play anything but the drums, he certainly had some ready and willing friends who could and did, on his behalf. The other three were having their own problems, though. George finally reappeared with a new LP, **Living In The Material World**, which merely seemed to be his equivalent of John's earlier problem; that is, giving in to a current obsession -- in this case, spiritualism – and letting it overshadow and ultimately defeat the music. Nonetheless, it seemed to sell well. John, still enmeshed in his deportation saga, had a falling out with Yoko, beginning over a year of genuine lethargy and depression for him. Lennon's album for that year, **Mind Games**, just seemed like **Imagine** with different words. It was Paul who scored the rebound of the year. Beginning with a weak but much bally-hooed LP, **Red Rose Speedway**, and a very mediocre TV special, Paul hit rock bottom in September when, about to depart to Nigeria to record a new album, two--thirds of his back--up band quit. Somehow, without so much as a pause, he, Linda and Denny Laine recorded **Band On The Run**, which re-ceived both universal critical praise and a top place on the charts. McCartney, who for three years had been pictured as a cute but es-sentially vapid talent, suddenly leapfrogged to the "head of the class" for those who were keeping track of post--Beatle break--up activities.

Goodnight Vienna   **Apple SW 3417 (LP)**

Recommended Recordings: The superb *McGear album (produced by Paul); George's initial offering on Dark Horse, Splinter's **The Place I Love**; Paul's tune for Rod Stewart: *Mine For Me*; three off-beat McCartney instrumentals: *Zoo Gang* (British flip of *Band On The Run*), and two sides of a single by the Country Hams (Wings): *Walking In The Park With Eloise* (written by Paul's dad) and *Bridge On The River Suite*. **Three terrible records to avoid:** John Christie's *4th Of July* (written by Paul and Linda), Adam Faith's *I Survive* (backed by Paul and Linda) and Thronton, Fradkin & Unger's **Pass On This Side** (also backed by Paul and Linda).

1974

January. Jimmy McCulloch and Geoff Britton join Wings.

January. John asks the Queen for a Royal Pardon of his 1968 drug conviction.

February. Paul producing tracks for his brother, Mike McGear.

March. John ejected from the L.A. Troubadour after heckling the Smothers Brothers in their opening night performance.

March--May. John produces an LP for Harry Nilsson, **Pussycats**.

May 25. George forms the Dark Horse label.

Summer. Paul and Wings in Nashville.

Mid June. Paul writes and produces a track for Peggy Lee, *Let's Love*.

July 17. John ordered by the Justice Department to leave the U.S. in sixty days. He hears the news in a cab and jokingly orders the cabbie to drive him to the airport to catch the next plane out.

August. John records **Walls And Bridges** in New York. Elton John joins the sessions. John returns the favor by playing on Elton's *Lucy In The Sky With Diamonds* single. The album, the single (*Whatever Gets You Through The Night*), and Elton's *Lucy* all hit number one.

September. Board of Immigration Appeals orders John to leave the U.S. by September 8. He appeals.

October 8. Lennon and Morris Levy meet at the Club Cavallero in Manhattan. Lennon mentions perhaps putting out his oldies LP as a TV promo.

November 2. George Harrison begins a solo--tour of America.

November 28. John joins Elton John on stage at his Madison Square Garden concert. Backstage, he meets Yoko Ono.

December 13. George and his dad and some touring mates visit the White House.

1974

The first half of 1974 was made up almost solely of echoes. Successful singles were continually peeled off the 1973 albums re-leased by Paul and Ringo. John seemed unable to get out of the mental and musical rut he was in. He got plenty of unwanted publicity by getting into a drunken shouting match at a Los Angeles club. He produced an album for Harry Nilsson, who succeeded in sounding more burned-out than John was acting, and then put out an album of his own, **Walls And Bridges**, which was OK, but nothing more. When they ran out of singles from "**Ringo**", the world's favorite drummer turned out **Goodnight Vienna**, which had prac-tically the same cast of characters but wasn't as inventive. The only real accomplishments came from Paul and George, and even so, these were mostly side-bar actions. Wings turned out two fine singles, but Paul's real gem was the LP (*McGear) he produced and mostly wrote for his brother Mike. Unencumbered by the burden of having to turn out new "Beatle product," Paul loosened up and injected more humor and slicker production tricks than he usually dared on his own albums. George had a very ambitious year, but not a totally successful one. He became the first of the ex--Beatles to tour America, and even showed up at the White House, but the rush to record an album before the tour's commencement, and setting up the tour's logistics, combined to effectively cancel out George's voice by the time the tour actually began. That, George's insistence on a heavy dose of Indian music, and his dogged refusal to showcase much of his Beatle era work, cast a pallor over the tour which never lifted. George's real accomplishment of the year was the successful launch-ing of his own record label, Dark Horse. Apple, by this time, was an empty vessel used only as the means to transmit the Beatles' music until their contract ran out. Like Apple, Dark Horse got off to a fairly good start, and then seemed to stagnate. One of the first groups to record for the label, Splinter, met with a friendly recep-tion. Finally, the removal of Richard Nixon from the presidency marked the beginning of the end of John's immigration problems.

Recommended Recordings:
John's **Rock 'n' Roll** LP plus
his tune *Move Over Ms. L* (the
flip of *Stand By Me* and also
done by Keith Moon on his
Two Sides Of The Moon LP):
I Saw Her Standing There (the

Venus And Mars   Capitol SMAS 11419 (LP)

January. A High Court in London finally dissolves the Beatles.
January. John and Yoko reunited.
February. Unauthorized **Roots** LP of Lennon oldies appears as a
TV promo.
February 17. Apple rush–releases **Rock 'n' Roll** LP of Lennon
oldies.
February. Paul and Wings in New Orleans.
March 1. John appears on the Grammy Awards presentation with
Paul Simon. John and Yoko also appear in public for the first time
since their reconciliation.
March. Joe English joins Wings, replacing Geoff Britton.
May. Paul releases **Venus And Mars**, the first album in a new, in–
dependent deal with Capitol records.
September. Wings begins a year–long world tour.
October 7. U.S. Court of Appeals overturns the order to deport
John.
October 9. Sean Ono Lennon is born on John's birthday.
October 24. John releases his **Shaved Fish** collection of greatest
hits to celebrate.
November 20. Ringo releases his greatest hits collection **Blast From
Your Past.**
December 8. George's *This Guitar* released as a single. It becomes
the first Beatle solo single to fail to make the U.S. charts.

1975

Extra Texture   Apple SW 3420 (LP)

flip of Elton John's *Philadelphia Freedom*), featuring John
and Elton John live at Madison Square Garden; Monty
Python's *Lumberjack Song*
produced by George; and also
George's own *This Guitar* (lost
on **Extra Texture**).

1975

1975 was a great year for transitions. It marked the end of many phases of the Beatles' careers and the starts of others. The Beatles' long--time contract with Capitol Records expired at year's end, and they began to fend for themselves. Individual *Best Of* albums (**Shaved Fish, Blast From Your Past**) began to appear. The Apple legal log–jam began to break up, and the company was ef--fectively dissolved. John, with some nudging from a bootlegger, finally released his long--dreamed–of oldies LP. John and Yoko re-united, and at the end of the year, literally as a birthday present, Yoko successfully delivered a son, Sean. To celebrate, John released the **Shaved Fish** collection of his hits, then he, Yoko and his new son virtually dropped from public sight. George completed his require-ments to Capitol Records with **Extra Texture**, a slightly slapdash affair, and signed up a number of new artists to his Dark Horse label. Ringo milked a few more singles from his 1974 album, and actually set up *his* own record company, Ring O' Records, which has yet to be truly heard from. Paul was the first of the four to get completely out from the Apple umbrella, signing an independent deal with Capitol Records. He finally worked up the nerve to record a follow--up LP to **Band On The Run**: **Venus And Mars**. While not a work for the ages, it was quite all right, thank you, and served as a launching pad to the culmination of his four--year steady incubation method of growing a new band. In September, Paul and Wings began an unprecedented, mammoth world–wide tour which, in effect, lasted a full twelve months. The 1975 segment, still modeled on the "warm–up" theory, began in Britain, moved to the "outer suburbs" (Australia) with sights set, at year's end, for the European continent and, finally, everybody's promised land, America.

The Best of
George Harrison

Capitol ST 11578 (LP)

The Best of
George Harrison

EMI PAS 10011 (LP)

1976

January 5. Mal Evans dies.
February 6. Beatles' contract with EMI expires.
February. George moves over to his own Dark Horse label.
February. Promoter Bill Sargent offers the Beatles $50 million for a single reunion concert.
March 5. EMI releases *Yesterday* as a single in Britain, spear--heading the reservice on all 22 old Beatle singles. *Yesterday* hits top ten; all 23 discs hit the British top one hundred.
March 10. In a ceremony in Amsterdam, Ringo signs with Atlantic/ Polydor records.
April. John wins the court battle against Morris Levy.
May. *Beatles Monthly Magazine* resumes publication in Britain.
May 3--June 23. Paul McCartney tours the U.S. with Wings.
June 7. Capitol releases the **Rock 'n' Roll Music** repackage LP.
June. Two suits in the ABKCO--Beatles controversy settled.
July 27. John Lennon receives his green card.
July. *Got To Get You Into My Life*, released as a single, hits top ten in the U.S.
August. George and Ringo fail in their attempt to block the release of David Wigg's album of Beatle interviews.
August. Paul releases **Band On The Run** in the U.S.S.R. on the Melodiya label.
September 11. George found guilty in the *My Sweet Lord* suit.
November. George moves Dark Horse from A&M to Warner Brothers.

Recommended Recordings: George's very upbeat **33 1/3** LP; Paul's mammoth **Wings Over America** 3—LP set; Ringo's very own composition *Band of Steel* on Guthrie Thomas' **Lies And Alibis** LP (Ringo even joins in on vocals); Wings' excellent song *Beware My Love*.

1976

The Beatles became nostalgia 1976. After all, they had been world–wide stars for six years, and now six more years had passed since their break–up. In January, they lost control of their old re-cordings and the process began which will lead, no doubt, to (soon enough) late–night television commercials with perhaps Ringo say-ing: "Hi! Remember me! I'm a famous Pop Star of the Sixties! Now you can get, on one disc . . . " It began in Britain in March. *Yesterday*, a song never released on a single over there, was treated like a new release and used to spearhead a promotion to reservice the twenty–two older Beatle singles. To the surprise of almost every-body, not only did *Yesterday* do well, but a mild wave of Beatle-mania resurfaced with *all* twenty–two oldies crashing into the top 100. Perhaps it was a whole new generation to whom the Beatles had been merely a name. Or, perhaps, a resurgence of feeling by the original Beatle fans for the group that had altered the world of music over a decade before. What difference did it make? The records were selling. A new double *Best Of* album, **Rock'n'Roll Music**, came out in America in June, with very confusing artwork. The al-bum looked like nothing so much as a Chuck Berry retrospective, even down to the heavy use of coca--cola imagery. It all seemed to say that the 50's and 60's were now interchangeable, all one big *Happy Days* bucolic memory. In truth, of course, the changes that came with the Beatles' arrival were in many ways the complete antithesis of the late 50's mentality. Such philosophical meander-ings aside, the floodgate on Beatle memorabilia was opened. Their 1961 recordings with Tony Sheridan were reissued in Britain. Three successful singles were pulled from the old Beatle catalogue. Britain finally got around to releasing the **Magical Mystery Tour** album, which had been a mere double EP back in 1967. Material only secondarily relating to the Beatles came out using their name. David Wigg, a British music writer, released a double LP set, after some minor legal obstructions, of taped highlights of interviews he had conducted with the four individual Beatles between 1968 and 1973.

41

Lou Reizer, who brought us the orchestrated version of **Tommy**, came out with the slightly daft notion of marrying World War II newsreel clips to cover versions of Beatle songs by well--known rock artists, calling it (surprise!) *All This And World War II*. It even seem--ed as if the long–ignored tape of the Beatles performing live in Hamburg would finally reach the public.

For being the components of a supposedly dead giant, most of the former members of the Beatles were carrying on energetically on their own, as if to specifically refute their image as denizens of the past. Paul and Wings seemed to be on the cover of every weekly magazine. Only taking a two month break to record their new LP, **At The Speed Of Sound**, the group kept sharpening their road per--formance (becoming one of the most elaborate in rock history) and after a swing through Europe, finally challenged, and conquered, the American continent. Performing in 21 cities over 52 days, Paul and Wings completely charmed America and finally won his long--sought crown as one of the major components of 70's rock, independent of his past. After a brief rest, they made a final sweep through Europe, then concluding their year--long world tour where it began, in London. As a capstone to the whole mammoth project, an appro--priately mammoth three record set, **Wings Over America**, came out just in time for Christmas. Back in 1975, Paul's publishing company acquired rights to the Buddy Holly songbook. During the summer, Paul and Denny Laine began working on an album of Buddy Holly songs. Delays kept popping up, and only a single from these sessions came out in 1976, with the album delayed until the next year. Even Jimmy McCulloch formed his own side bar group, White Line, and put out a single.

George managed to weather numerous setbacks in 1976 and somehow came out of it all on top. Dragged into court and even--tually found "sort--of" guilty on the old *My Sweet Lord/He's So Fine* plagarism case, Harrison turned the whole event into a hit song, *This Song*. It was virtually hopping from one courtroom to another all year for George, with A&M records, the distributor of his new home, Dark Horse Records, suing him for delay of delivery of his first album. He had been sick, George explained, but it could be that A&M wanted to unload the label which, aside from Harrison, didn't seem to be going anywhere. An out--of--court settlement ensued and Warner Brothers more--than--happily took over auspices of Dark Horse. George's album, 33 1/3 (both his age during its re--cording and the speed of a turntable) was his most upbeat release in years, revealing a lightness of touch long hoped for. George even broke his reclusive habits and made a nationwide publicity tour to push the new LP, highlighted by an appearance with Paul Simon on *NBC's Saturday Night* in November.

You may, by now, be detecting the trend that the *real* stars in Beatle affairs of 1976 were the lawyers. The various suits and counter--suits with Allen Klein were finally cleared up, after Kissenger--like diplomacy by Yoko Ono. The Apple money, frozen for so many years, now seemed free to flow. John also spent more than his share of days in court. A messy and complicated case dating back to the supposed copying of Chuck Berry's *You Can't Catch Me* in **Abbey Road's** *Come Together*, which was all tied up in the **Rock 'n' Roll** LP and its bootleg companion, **Roots**, was finally disposed of. John, amazingly, won the case and actually received money. More impor--tantly, the equally interminable deportation proceedings against John were closed down and, after having his character attested to, he received the long sought--after green card, which is actually blue, but allows him permanent residence status in the U.S., regardless of color. John then retired to enjoy parenthood and consider what he wants to do next. His contract with Capitol has, of course, expired, and he is, as of this writing, a free agent. His only recording work in 1976 was contributing a song and some back--up musicianship to Ringo's new LP.

Ringo, who signed with Polydor (worldwide, except the U.S. and Canada) and Atlantic (in the United States and Canada) came out with a traditional super--star--studded LP called **Rotogravure**. It just didn't seem to catch on, though. The first single, *A Dose Of Rock 'n' Roll*, did all right, but the follow--up, *Hey Baby*, barely made its way onto the charts at all. As usual, Ringo spent a lot of time working on sessions with friends, helping out (or at least hang--ing around) Harry Nilsson, Lynsey de Paul, Vera Lynn, Guthrie Thomas, Manhattan Transfer and Kinky Friedman.

In this year of Beatle revival, with many diverse people finally cashing in on the Beatles' legacy, it was more than tragic that Mal Evans, long time road manager and go--fer, who more than anybody else probably deserved some fame, died in January just before finishing his book of memoirs.

501.   JAN 5, 1976 (US) Ode 66118
by Tom Scott Prod: Tom Scott and Hank Cicalo
B: *APPOLONIA (FOXTRATA)*—Tom Scott—*3:59*
   George: Slide Guitar
A: *(uptown and country)*

502.   JAN 9, 1976 (UK) Apple R 6011
by Ringo Starr Prod: Richard Perry
A: *OH MY MY*—-Starkey—Vini Poncia—*3:19*
B: *NO NO SONG*—-Hoyt Axton—David P. Jackson—*2:30*

503.   FEB 6, 1976 (US) Dark Horse SP 22007 (LP)
MAR 19, 1976 (UK) Dark Horse AMLH 22007 (LP)
by Ravi Shankar
RAVI SHANKAR'S MUSIC FESTIVAL FROM INDIA Prod:
   George Harrison
side one
   Vandana—Ravi Shankar—*2:35*
   Dhamar—Ravi Shankar—*5:20*
   Tarana—Ravi Shankar—*3:50*
   Chaturang—Ravi Shankar—*2:00*
   Raga Jait—Ravi Shankar—*9:41*
side two
   Kajri—Ravi Shankar—*4:45*
   Bhajan—Ravi Shankar—*3:50*
   Naderdani—Ravi Shankar—*4:40*
   Dehati—-Ravi Shankar—*10:04*
Musicians performing on the Ravi Shankar album listed above include
Ravi Shankar:*Conductor, Composer and Arranger;* Lakshmi Shankar:
Lead Vocals and Swaramandal; Vijji Shankar and Kamala:*Vocals and
Tanpura;* Alarakha:*Tabla;* Kartick Kumar:*Sitar;* L. Subramaniam:
Violin; Sultan Khan:*Sarangi;* Kamlesh Maitra:*Sarod, Madal, Tabla
Tarang, Duggi Tarang, and Ek Tara;* Satyadev Pawar:*Violin;* Harihar
Rao:*Kartal, Manuira, Dholak, Vocals and Gub Gubi;* T.V. Gopalkrish-
nan:*Mridagam, Khanjira and Vocals;* Gopal Kishan Veenkar:*Vichitra
Veena and Vocals;* Anantlal:*Shahnai;* Rijram Desad:*Pakahwaj, Nal, Mag-
ade, Madal Tarang, Huduk and Duff;* Shivkumar Sharma:*Santoor, Ka-
noon and Vocals;* and Hariprasad Chaurasia:*Flutes.*

504.   FEB 9, 1976 (US) Blue Sky PZ 33944 (LP)
MAR 12, 1976 (UK) Blue Sky 69230 (LP)
Recorded live in California 1975
by Johnny Winter
JOHNNY WINTER CAPTURED LIVE Prod: Johnny Winter
side one
   cut three: *Rock 'n' Roll People*—-Lennon—*5:39*

Musicians performing on the Johnny Winter album listed above include Johnny Winter:*Vocals, Guitar, Slide Guitar;* Randy Jo Hobbs:*Bass, Background Vocals;* Richard Hughes:*Drums;* and Floyd Radford:*Guitar.*

505. FEB 20, 1976 (UK) EMI 2413
     by Vera Lynn Prod: Lynsey de Paul
    *A: Don't You Remember When—Lynsey de Paul—Barry Blue—
        5:00* Ringo: Tambourine
    B: (that old feeling)

506. MAR   5, 1976 (UK) Parlophone R 6013
     by The Beatles Prod: George Martin
    A: YESTERDAY—2:04
    B: I SHOULD HAVE KNOWN BETTER—2:42

507. MAR 22, 1976 (US) A&M SP 3528 (2 LPs)
     by Gary Wright Prod: Gary Wright
      George (as George O'Hara): Guitar, Slide Guitar
    THAT WAS ONLY YESTERDAY
    side one
      cut five: *TWO FACED MAN—Gary Wright—3:40*
    side two
      cut one: *LOVE TO SURVIVE—Gary Wright—4:48*
      cut five: *I CAN'T SEE THE REASON—Gary Wright—4:24*
    side three
      cut three: *FASCINATING THINGS—Gary Wright—5:05*
    side four
      cut two: *STAND FOR OUR RIGHTS—Gary Wright—3:32*

508 MAR 25, 1976 (US) Capitol SW 11525 (LP)
    MAR 26, 1976 (UK) Capitol PAS 10010 (LP)
    Recorded: January and February 1976
    by Wings
    WINGS AT THE SPEED OF SOUND Prod: Paul McCartney
    side one
    Let 'Em In—McCartney—5:08
    The Note You Never Wrote—McCartney—4:18
    She's My Baby—McCartney—3:08
    Beware My Love—McCartney—6:05
    Wino Junko—Jimmy McCulloch—Colin Allen—5:15
    side two
    Silly Love Songs—McCartney—5:54
    Cook Of The House—McCartney—2:37
    Time To Hide—Denny Laine—4:33
    Must Do Something About It—McCartney—3:22

San Ferry Anne—McCartney—*2:02*
Warm and Beautiful—McCartney—*3:08*

Musicians performing on the Wings album listed above include Paul McCartney:*Vocals, Bass, Piano, Acoustic Guitar, Guitar;* Linda McCartney: *Vocals, Keyboards;* Denny Laine:*Vocals, Electric Guitar, Acoustic Guitar, Piano, Bass;* Jimmy McCulloch:*Electric Guitar, Vocals, Acoustic Guitar, Bass;* Joe English:*Drums, Vocals.* Paul McCartney:All *Lead Vocals* except *The Note You Never Wrote* and *Time To Hide* (Denny), *Wino Junko* (Jimmy), *Must Do Something About It* (Joe), and *Cook Of The House* (Linda). Oddities:Paul plays *Drums* on *Must Do Something About It*, and plays the *Acoustic Bass* used by Bill Black on *Heartbreak Hotel* on *Cook Of The House.* The album's Horn Section includes:Tony Dorsey:*Trombone;* Howie Casey:*Saxophone;* Steve Howard:*Trumpet, Flugelhorn;* and Thadeus Richard:*Saxophones, Clarinet, Flute.*

509. APR 1, 1976 (US) Capitol 4256
APR 30, 1976 (UK) Capitol R 6014
by Wings Prod: Paul McCartney
A: *SILLY LOVE SONGS*—McCartney—*5:54*
B: *COOK OF THE HOUSE*—McCartney—*2:37*

510. APR 29, 1976 (US) Mercury SRM 2-7507 (2 LPs)
JUN 18, 1977 (UK) Mercury 6643 030 (2 LPs)
by Rod Stewart Prod: Rod Stewart
BEST OF ROD STEWART
side four
cut five: *MINE FOR ME*—McCartney—*4:02*

511. MAY 3, 1976 (US) Capitol ST 11519 (LP)
Recorded: February 1976
by Guthrie Thomas
Ringo: Drums and † Vocal
LIES AND ALIBIS
side one
cut two: *Good Days Are Rollin' In*—Guthrie Thomas—*3:24*
†cut three: *Band Of Steel*—Starkey—*5:20*
side two
cut five: *Ramblin' Cocaine Blues*—Luke Jordan—Guthrie Thomas—*4:42*

Musicians performing on the Guthrie Thomas songs listed above include on *Good Days Are Rollin' In* Guthrie Thomas:*Acoustic Lead and Vocal;* Ringo Starr and Jim Keltner:*Drums;* Lyle Ritz:*Bass;* Roger Johnson: *Electric Guitar;* Marc Edelsen:*Acoustic Rhythm;* David Foster:*Piano;* David Paich:*Organ;* and *Harmony Vocals* by Mark Dawson, Brooks Cropper and Renee Armand;
on *Band Of Steel* Guthrie Thomas, Ringo Starr, Steve Cropper and Lee Montgomery:*Vocals;* Guthrie Thomas:*Acoustic Guitar;* Ringo Starr and Jim Keltner:*Drums;* Lyle Ritz:*Bass;* John Hartford:*Fiddle;* David

Paich:*Piano*; Tom Brumley:*Pedal Steel*; and Roger Johnson:*Electric Guitar*;

on *Ramblin' Cocaine Blues* Guthrie Thomas:*Acoustic Guitar and Vocals*; Ringo Starr and Jim Keltner:*Drums*; Lyle Ritz:*Bass*; David Foster: *Piano*; David Paich:*Organ*; John Hartford:*Fiddle*; Roger Johnson: *Electric Guitar*; and *Singers* Lee Montgomery, Mark Dawson, Nicolette Larson, Bill Harring, David Jackson, Denny Brooks and Ginny Vick.

512. MAY 21, 1976 (UK) RCA RS 1055 (LP)
MAY 31, 1976 (UK) RCA APL 1–1732 (LP)
by David Bowie Prod: David Bowie and Harry Maslin
CHANGESONEBOWIE .
side two
  cut four: *FAME*—Lennon—David Bowie—Luther Andross—*4:12*

513. MAY 31, 1976 (US) Capitol 4274
by The Beatles Prod: George Martin
A: GOT TO GET YOU INTO MY LIFE—2:31
B: HELTER SKELTER—4:30

514. JUN 4, 1976 (UK) Contour CN 2007 (LP)
by Tony Sheridan and The Beatles, and †The Beatles Prod: Bert Kaempfert (Additional cuts by %Tony Sheridan and the Beat Brothers)
THE BEATLES FEATURING TONY SHERIDAN
side one
  †AIN'T SHE SWEET—Jack Yellen—Milton Ager—*2:12*
  †CRY FOR A SHADOW—Lennon—Harrison—*2:22*
  %(let's dance)
  MY BONNIE—Charles Pratt—*2:06*
  TAKE OUT SOME INSURANCE ON ME, BABY—Charles Singleton—Waldenese Hall—*2:52*
  %(what'd i say)
side two
  SWEET GEORGIA BROWN—Ben Bernie—Maceo Pinkard—Kenneth Casey—*2:03*
  THE SAINTS—P.D.—*3:19*
  %(ruby baby)
  WHY—Tony Sheridan—Bill Crompton—*2:55*
  NOBODY'S CHILD—Mel Foree—Cy Coben—*3:52*
  %(ya ya)

515. JUN 7, 1976 (US) Capitol SKBO 11537 (2 LPs)
JUN 11, 1976 (UK) Parlophone PCSP 719 (2 LPs)
by The Beatles

ROCK 'N' ROLL MUSIC   Prod: George Martin except † George Martin (January 1969) and Phil Spector (March 1970)

side one
TWIST AND SHOUT—Bert Russell—Phil Medley—*2:32*
I SAW HER STANDING THERE—*2:50*
YOU CAN'T DO THAT—*2:33*
I WANNA BE YOUR MAN—*1:59*
I CALL YOUR NAME—*2:02*
BOYS—Luther Dixon—Wes Farrell—*2:24*
LONG TALL SALLY—Enotris Johnson—Richard Penniman—Robert Blackwell—*1:58*

side two
ROCK AND ROLL MUSIC—Chuck Berry—*2:02*
SLOW DOWN—Larry Williams—*2:54*
MEDLEY: 2:30
  KANSAS CITY—Jerry Leiber—Mike Stoller—*1:21*
  HEY!-HEY!-HEY!-HEY!—Richard Penniman—*1:18*
MONEY (THAT'S WHAT I WANT)—Berry Gordy—Janie Bradford—*2:47*
BAD BOY—Larry Williams—*2:17*
MATCHBOX—Carl Perkins—*1:37*
ROLL OVER BEETHOVEN—Chuck Berry—*2:44*

side three
DIZZY MISS LIZZIE—Larry Williams—*2:51*
ANY TIME AT ALL—*2:10*
DRIVE MY CAR—*2:25*
EVERYBODY'S TRYING TO BE MY BABY—Carl Perkins—*2:24*
THE NIGHT BEFORE—*2:33*
I'M DOWN—*2:30*
REVOLUTION—*3:22*

side four
BACK IN THE U.S.S.R.—*2:45*
HELTER SKELTER—*4:30*
TAXMAN—Harrison—*2:36*
GOT TO GET YOU INTO MY LIFE—*2:31*
HEY BULLDOG—*3:09*
BIRTHDAY—*2:40*
†*GET BACK (version two)*—*3:09*

516. JUN 25, 1976 (UK) Parlophone R 6016
by The Beatles Prod: George Martin
A: BACK IN THE U.S.S.R.—*2:45*
B: TWIST AND SHOUT—Bert Russell—Phil Medley—*2:32*

517.   JUN 28, 1976 (US) Capitol 4293
         JUL 23, 1976 (UK) Capitol R 6015
         by Wings Prod: Paul McCartney
         A: LET 'EM IN—McCartney—*5:08*
         B: BEWARE MY LOVE—McCartney—*6:05*

518.   JUL 6, 1976 (US) Shelter 62001
         by Larry Hosford Prod: Dino Airali and Larry Hosford
         A: Wishing I Could—Larry Hosford—*3:14*
            George: Harmony Vocals
         B: (nobody remembers the losers)

519.   JUL 30, 1976 (UK) Polydor 2683 068 (2 LPs)
         by The Beatles; Interviews Conducted and Edited by David
            Wigg (Incidental instrumental cuts produced and conduct–
            ed by Martyn Ford)
         **THE BEATLES TAPES FROM THE DAVID WIGG INTER–
         VIEWS**
         side one: John Lennon with Yoko Ono
         Interview: June 1969—*3:26*
         (Give Peace A Chance)
         Interview: June 1969—*8:41*
         (Imagine)
         Interview: June 1969—*8:12*
         (Come Together)
         Interview: October 1971—*9:16*
         side two: Paul McCartney
         Interview: March 1970—*1:25*
         (Because)
         Interview: March 1970—*10:21*
         (Yesterday)
         Interview: March 1970—*1:33*
         side three: George Harrison
         Interview: September 1969—*14:14*
         (Here Comes The Sun)
         Interview: September 1969—*5:31*
         (Something)
         side four: Ringo Starr
         Interview: December 1968—*3:23*
         Interview: July 1970—*6:32*
         Interview: December 1973—*4:40*
         (Octopus's Garden)
         Interview: December 1973—*3:37*
         (Yellow Submarine)

520. AUG 2, 1976 (US) Shelter 52003 (LP)
by Larry Hosford
CROSSWORDS Prod: Dino Airali and Larry Hosford
side one
  cut three: *Direct Me—Larry Hosford—3:30*
  George: Slide Guitar
  cut five: *Wishing I Could—Larry Hosford—3:14*
  George: Harmony Vocals
Musicians performing on the Larry Hosford cuts listed above include
on *Direct Me* Larry Hosford:*Vocal*; Doug Haywood and Dino Airali:
Harmony Vocals; George Harrison:*Slide Guitar*; Leon Russell:*Piano
and Vibes*; Frank Reckard:*Acoustic Guitar*; and the "Fly By Night"
section of Gary Roda:*Pedal Steel Guitar*; Duane Sousa:*Bass*; Pat
Hubbard:*Piano*; Ann Hughes:*Flute*; and Jim Norris:*Drums*;
on *Wishing I Could* Larry Hosford:*Lead Vocal*; George Harrison and
Leon Russell:*Harmony Vocals*; Jerry Miller:*Acoustic Guitar*; Tom
Scribner:*"The Lost Sound Of The Musical Saw"*; Jeff Gylkinson:
Harmonica; and the "Owens A Team" section of Harold Bradley and
Billy Sanford:*Acoustic Guitar*; Bob Moore:*Bass*; and Buddy Harman:
Drums.

521. AUG 27, 1976 (UK) Atlantic K 50291 (LP)
AUG 30, 1976 (US) Atlantic SD 18183 (LP)
by Manhattan Transfer
  Ringo: Drums
COMING OUT Prod: Richard Perry
side one
  cut two: *Ziny Lou—Johnny Moore—Eddie Smith—2:50*
side two
  cut two: *S.O.S.—Gerry Shury—Phillip Swern—3:10*
Musicians performing on the Manhattan Transfer cuts listed above
include on *S.O.S.* Ringo Starr and Jim Keltner:*Drums*; Clarence
MacDonald:*Piano*; Andy Muson:*Bass*; Ira Newbom:*Guitar*; and
Jackie Kelso:*Tenor Sax Solo;*
on *Zindy Lou* Ringo Starr and Jim Keltner:*Drums;*Mac Rebennack:
*Piano;*Andy Muson:*Bass*; Ira Newbom:*Guitar*; and Doug Throngren:
Percussion. Vocals are by the members of Manhattan Transfer.

522. SEP 3, 1976 (UK) EMI 2523
OCT 4, 1976 (US) Capitol 4340
by Denny Laine Prod: Paul McCartney
A: medley: 2:17
      It's So Easy—Buddy Holly—Norman Petty
      Listen To Me—Charles Hardin—Norman Petty
  B: I'm Lookin' For Someone To Love—Buddy Holly—Norman
    Petty—3:57

523. SEP 10, 1976 (UK) RCA MAXI 2733
by Harry Nilsson Prod: Harry Nilsson
side one
(without you)
side two
(everybody's talkin')
KOJAK COLUMBO—Harry Nilsson—*3:23*
Ringo: Drums

524. SEP 17, 1976 (UK) Polydor 2382 040 (LP)
SEP 27, 1976 (US) Atlantic SD 18193 (LP)
Recorded: April–May 1976
by Ringo Starr
RINGO'S ROTOGRAVURE Prod: Arif Mardin
side one
A Dose Of Rock 'n' Roll—Carl Grossman—*3:24*
Hey Baby—Bruce Channel—Margaret Cobb—*3:10*
Pure Gold—McCartney—*3:13*
Cryin'—Starkey—Vini Poncia—*3:17*
You Don't Know Me At All—Dave Jordan—*3:15*
side two
Cookin' (In The Kitchen Of Love)—Lennon—*3:37*
I'll Still Love You—Harrison—*2:56*
This Be Called A Song—Eric Clapton—*3:13*
Las Brisas—Starkey—Nancy Andrews—*3:33*
Lady Gaye—Starkey—Vini Poncia—Clifford T. Ward—*2:56*
Spooky Weirdness—*1:25*

Musicians performing on the Ringo Starr album listed above include
Ringo on *Vocals and Drums*, joined by Jim Keltner on *Drums* for every
song except *Las Brisas*. Personnel for the individual tracks include:
on *A Dose Of Rock 'n' Roll* Peter Frampton, Danny Kortchmar and
Jesse Ed Davis:*Guitars*; Klaus Voorman:*Bass*; Mac Rebennack:*Keyboards*; Melissa Manchester, Duitch Helmer, Joe Bean and Vini Poncia:
Background Vocals; and a Horn Section of Randy Brecker and Alan
Rubin:*Trumpets*; Michael Brecker and George Young:*Tenor Sax*;
and Lewis Delgatto:*Baritone Sax*;
on *Hey Baby* Lon Van Eaton:*Guitar*; Cooker Lo Presti:*Bass*; John
Jarvis:*Keyboards*; The Mad Mauries:*Background Vocals & Claps*;
and the same Horn Section as in *A Dose Of Rock 'n' Roll*;
on *Pure Gold* Ringo and Vini Poncia:*Vocals*; Lon Van Eaton:*Guitar*;
Klaus Voorman:*Bass*; Jane Getz and John Jarvis:*Keyboards*; George
Devens:*Congas*; Paul and Linda McCartney:*Background Vocals*; and
Strings by Gene Orloff;
on *Cryin'* Lon Van Eaton:*Guitar*; Cooker Lo Presti:*Bass*; John Jarvis:
Piano; Sneaky Pete:*Pedal Steel* and Arif Mardin:*Electric Piano*;
on *You Don't Know Me At All* Lon Van Eaton:*Guitar*; Cooker Lo
Presti:*Bass*; John Jarvis:*Keyboards*; Duitch Helmer and Vini Poncia:

Background Vocals; and *Strings* by Gene Orloff;
on *Cookin' (In The Kitchen Of Love)* Mac Rebennack:*Guitar and Organ*; Danny Kortchmar:*Guitar*; Will Lee:*Bass*; John Lennon:*Piano*; King Errisson:*Percussion*; and Melissa Manchester and Duitch Helmer: *Background Vocals*;
on *I'll Still Love You* Lon Van Eaton:*Guitar*; Klaus Voorman:*Bass*; Jane Getz:*Piano*; David Lasley:*Background Vocals*; and *Strings* by Gene Orloff;
on *This Be Called A Song* Eric Clapton and Lon Van Eaton:*Guitars*; Klaus Voorman:*Bass*; Jane Getz:*Piano*; Robert Greenidge:*Steel Drums*; and Melissa Manchester, Vini Poncia and Joe Bean:*Background Vocals*;
on *Las Brisas* it's just Ringo *(Maracas)* and Vini Poncia on *Vocals*, joined by the Los Galleros Mariachi Band;
on *Lady Gaye* Danny Kortchmar and Jesse Ed Davis:*Guitars*; Klaus Voorman:*Bass*; Mac Rebennack:*Keyboards*; George Devens:*Marimba*; Harry Nilsson and David Lasley:*Background Vocals*; and a Horn Section of Michael Brecker and Lou Marini:*Tenor Sax* and Lewis Delgatto:*Baritone Sax*;
and *Spooky Weirdness* is merely a collage of extraneous sounds and voices.

525.   SEP 20, 1976 (US) Atlantic 45--3361
OCT 15, 1976 (UK) Polydor 2001 694
by Ringo Starr Prod: Arif Mardin
A: A Dose Of Rock 'n' Roll--Carl Grossman---*3:24*
B: Cryin'--Starkey--Vini Poncia--*3:17*

526.   OCT   1, 1976 (US) Shelter SRL 52007 (LP)
DEC   3, 1976 (UK) Shelter ISA 5013 (LP)
by Leon Russell
  Ringo: Drums
BEST OF LEON Prod: Denny Cordell and Leon Russell
side one
    cut two: *DELTA LADY*--Leon Russell---*4:00*
    cut five: *SHOOT OUT ON THE PLANTATION*--Leon Russell--*3:10*

527.   OCTOBER 1976 (JAPAN) Dark Horse CM 2006
by Splinter Prod: George Harrison and Tom Scott
A: Lonely Man (in Japanese)--M. Nakamura--Robert J. Purvis--Mal Evans--*4:15*
B: LONELY MAN--Robert J. Purvis--Mal Evans--*4:15*

528.   OCT 15, 1976 (UK) EMI 2546
by Billy J. Kramer with The Dakotas Prod: George Martin
B: BAD TO ME--L-McC---*2:18*
A: (little children)

52

529. OCT 25, 1976 (US) 20th Century 2T–522 (2 LPs)
Reissued as 20th Century 2T–540 on June 16, 1977:
The Songs of John Lennon and Paul McCartney Performed by The
World's Greatest Rock Artists
NOV 5, 1976 (UK) Riva RVLP 2 (2 LPs)
by Various Artists
ALL THIS AND WORLD WAR II
side one
  cut two: *LUCY IN THE SKY WITH DIAMONDS*–L-McC–
  6:11
    by Elton John Prod: Gus Dudgeon
    John: Guitars and Backing Vocal

530. NOV 5, 1976 (UK) Charisma MP 001 (2 45s)
by Monty Python Prod: George Harrison
PYTHON ON SONG
record one
*A: LUMBERJACK SONG—Monty Python–3:17
B: (spam song)
record two
A: (bruce's song)
B: (eric the half–a–bee)

531. NOV 5, 1976 (US) Epic PE 34304 (LP)
FEB 25, 1977 (UK) Epic EPC 81640 (LP)
by Kinky Friedman Prod: Kinky Friedman and Huey P.
  Meaux
LASSO FROM EL PASO
side two
  cut two: *Men's Room, L.A.—Buck Fowler–2:10*
    Ringo: The Voice of Jesus

532. NOV 8, 1976 (US) Capitol 4347
by The Beatles Prod: George Martin
A: OB–LA–DI, OB–LA–DA–3:10
B: JULIA–2:57

533. NOV 8, 1976 (US) Capitol ST 11578 (LP)
NOV 20, 1976 (UK) Parlophone PAS 10011 (LP)
by The Beatles (side one) and George Harrison (side two)
THE BEST OF GEORGE HARRISON Prod: George Martin
  except † George Harrison, %George Harrison and Phil
  Spector, $ George Martin (January 1969) and Phil Spector
  (March 1970)
side one: The Beatles
  SOMETHING—Harrison–2:59
  IF I NEEDED SOMEONE—Harrison–2:19

HERE COMES THE SUN—Harrison—*3:04*
TAXMAN—Harrison—*2:36*
THINK FOR YOURSELF—Harrison—*2:16*
$FOR YOU BLUE—Harrison—*2:33*
WHILE MY GUITAR GENTLY WEEPS—Harrison—*4:46*
side two: George Harrison
%MY SWEET LORD—Harrison—*4:39*
†GIVE ME LOVE (GIVE ME PEACE ON EARTH)—Harrison—
    3:32
† YOU—Harrison—*3:40*
%BANGLA DESH—Harrison—*3:52*
†DARK HORSE—Harrison—*3:50*
%WHAT IS LIFE—Harrison—*4:18*

533a. NOV 19, 1976 (UK) Parlophone PCTC 255 (LP)
       by The Beatles
       MAGICAL MYSTERY TOUR Prod: George Martin
       side one: Songs from the film *Magical Mystery Tour*
       MAGICAL MYSTERY TOUR—*2:48*
       THE FOOL ON THE HILL—*3:00*
       FLYING—Lennon—McCartney—Harrison—Starkey—*2:16*
       BLUE JAY WAY—Harrison—*3:50*
       YOUR MOTHER SHOULD KNOW—*2:33*
       I AM THE WALRUS—*4:35*
       side two
       HELLO GOODBYE—*3:24*
       STRAWBERRY FIELDS FOREVER—*4:05*
       PENNY LANE—*3:00*
       BABY, YOU'RE A RICH MAN—*3:07*
       ALL YOU NEED IS LOVE—*3:57*

534.   NOV 15, 1976 (US) Dark Horse DRC 8294
       NOV 19, 1976 (UK) Dark Horse K 16856
       by George Harrison Prod: George Harrison assisted by Tom
         Scott
       A: This Song—Harrison—*3:45*
       B: Learning How To Love You—Harrison—*4:15*

535.   NOV 19, 1976 (UK) Dark Horse K 56319 (LP)
       NOV 24, 1976 (US) Dark Horse DH 3005 (LP)
       Recorded: Mid 1976
       by George Harrison
       THIRTY THREE & 1/3 Prod: George Harrison assisted by
         Tom Scott

side one

Woman Don't You Cry For Me—Harrison—*3:15*
Dear One—Harrison—*5:08*
Beautiful Girl—Harrison—*3:38*
This Song—Harrison—*4:11*
See Yourself—Harrison—*2:48*

side two

It's What You Value—Harrison—*5:05*
True Love—Cole Porter—*2:34*
Pure Smokey—Harrison—*3:52*
Crackerbox Palace—Harrison—*3:52*
Learning How To Love You—Harrison—*4:15*

Musicians performing on the George Harrison album listed above include George Harrison:*Guitars, Vocals, Synthesizers and Percussion;* Tom Scott:*Saxophone, Flute, Lyricon;* Alvin Taylor:*Drums;* Gary Wright: *Keyboards;* Richard Tee:*Piano, Organ, Fender Rhodes;* David Foster: *Fender Rhodes, Clavinet;* and Emil Richards:*Mirimba.* Billy Preston overdubbed *Piano, Organ and Synthesizer* on three cuts, *Beautiful Girl, This Song* and *See Yourself.*

536.   NOV 22, 1976 (US) Atlantic 45–3371
NOV 26, 1976 (UK) Polydor 2001 699
by Ringo Starr Prod: Arif Mardin
A: HEY BABY—Bruce Channel—Margaret Cobb—*3:10*
B: LADY GAYE—Starkey—Vini Poncia—Clifford T. Ward—
2:56

537.   DEC 3, 1976 (UK) NUTS NUT 1 (LP)
by Various Artists
(By Billy J. Kramer with The Dakotas Prod: George Martin;
† Cilla Black; % Cilla Black Prod: George Martin; $ The
Fourmost)
HISTORY OF THE MERSEY ERA---VOL. I
side one
cut two: *DO YOU WANT TO KNOW A SECRET*—L-McC—
1:59
†cut four: *LOVE OF THE LOVED*—L-McC—*2:00*
side two
%cut four: *IT'S FOR YOU*---L-McC—*2:20*
$cut five: *HELLO LITTLE GIRL*—L-McC—*1:50*

538.   DEC 10, 1976 (US) Capitol SWCO 11593 (3 LPs)
DEC 10, 1976 (UK) Capitol PCSP 720 (3 LPs)
Recorded live in America May 3–June 23, 1976
by Wings

WINGS OVER AMERICA Prod: Paul McCartney
side one
  medley: 10:05
    Venus And Mars—McCartney—*1:29*
    Rock Show—McCartney—*4:26*
    Jet—McCartney—*4:10*
  Let Me Roll It—McCartney—*3:40*
  Spirits Of Ancient Egypt—McCartney—*3:59*
  Medicine Jar—Jimmy McCulloch—Colin Allen—*3:59*
side two
  Maybe I'm Amazed—McCartney—*5:15*
  Call Me Back Again—McCartney—*5:07*
  Lady Madonna—L-McC—*2:19*
  The Long And Winding Road—L-McC—*3:59*
  Live And Let Die—McCartney—*3:08*
side three
  medley: 4:40
    Picasso's Last Words—McCartney—*1:48*
    Richard Corey—Paul Simon—*2:52*
  Bluebird—McCartney—*3:40*
  I've Just Seen A Face—L-McC—*1:55*
  Blackbird—L-McC—*2:30*
  Yesterday—L-McC—*1:43*
side four
  You Gave Me The Answer—McCartney—*1:49*
  Magneto And Titanium Man—McCartney—*3:20*
  Go Now—Larry Banks—Milton Bennet—*3:30*
  My Love—McCartney—*4:10*
  Listen To What The Man Said—McCartney—*3:20*
side five
  Let 'Em In—McCartney—*4:05*
  Time To Hide—Denny Laine—*4:50*
  Silly Love Songs—McCartney—*5:55*
  Beware My Love—McCartney—*4:55*
side six
  Letting Go—McCartney—*4:30*
  Band On The Run—McCartney—*5:05*
  Hi Hi Hi—McCartney—*3:03*
  Soily—McCartney—*5:12*

Musicians performing on the Wings album listed above include Paul
McCartney:*Vocals, Bass, Piano* (sides 2, 4 and *Let 'Em In*), *Acoustic
Guitar* (side 3), *Keyboards (Magneto And Titanium Man), Guitar*;
Linda McCartney:*Keyboards, Vocals, Flowers* (side 3), *Tambourine
(Hi Hi Hi)*; Denny Laine:*Vocals, Electric Guitar, Acoustic Guitar*
(side 3), *Piano (Silly Love Songs), Keyboards (Letting Go), Snare Drum*

(Let 'Em In), Bass; Jimmy McCulloch:*Electric Guitar, Vocals, Acoustic Guitar* (side 3), *Bass;* Joe English:*Drums, Vocals;* and a Horn Section including Tony Dorsey:*Trombone;* Howie Casey:*Saxophone;* Steve Howard:*Trumpet, Flugelhorn;* and Thadeus Richard:*Saxophones, Clarinet, Flute.* Paul McCartney:All *Lead Vocals* except *Spirits of Ancient Egypt* (Paul & Denny), *Medicine Jar* (Jimmy), and *Richard Corey, Go Now* and *Time To Hide* (Denny).

539.   DEC 13, 1976 (US) Atlantic SD 18201 (LP)
DEC 17, 1976 (UK) Atlantic K 50327 (LP)
by Stephen Stills Prod: Steve Stills and Bill Halverson
THE BEST OF STEPHEN STILLS
side one
  cut three: *WE ARE NOT HELPLESS*---Steve Stills—*4:17*
    Ringo: Drums

1977

January 10. Apple–ABKCO suit officially settled. Approximate figures: ABKCO pays Apple about $800,000; Apple pays Allen Klein $5 million.

March. Klaatu rumors sweep the country.

April 6. Beatles and Apple fail in their attempt to stop the release of the Hamburg Star Club tapes from 1962.

April 8. Hamburg tapes released in Germany. Release in Britain and America follows in May and June.

May. EMI issues the Hollywood Bowl live concert recording from 1964/1965.

May. Suzy and the Redstripes recording of *Seaside Woman* finally issued -- on Epic records.

June. George and Patti Harrison granted a divorce.

June. Ringo's Ring O' Jabel reactivated in Britain.

August. EMI acknowledges that sales of the **Hollywood Bowl** album fell below their original expectations. Though the disc reached top five on both the British and American charts, it quickly dropped from both.

September. Jimmy McCulloch quits Wings to join Small Faces.

October 19. By an 11 to 9 vote, the city council of Liverpool rejects a plan to build a monument to the Beatles.

The Beatles   Capitol SWCO 11593 (LP)
At The Hollywood Bowl

Ringo The 4th   Atlantic SD 19108 (LP)

Recommended Recordings: The long-awaited **Hamburg Star Club LP** (foreign and domestic pressings); Paul's *Giddy* for Roger Daltrey's **One Of The Boys** LP; and several other long-awaited (sometimes disappointing) discs: **Holly Days** (Paul and Denny Laine); *Seaside Woman* (Paul and Linda); **The Beatles At The Hollywood Bowl** (the Beatles and a cast of thousands).

1977

The first half of 1977 was a collective period of relief for all four ex–Beatles, after the hectic days of 1976. Paul, who seems physically incapable of resting, finally got the Denny Laine album out, and did some work with Roy Harper and the Who's Roger Daltrey. June finally saw the realization of a long threatened . . . rather, promised event: the release of Linda's famed Suzy and the Red Stripes recording, *Seaside Woman*. Originally begun in late 1973, right after **Band On The Run**, Linda was to release a few songs under the guise of Suzy and the Red Stripes (named after a Jamaican beer), but for some reason, these were constantly held up. Suddenly, Epic records announced a special single release by the ubiquitous Suzy. The flip side, *B–Side To Seaside*, might be considered a classic in the Phil Spector tradition (*Tedesco And Pitman*) of fatuous flips. Nonetheless, *Seaside Woman* slipped comfortably into the lower half of the charts upon release, a sure sign that there's more to come from Suzy. George's Dark Horse records pushed a–head in its efforts to have a success apart from George. Keni Burke, from Stairsteps, released his first solo album. Splinter released a new album, **Two Man Band**, once again including George himself helping out on guitar. Attitude's 1976 hit *Sweet Summer Music* was re–released by Warner Brothers for the summer of 1977, and also wound up on their long–postponed second album, **Good News**, which included a guest appearance by Ringo. Ringo, by the way, began to reactivate his Ring O' Records, with *It's All Over Now, Baby Blue* by Graham Bonnet as its first new release. We can't wait for the rest.

More of the previously withheld recorded history of the Beatles made its way to the public in early 1977. The practically legendary Hamburg Star Club tapes, recorded at Christmas 1962, survived a last–minute legal challenge and appeared as a double album first in Germany and then, with four different cuts!, in the U.S. in June on Atlantic. Containing many songs previously only available by the Beatles on bootlegs, the album, while certainly not up to modern recording standards, is an interesting souvenir. The long–dreamed–of live Beatle album finally became a reality in May when Capitol re--

cords, with the technical assistance of George Martin, released an album of highlights of the 1964 and 1965 Hollywood Bowl Beatle concerts. It may not be the next--best--thing-to--being--there, but after years of listening to barely comprehensible live bootlegs, the Capitol release was a blessed relief. A blessed relief to fans, but certainly not to the EMI sales staff, since the **Hollywood Bowl** LP came nowhere near the smash status expected of it. They didn't even pull a single from the album. This does not auger well for the possible future release by EMI of previously unissued Beatle tracks. If a live concert recording from the height of the Beatles' touring career can't sell that well, how will those infamous out-takes ("Take 25" of *Get Back* or the two-track drum-and-bass portion of some unfinished songs) do any better?

Jimmy McCulloch, after toying with the idea of going it alone with his own group, left Wings and joined the newly re-formed Small Faces. Paul, aside from finding a new guitarist, has only one more record to deliver to fulfill his Capitol records contract. He claims he has no intention of leaving the EMI/Capitol fold, but veteran legal observers know such protestations mean nothing when it comes time to talk turkey. George had a successful follow-up single to *This Song* (*Crackerbox Palace*), but in Britain a pair of successors failed to make the charts. Ringo inaugurated the fall with a highly publicized new LP, **Ringo The 4th**, which had a slightly disasterous send-off with an *el-floppola* single, *Wings* (no relation, he assures us). John and Yoko continue to stay out of the limelight. In fact, they spent most of the summer in Japan. Every few months, a new rumor will surface implying John is about to resume recording or even sign a record contract.

The Beatles, however, live on, almost eight years after their death, through the holiday season beneficence of EMI/Capitol. An otherwise pointless two record compilation, the Beatles' **Love Songs** was released (with a 28 page lyric booklet) just in time for Christmas ("Christmas time is here again, ain't been 'round since . . . **Wings Over America!**"). If repackaged albums like this can turn a reasonable profit (and with next to no production cost, it's hard to see how they couldn't), the future seems to promise an unbroken chain of repackaged Beatle hits. It may still be awhile before Ringo (or one of the others) turns up on those late-night TV record ads but, for better or worse, the Beatles as a group (a group more and more associated with the past, not the present) have begun that long journey into history.

540. JAN 24, 1977 (US) Dark Horse DRC 8313
by George Harrison Prod: George Harrison assisted by Tom
  Scott
A: CRACKERBOX PALACE--Harrison--*3:52*
B: LEARNING HOW TO LOVE YOU--Harrison--*4:15*

541. FEB 4, 1977 (UK) Harvest 5120
by Roy Harper Prod: Roy Harper and Peter Jenner
A: One Of Those Days In England (Part 1)--Roy Harper--*3:25*
    Paul: Backing Vocal
B: (watford gap)

542. FEB 4, 1977 (UK) Capitol R 6017
FEB 7, 1977 (US) Capitol 4385
by Wings Prod: Paul McCartney
A: MAYBE I'M AMAZED--McCartney--*5:15*
B: SOILY--McCartney--*5:12*

543. FEB 11, 1977 (UK) Harvest SHSP 4060 (LP)
MAR 21, 1977 (US) Chrysalis CHR 1138 (LP)
by Roy Harper Prod: Roy Harper and Peter Jenner
ONE OF THOSE DAYS IN ENGLAND (BULLINAMINGVASE)
side one
  cut one: *One Of Those Days In England (Part 1)*--Roy
  Harper--*3:25*
  Paul: Backing Vocal
Musicians performing on the Roy Harper album listed above include
Roy Harper:*Guitars and Vocals;* Andy Roberts and Henry McCullough:
Guitars; David Lawson:*Keyboards;* Dave C. Drill:*Bass;* and Admiral
John Halsey:*Drums;* additionally, Paul and Linda McCartney join in on
Backing Vocals for *One Of Those Days In England (Part 1).*

544. FEB 18, 1977 (UK) Dark Horse K 16896
by George Harrison Prod: George Harrison assisted by Tom
  Scott
A: TRUE LOVE--Cole Porter--*2:34*
B: PURE SMOKEY--Harrison--*3:52*

545. MAR 7, 1977 (US) Columbia 34467 (LP)
by David Bromberg Prod: David Bromberg
OUT OF THE BLUES (BEST OF DAVID BROMBERG)
side one
  cut one: *THE HOLDUP*--Harrison--David Bromberg--*3:00*

546. MAR 18, 1977 (UK) Music For Pleasure MFP 50317 (LP)
by Various Artists
ORIGINAL ARTISTS HITS OF THE 60'S
side one
    cut five: *I'LL KEEP YOU SATISFIED*---L-McC—*2:04*
    by Billy J. Kramer with The Dakotas Prod: George Martin
side two
    cut six: *GOT TO GET YOU INTO MY LIFE*---L-McC—*2:29*
    by Cliff Bennett and The Rebel Rousers Prod: Paul
    McCartney

547. MAR 25, 1977 (UK) Capitol EST 24058 (LP)
by The Steve Miller Band Prod: Glyn Johns and Steve Miller
BEST OF STEVE MILLER 1968–1973
side two
    cut three: *MY DARK HOUR*---Steve Miller—*3:05*
    Paul: Bass Guitar, Drums and Backing Vocal

548. APR 1, 1977 (UK) Sunset SLS 50404 (LP)
by P.J. Proby Prod: Ron Richards
SOMEWHERE
side two
    cut five: *THAT MEANS A LOT*---L-McC—*2:31*

549. APR 4, 1977 (US) Capitol 6244
by John Lennon Prod: John Lennon (A side); John Lennon,
    Yoko Ono and Phil Spector (B side)
A: *STAND BY ME*—Ben E. King—Jerry Leiber—Mike Stoller—
    3:29
B: *WOMAN IS THE NIGGER OF THE WORLD*--Lennon—
    Yoko Ono—*5:15*

550. APR 4, 1977 (US) Capitol 6245
by George Harrison Prod: George Harrison
A: *DARK HORSE*—Harrison—*3:50*
B: *YOU*--Harrison—*3:40*

551. APR 8, 1977 (GERMANY) Bellaphon BLS 5560 (2 LPs)
MAY 25, 1977 (UK) Lingasong LNL 1 (2 LPs)
Recorded Live in December 1962 at the Star Club, Hamburg,
Germany
by The Beatles
**THE BEATLES LIVE! AT THE STAR CLUB IN HAMBURG,
GERMANY, 1962**
    Album produced by Larry Grossberg, assisted by Mitchell
    Margo and Larry Halpern, from a concert recorded by Ted
    "Kingsize" Taylor

side one: *14:48*

Introduction Of The Band—0:34
I Saw Her Standing There—2:22
*Roll Over Beethoven—*Chuck Berry*—2:15*
*Hippy Hippy Shake—*Chan Romero*—1:42*
*Sweet Little Sixteen—*Chuck Berry*—2:45*
*Lend Me Your Comb—*Kay Twomey—Fred Wise—Ben
   Weisman*—1:44*
*Your Feet's Too Big—*Ada Benson—Fred Fisher*—2:18*

side two: *14:49*

*Twist And Shout—*Bert Russell—Phil Medley*—2:03*
*Mr. Moonlight—*Roy Lee Johnson*—2:06*
*A Taste Of Honey—*Ric Marlow—Bobby Scott*—1:45*
*Besame Mucho—*Consuelo Velazquez—Selig Shaftel*—2:36*
*Reminiscing—*King Curtis*—1:41*
medley: 2:09
   *Kansas City—*Jerry Leiber—Mike Stoller*—1:04*
   *Hey—Hey—Hey—Hey—*Richard Penniman*—1:05*

side three: *18:39*

*Nothin' Shakin' (But The Leaves On The Trees)—*Cirino
   Colacrai—Eddie Fontaine—Dianne Lampert—Jack
   Cleveland*—1:15*
*To Know Her Is To Love Her—*Phil Spector*—3:02*
*Little Queenie—*Chuck Berry*—3:51*
*Falling In Love Again (Can't Help It)—*Sammy Lerner—
   Frederick Hollander*—1:57*
Ask Me Why—2:26
*Be—Bop—A—Lula—*Gene Vincent—Tex Davis*—2:29*
*Hallelujah, I Love Her So—*Ray Charles*—2:10*

side four: *16:28*

*Red Sails In The Sunset—*Jimmy Kennedy—Will Grosz*—2:00*
*Everybody's Trying To Be My Baby—*Carl Perkins*—2:25*
*Matchbox—*Carl Perkins*—2:35*
*I'm Talking About You—*Chuck Berry*—1:48*
*Shimmy Shake—*Joe South—Billy Land*—2:17*
*Long Tall Sally—*Enotris Johnson—Richard Penniman—
   Robert Blackwell*—1:45*
*I Remember You—*Johnny Mercer—Victor Schertzinger*—1:54*

Musicians performing on the Star Club live recording include the four
Beatles in their usual line--up:George:*Lead Guitar;* John:*Rhythm
Guitar;* Paul:*Bass Guitar;* and Ringo:*Drums.*
German waiter Horst Obber joins them for two numbers, doing the
lead vocal on *Be--Bop--A--Lula* and *Hallelujah, I Love Her So.* Ringo
does lead vocal on *Matchbox;* George does lead vocal on *Everybody's
Trying To Be My Baby, Lend Me Your Comb, Nothin' Shakin',
Reminiscing* and *Roll Over Beethoven;* John does the lead vocal on

63

Ask Me Why I'm Talking About You, Mr. Moonlight, Sweet Little Sixteen,
and *Twist And Shout*; Paul does lead vocal on the remaining tracks
*Besame Mucho, Falling In Love Again, Hippy Hippy Shake, I Remember
You* (John on *Harmonica*), *I Saw Her Standing There, Kansas City/Hey Hey
Hey Hey, Little Queenie, Long Tall Sally, Red Sails In The Sunset,
Shimmy Shake, A Taste Of Honey, To Know Her Is To Love Her,* and
Your Feet's Too Big.

552.　　APR 15, 1977　(UK)　EMI 2588
　　　　MAY 31, 1977　(US)　Capitol 4425
　　　　by Denny Laine　Prod: Paul McCartney
　　　　A: Moondreams—Norman Petty—*2:41*
　　　　B: Heartbeat—Bob Montgomery—Norman Petty—*2:37*

553.　　MAY　4, 1977　(US)　Capitol SMAS 11638　(LP)
　　　　MAY　6, 1977　(UK)　EMI EMTV 4　(LP)
　　　　*Recorded Live: August 23, 1964 and August 30, 1965 at
　　　　the Hollywood Bowl, Los Angeles, California*
　　　　by The Beatles
　　　　THE BEATLES AT THE HOLLYWOOD BOWL　Prod: George
　　　　Martin
　　　　side one: *17:44*
　　　　†*Twist And Shout*—Bert Russell—Phil Medley—*1:20*
　　　　†*She's A Woman*—*2:45*
　　　　†*Dizzy Miss Lizzie*—Larry Williams—*3:00*
　　　　†*Ticket To Ride*—*2:18*
　　　　†*Can't Buy Me Love*—*2:08*
　　　　　Things We Said Today—*2:07*
　　　　　Roll Over Beethoven—Chuck Berry—*2:10*
　　　　side two
　　　　　Boys—Luther Dixon—Wes Farrell—*1:57*
　　　　†*A Hard Day's Night*—*2:30*
　　　　†*Help*—*2:16*
　　　　　All My Loving—*1:55*
　　　　　She Loves You—*2:10*
　　　　　Long Tall Sally—Enotris Johnson—Richard Penniman—
　　　　　Robert Blackwell—*1:54*
　　　　Musicians performing on the Beatles album listed above include the
　　　　four Beatles in their usual line--up:George:*Lead Guitar;* John:*Rhythm
　　　　Guitar;* Paul:*Bass Guitar;* and Ringo:*Drums.* Ringo does the lead
　　　　vocal on *Boys;* George does the lead vocal on *Roll Over Beethoven;*
　　　　John and Paul share the lead on *She Loves You;* John does the lead
　　　　vocal on *Dizzy Miss Lizzie, A Hard Day's Night, Help, Ticket To Ride*
　　　　and *Twist And Shout;* Paul does the lead vocal on *All My Loving,
　　　　Can't Buy Me Love, Long Tall Sally, She's A Woman,* and *Things We
　　　　Said Today.*

554. MAY 5, 1977 (US) Dark Horse DH 3021 (LP)
JUN 3, 1977 (UK) Dark Horse K 56385 (LP)
by Attitudes
GOOD NEWS Prod: Jay Lewis and Attitudes
side two
   cut five: *Good News*--Paul Stallworth--*3:45*
    Ringo: Drums
Musicians performing on the Attitudes cut listed above include Paul
Stallworth:*Bass;* David Foster:*Keyboards;* Danny Kootch:*Guitar;*
and Jim Keltner:*Drums* (Attitudes) joined by Ringo Starr:*Drums;*
Booker T. Jones:*Organ;* Jorge Calderon & Y. Rankin:*Background
Vocals;* and the Tower of Power Horn Section.

555. MAY 6, 1977 (UK) EMI EMA 781 (LP)
MAY 19, 1977 (US) Capitol ST 11588 (LP)
by Denny Laine
HOLLY DAYS Prod: Paul McCartney
side one
   Heartbeat—Bob Montgomery—Norman Petty—*2:37*
   Moondreams--Norman Petty—*2:41*
   Rave On--Norman Petty—Bill Tilghman—Sunny West—*1:53*
   I'm Gonna Love You Too—Joe Mauldin—Norman Petty—
    Niki Sullivan—*2:15*
   Fool's Paradise—Norman Petty—Sonny LeGlaire—Horace
    Linsley—*2:46*
   Lonesome Tears--Buddy Holly—*3:05*
side two
   MEDLEY: 3:47
    IT'S SO EASY--Buddy Holly—Norman Petty
    LISTEN TO ME--Norman Petty—Charles Hardin
   Look At Me—Jerry Allison—Buddy Holly—Norman Petty—
    3:10
   Take Your Time--Norman Petty—Buddy Holly—*3:38*
   I'M LOOKING FOR SOMEONE TO LOVE—Norman Petty—
    Buddy Holly—*3:57*
Musicians performing on the Denny Laine album listed above include
Paul McCartney:*Drums, Guitars and Harmony Vocals;* Denny Laine:
Lead Vocals; and Linda McCartney:*Harmony Vocals.* Two cuts,
Lonesome Tears and *I'm Looking For Someone To Love,* are
instrumentals.

556. MAY 13, 1977 (UK) Polydor 2442 146 (LP)
JUN 16, 1977 (US) MCA 2271 (LP)
by Roger Daltrey
ONE OF THE BOYS Prod: David Courtney and Tony Meehan

side two
  cut two: *Giddy*—McCartney—*4:46*
Musicians performing on the Roger Daltrey album listed above include
Roger Daltrey:*Lead Vocals;* Brian Odgers and John Entwistle:*Bass;*
Stuart Tosh:*Drums;* Jimmy McCulloch and Paul Keogh:*Guitars;*
Rod Argent:*Keyboards;* Phil Kenzie and Jimmy Jewell:*Saxophones;*
and Tony Rivers, John Perry and Stuart Calver:*Backing Vocals.*

557.   MAY 31, 1977 (US) Epic 8--50403
      by Suzy and The Red Stripes Prod: Paul McCartney
      *A: Seaside Woman—McCartney—*3:36*
      *B: B—Side to Seaside--McCartney—*2:36*
Musicians performing on the Suzy and the Red Stripes songs above
include Linda McCartney:*Lead Vocals,* backed by various members
of Wings.

558.   JUN 10, 1977 (UK) Dark Horse K 16967
      by George Harrison Prod: George Harrison assisted by Tom
      Scott
      A: IT'S WHAT YOU VALUE--Harrison—*5:05*
      B: WOMAN DON'T YOU CRY FOR ME—Harrison—*3:15*

559.   JUN 13, 1977 (US) Lingasong LS 2 7001 (2 LPs)
      by The Beatles
      **THE BEATLES LIVE! AT THE STAR CLUB IN HAMBURG,
      GERMANY; 1962**
        Album produced by Larry Grossberg, assisted by Mitchell
        Margo and Larry Halpern, from a concert recorded by Ted
        "Kingsize" Taylor
      side one: *14:53*
      Introduction Of The Band—*0:21*
      I'm Gonna Sit Right Down And Cry (Over You)--Joe
        Thomas—Howard Biggs—*2:43*
      Roll Over Beethoven—Chuck Berry—*2:15*
      Hippy Hippy Shake—Chan Romero—*1:42*
      Sweet Little Sixteen—Chuck Berry—*2:45*
      Lend Me Your Comb—Kay Twomey—Fred Wise—Ben
        Weisman—*1:44*
      Your Feet's Too Big—Ada Benson—Fred Fisher—*2:18*
      side two: *14:13*
      Where Have You Been All My Life?--Barry Mann—Cynthia
        Weil—*1:55*
      Mr. Moonlight—Roy Lee Johnson—*2:06*
      A Taste Of Honey—Ric Marlow—Bobby Scott—*1:45*
      Besame Mucho—Consuelo Velazquez—Selig Shaftel—*2:36*
      'Till There Was You—Meredith Willson—*1:59*

medley: 2:09
  Kansas City—Jerry Leiber—Mike Stoller—*1:04*
  Hey—Hey—Hey—Hey—Richard Penniman—*1:05*
side three: *18:01*
  Nothin' Shakin' (But The Leaves On The Trees)—Cirino
    Colacrai—Eddie Fontaine—Dianne Lampert—Jack Cleveland—
    1:15
  To Know Her Is To Love Her—Phil Spector—*3:02*
  Little Queenie—Chuck Berry—*3:51*
  Falling In Love Again (Can't Help It)—Sammy Lerner—
    Frederick Hollander—*1:57*
  Shella—Tommy Roe—*1:56*
  Be—Bop—A—Lula—Gene Vincent—Tex Davis—*2:29*
  Hallelujah, I Love Her So—Ray Charles—*2:10*
side four: *16:28*
  Red Sails In The Sunset—Jimmy Kennedy—Will Grosz—*2:00*
  Everybody's Trying To Be My Baby—Carl Perkins—*2:25*
  Matchbox—Carl Perkins—*2:35*
  I'm Talking About You—Chuck Berry—*1:48*
  Shimmy Shake—Joe South—Billy Land—*2:17*
  Long Tall Sally—Enotris Johnson—Richard Penniman—
    Robert Blackwell—*1:45*
  I Remember You—Johnny Mercer—Victor Schertzinger—*1:54*
Musicians performing on the American edition of the Star Club live
recording are the same as the original German and British editions with
these additional vocals:John does lead on:*I'm Gonna Sit Right Down
and Cry (Over You)* and *Where Have You Been All My Life?;* Paul does
lead vocal on *'Till There Was You;* and George does lead vocal on *Shelia.*

560. JUN 24, 1977 (UK) Lingasong NB 1
  by The Beatles From an album produced by
  Larry Grossberg, assisted by Mitchell Margo and
  Larry Halpern, from a concert recorded by Ted
  "Kingsize" Taylor
  A: TWIST AND SHOUT—Bert Russell—Phil Medley—*2:03*
  B: FALLING IN LOVE AGAIN (CAN'T HELP IT)—Sammy Lerner—
    Frederick Hollander—*1:57*

561. JULY 1977 (US MAIL ORDER) ABKCO DVL 2-0268 (2 LPs)
  by The Rolling Stones Prod: Andrew Loog Oldham
  THE ROLLING STONES GREATEST HITS
  side three
    cut five: *WE LOVE YOU*—Mick Jagger—Keith Richard—*4:39*
    John and Paul: Backing Vocals

562.   AUG 5, 1977 (UK) NUTS NUT 8 (LP)
      by Peter and Gordon †Prod: Norman Newell
      THE BEST OF PETER AND GORDON
        †I DON'T WANT TO SEE YOU AGAIN---L-McC---*1:59*
        †NOBODY I KNOW---L-McC---*2:27*
        WOMAN---Paul McCartney---*2:21*
        A WORLD WITHOUT LOVE---L-McC---*2:38*

563.   AUG 5, 1977 (UK) NUTS NUT 9 (LP)
      by Billy J. Kramer with The Dakotas Prod: George Martin
      THE BEST OF BILLY J. KRAMER WITH THE DAKOTAS
      side one
        cut one: *I'LL KEEP YOU SATISFIED*---L-McC---*2:04*
        cut two: *DO YOU WANT TO KNOW A SECRET*---L-McC--*1:5*
        cut four: *I CALL YOU NAME*---L-McC---*2:00*
        cut five: *FROM A WINDOW*---L-McC---*1:55*
        cut ten: *I'LL BE ON MY WAY*---L-McC---*1:38*
      side two
        cut one: *BAD TO ME*---L-McC---*2:18*

564.   AUG 25, 1977 (US) Atlantic 3429
      by Ringo Starr Prod: Arif Mardin
      A: Wings---Starkey—Vini Poncia---*3:03*
     B: Just A Dream---Starkey—Vini Poncia---*4:23*

565.   AUG 26, 1977 (US) EMI M 11690 (LP)
      by Various Artists
        (By Cilla Black;† Billy J. Kramer with The Dakotas Prod:
        George Martin
      HITS OF THE MERSEY ERA VOLUME 1
      side one
      †cut two: *DO YOU WANT TO KNOW A SECRET*---L-McC---*1:5*
        cut four: *LOVE OF THE LOVED*---L-McC---*2:00*
      side two
        cut three: *IT'S FOR YOU*---L-McC---*2:20*

566.   SEP 6, 1977 (US) Dark Horse DRC 8439
      by Splinter Prod: Norbert Putnam
      George: Guitar
      A: Round And Round---Parker McGee---*3:04*
     B: I'll Bend For You---Robert J. Purvis---*3:48*

567.   SEP 6, 1977 (US) Dark Horse DRC 8452
        by Attitudes Prod: Jay Lewis and Attitudes
        B: GOOD NEWS---Paul Stallworth---*3:45*
            Ringo: Drums
        A: (in a stanger's arms)

568.   SEP 16, 1977 (UK) Polydor 2001 734
        OCT 18, 1977 (US) Atlantic 3412
        by Ringo Starr Prod: Arif Mardin
        A: Drowning In The Sea Of Love---Kenny Gamble—Leon
            Huff---*5:08*
        B: Just A Dream---Starkey—Vini Poncia---*4:23*

569.   SEP 26, 1977 (US) Arista AB 4145 (LP)
        by The Alpha Band
          Ringo: Drums
        SPARK IN THE DARK Prod: Steven Soles
        side one
            cut two: *Born In Captivity*---Arthur B. Stahr---*3:44*
        side two
            cut two: *You Angel You*---Bob Dylan---*2:44*
        Musicians performing on the Alpha Band album listed above include mem--
        bers Steven Soles and "T" Bone Burnett:*Vocals, Guitars and Pianos* and
        David Mansfield:*Mandolin, Guitar, Dobro, Violin, Viola, Steel Guitar,
        Cello, Hanging Bells, and Piano,* supplemented on *Born In Captivity* and
        You Angel You by:
        on *Born In Captivity* Ringo Starr and Matt Betton:*Drums;* K.O.
        Thomas:*Piano;* and David Miner:*Bass;*
        and on *You Angel You* Ringo Starr and Matt Betton:*Drums;* David
        Miner:*Bass;* and Candy Bullens:*Harmony.*

Continued on page 255

THE BEATLES

Live!

INCLUDES
15
NEVER BEFORE
RELEASED TRACKS
2 LP's

at the Star-Club

in Hamburg,

Germany;

1962.

A PIECE OF HISTORY
BEATLES
LINGASONG

The Beatles Live!
   At The Star Club in Hamburg, Germany; 1962

Lingasong LS-2-7001 (LP)

The Case of the
Belittled Beatles Tapes*

A television producer, hitting paydirt after numerous flops, once complained that failure brings the balm of anonymity, while success brings lawsuits. Nowhere has this been more apparent than in rock music. Rock musicians have spent so much time in court lately that it's only a matter of time before albums like **Bruce Springsteen Alive and Well At District Appeals Court 263** top the charts.

Oddly enough, the Beatles, the most popular rock group ever, were somehow able to ward off the bulk of such lawsuits during the 60's, even while they were leading the gravy train of profit. Since their break-up in 1969, however, they have joined the 70's litany of suits and counter-suits: they sued each other, Allen Klein sued them, they sued Allen Klein, the US Government tried to deport John and Yoko, George was accused of stealing *My Sweet Lord* from *He's So Fine*, John was accused of stealing *Come Together* from *You Can't Catch Me*, an independent record producer was accused of stealing the tracks from John's **Rock 'n' Roll** album, and on and on. Unfortunately most of these court cases, though involving sums up to $1 million, are usually steeped in extremely technical claims and counter-claims. Not very exciting to a fan of the legal process, weaned on reruns of Perry Mason.

One case with a better-than-average plot has been that of the Hamburg tapes.

These Hamburg tapes were made at the behest of Ted "Kingsize" Taylor, who was performing at Hamburg's Star Club in 1962 along with the Beatles. Taylor had a friend record a few nights' shows on a mono Grundig tape recorder, with a low-fi mono handheld microphone. Along with Taylor's group, the Dominoes, the tape featured the Beatles' performance. A few years later, when the Beatles were well on the way to topping Jesus Christ in the world's popularity poll, Taylor realized he was sitting on a possible windfall. While other equally crude recordings existed of live Beatle performances, Taylor's was one of the earliest, and, more importantly, was the *only* known recording of the group in a club, as opposed to an

---

*First published, with slight editorial variations, in *Stereo Review*, November 1977, pages 66–68.

outdoor concert. Beatle scripture told of their club days as being the true molding era, when the staid Liverpool beat group was transformed into a hot, tight powerhouse band. A tape of such a performance would be an invaluable look at history in the making.

Taylor offered the tapes to Beatle manager Brian Epstein who turned him down, feeling they were of no commercial value, and that was the end of it for years. By the early 1970's, when the group had split up, interest in the Beatles as *history* (not just a regular act) picked up noticeably, and the market was ready for a "documentary" package like the Hamburg tapes. Allan Williams, who had briefly managed the Beatles around the time of the Hamburg performances, became the main driving force urging issuance of the old tapes. Finally, in 1976, a deal was made with Lingasong records in London and the Double H Licensing Corporation in New York City to release them as a double LP. Months of painstaking work followed to bring the muddy tapes as close to "modern" quality as possible. Earlier this year, just before the scheduled release, lawyers for the Beatles filed a dramatic last-minute claim to halt the tapes' issuance, but the judge ruled that Lingasong clearly marked the tapes for what they were, *old* tapes, and the Beatles had months to complain before, and didn't. So, in April, **The Beatles Live! At The Star Club in Hamburg, Germany; 1962** finally made it to the eager hands of Beatle aficionados around the world.

It seems, however, as if a major error was made by the legal eagles of EMI/Parlophone. Now, if Perry Mason had been handling their case, no doubt he would have realized that the prime question was *when* the tapes were recorded, to see if he could claim that Lingasong had no *right* to issue the LP because the Beatles were under exclusive contract to EMI when they were made. Far be it from us, who haven't even *applied* to law school to bring this up now, but the question of when the tapes were recorded has never, apparently, been answered. It seems everybody's assumed the Star Club tapes were made before the Beatles signed with EMI. The liner notes on the LP say as much, being quite vague as to an exact recording date. "Sometime" in 1962 is all one is led to assume. Since the Beatles signed with EMI in August of 1962, just *when* in 1962 is far from moot.

A brief historical investigation (the sort of thing Perry Mason franchised out to his flunky, Paul Drake) would turn up an easily traceable pattern. The Star Club *opened* in April of 1962 (so the tapes obviously were recorded no earlier). Ringo Starr did not officially replace Pete Best as the Beatles' drummer until August 1962, but Ringo had met the group almost two years earlier during early visits to Hamburg. In fact, Ringo "stood in" for Best every now and again. The Star Club liner notes say that Ringo just "happened" to be doing just that the night the tapes were made. So far, it all seems believable.

The Beatles made three visits to the Star Club during 1962. They played there from about April 23 to June 4, from November 1-14, and December 18-January 1, 1963. Since the Beatles' first EMI/Parlophone release (*Love Me Do/P.S. I Love You*) came out on October 4, 1962, Taylor obviously would have to have recorded the group sometime between April and June if the tapes *were* made *before* signing with EMI. Fine. Or is it?

Take a look at the *songs* played on the record. At the time, the Beatles did do some original numbers, but their stage act, like any bar band, was mostly made up of other people's hits (Chuck Berry's *Sweet Little Sixteen*, Little Richard's *Long Tall Sally*, etc.). The Beatles prided themselves on being able to pick up on the latest sounds that were big in the States, but if the Hamburg tape was made before June 4, John and Paul would have to have spent a lot of time monitoring a short wave set. Three songs they performed on the LP (the Isley Brother's *Twist and Shout*, Tommy Roe's *Sheila* and Arthur Alexander's *Where Have You Been All My Life?*) were only released in May of 1962.

Now if this *were* Perry Mason, Perry would begin pounding away at these inconsistencies:

"Do you mean to say that the Beatles besieged record shops in Hamburg, asking for import singles, and then spent hours listening to discs on record players they didn't own? Learning to mimic them, when they barely had enough time, after playing for hours, to eat and sleep? No, that seems unlikely. It's equally doubtful that they were prescient enough to know exactly how Frank Ifield would adapt *I Remember You* (an old war film hit from *The Fleet's In*), which he didn't release until June 20. The Beatles' version was a complete copy of Ifield's, even down to Lennon exaggerating the harmonica riff perfectly!"

At this point in our Mason script, it would now be five minutes before the hour. Perry would suddenly pull a copy of a Buddy Holly single from a bag delivered by Paul Drake moments earlier.

"No," Perry would say, "I doubt the Beatles were that far-sighted. In fact. . ."

At this point (there's only a minute or so left in the show), a record company executive would jump up from the audience and yell:

"Yes, it's true. That's a copy of the Buddy Holly single *Reminiscing*--Coral Q 72455--which wasn't released until September 7, 1962. Since the Beatles were in England then, and didn't return to Hamburg until two months later, the Hamburg tapes *couldn't* have been recorded before November of 1962, well after the Beatles were signed to EMI. In fact, *after* they released their first single! I admit it! Take me away!"

Here, Hamilton Burger would leap up, "But your honor, we are all familiar with Don McLean's *American Pie*. We all know Buddy Holly died in a plane crash in 1959. How could *Reminiscing* not have been released until 1962?"

Perry, with a slightly disdainful look, would respond: "Simple. Although *Reminiscing* was recorded in 1958, it was never released, while legal rights to it, and other Buddy Holly songs, were contested. In 1962, Norman Petty finally won the right to issue these songs. The first of the group, *Reminiscing*, was released in the United States on August 14, 1962, and in Britain three weeks later, on September 7. This was a full *two months* after the Beatles returned from Hamburg, almost on the very day they were in my client's studio, recording *Love Me Do*."

Judge bangs gavel, "Case closed."

Burger is seen sulking as scene fades to commercial.

Sixty seconds later, in the postscript back at the office, as Della brings in sandwiches, Paul asks:

"But Perry, how did you suspect Buddy Holly?"

Perry, ignoring the sandwiches while leafing through some *Law Review* digest, looks up and smiles.

"I didn't. I just listened to the album and heard two references to "the Holiday season" and "Christmas." Obviously, it *had* to be in November or December."

Fade to credit roll and to black.

If only life could imitate art, even old *Perry Mason* art, then it would be much easier to be a lawyer, and news reports of these suits would be a lot more fun to read. Needless to say, EMI didn't use our proposed scenario, with our very own "smoking gun." The Hamburg tapes *were* released on Lingasong. Perhaps EMI decided a lawsuit just wasn't worth it, what with their own **Hollywood Bowl** live LP doing better in sales. Of course, there's still time. Some budding legal wizard at EMI could study our script, memorize his lines, and come bounding into the courts with a nice, retroactive lawsuit demanding lost royalties. Lawyers cringe from ever *really* closing the book on any case, and this case, which began a full fifteen years ago, is truly ripe for a new addendum. A lawsuit, like a case of poison ivy, festers long after you've forgotten where it came from.

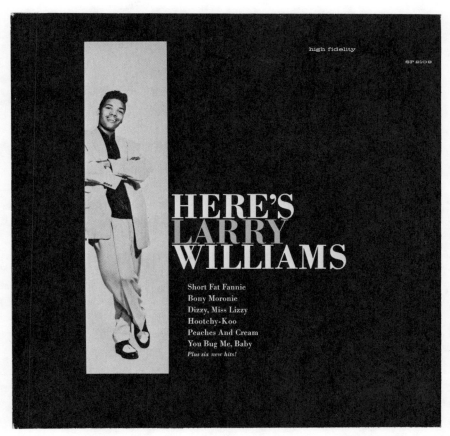

high fidelity

SP 2109

HERE'S LARRY WILLIAMS

Short Fat Fannie
Bony Moronie
Dizzy, Miss Lizzy
Hootchy-Koo
Peaches And Cream
You Bug Me, Baby
Plus six new hits!

Here's Larry Williams   **Specialty SP 2019 (LP)**

Little Richard — His Biggest Hits   Specialty SP 2111 (LP)

Little Richard's Grooviest
17 Original Hits   Specialty SPS 2113 (LP)

The Beatles
From Others

The release of the fifteen year old Hamburg tapes provided the public with a rare (possibly unique) glimpse of the Beatles *just* before they burst into mass popularity. They were right at the transitory point in which they were changing from a proficient "house" band, playing all your favorite hits along with a few originals, into a self-sufficient band whose performances were based solidly on songs written by the group.

The Beatles, like other mortals, developed their own style out of the music they grew up on and began playing. Unfortunately, many Beatle enthusiasts tend to ignore the well-known (and more obscure) artists and styles of an older era which heavily influenced the Beatles' musical tastes. Collectors will pay exorbitant amounts for rare pressings of Beatle songs they have three copies of already, but will ignore, for example, a mint condition copy of Arthur Alexander's *Anna*. As detailed in the "Beatles From Others" section of *All Together Now*, we have always strongly felt that no real appreciation of the Beatles is near complete without a cultivation of interest in these older rock classics. Accordingly, we exhumed more information on songs which were written by others but performed by the Beatles on their latest releases.

All songs recorded by The Beatles except % Tony Sheridan and The Beatles, † George Harrison, * Ringo Starr, and + Paul McCartney.
Sample:
Song Title--Authors
    Release Date and Performer
    Label, Number and *Flip Side*

Ain't She Sweet---Jack Yellen—Milton Ager
    Originally Performed—Early 1927 by Paul Ash and Orchestra
    Vaudeville Hit—Eddie Cantor
    Rock Version—August 30, 1956 by Gene Vincent
    Capitol T 764 (LP) **Bluejean Bop!**

Bad Boy---Larry Williams
    January 19, 1959 by Larry Williams
    Specialty 658 b/w *She Said "Yeah"*

Be-Bop-A-Lula---Gene Vincent—Tex Davis
    May 28, 1956 by Gene Vincent
    Capitol 3450 b/w *Woman Love*

Besame Mucho---Consuelo Velazquez—Selig Shaftel
    Originally—December 17, 1943 by Jimmy Dorsey and Orchestra
    (Vocals: Bob Eberle and Kitty Kallen)
    Rock Version—April 16, 1960 by The Coasters
    Atco 6163 b/w *Besame Mucho (Part II)*

Boys---Luther Dixon—Wes Farrell
    November 7, 1960 by The Shirelles
    Scepter 1211 b/w *Will You Still Love Me Tomorrow*

*Can She Do It Like She Dances—Steve Duboff—Gerry Robinson
    July 30, 1975 by Gold Rush
    Arista 0140 b/w *Jumbo Jack*

Dizzy Miss Lizzie---Larry Williams
    February 24, 1958 by Larry Williams
    Specialty 626 b/w *Slow Down*

*A Dose Of Rock 'n' Roll---Carl Grossman
    Given to Ringo—1976

*Drowning In The Sea Of Love—Kenny Gamble—Leon Huff
    November 8, 1971 by Joe Simon
    Spring 120 b/w *Let Me Be The One*

Everybody's Trying To Be My Baby---Carl Perkins
    August 18, 1958 by Carl Perkins
    Sun 1225 (LP) **Teen Beat---Carl Perkins**

Falling In Love Again (Can't Help It)---Sammy Lerner—Frederick Hollander
    Originally From the 1930 Film *The Blue Angel*, sung (in German) by
    Marlene Dietrich
    First English Recording—December 30, 1930 by Marlene Dietrich
    accompanied by Frederick Hollander and Sein Jazzsymphonicker
    Victor 22593 b/w *Ich Bin Die Fesche Lola*

+Go Now---Larry Banks—Milton Bennet
    Original—January 21, 1964 by Bessie Banks
    Tiger 102 b/w *It Sounds Like My Baby*
    Hit—January 12, 1965 by The Moody Blues
    London 9726 b/w *It's Easy Child*

Hallelujah, I Love Her So---Ray Charles
 May 14, 1956 by Ray Charles
 Atlantic 1096 b/w *What Would I Do Without You*

*Hey Baby---Margaret Cobb—Bruce Channel
 January 5, 1962 by Bruce Channel
 Smash 1731 b/w *Dream Girl*

Hey-Hey-Hey-Hey!---'Little' Richard Penniman
 January 13, 1958 by Little Richard
 Specialty 624 b/w *Good Golly, Miss Molly*

Hippy Hippy Shake---Chan Romero
 July 6, 1959 by Chan Romero
 Del-Fi 4110 b/w *If I Had A Way*

I Remember You---Johnny Mercer—Victor Schertzinger
 Originally From the 1942 Film *The Fleet's In*, sung by Dorothy Lamour
  with Jimmy Dorsey and the Band
 Cover Model—August 9, 1962 by Frank Ifield
  Vee Jay 457 b/w *I Listen To My Heart*

I'm Gonna Sit Right Down And Cry (Over You)---Joe Thomas—Howard
 Biggs
 January 25, 1954 by Roy Hamilton
  Epic 9015 b/w *You'll Never Walk Alone*
 Cover Model—September 10, 1956 by Elvis Presley
  RCA 6638 b/w *I'll Never Let You Go*

I'm Talking About You---Chuck Berry
 February 6, 1961 by Chuck Berry
 Chess 1779 b/w *Little Star*

Kansas City---Jerry Leiber—Mike Stoller
 Originally *K. C. Loving*—December 29, 1952 by Little Willie Littlefield
  Federal 12110 b/w *Pleading At Midnight*
 Cover Model—March 9, 1959 by Little Richard
  Specialty 2104 **(LP) The Fabulous Little Richard**
 Hit—March 23, 1959 by Wilbur Harrison
  Fury 1023 b/w *Listen My Darling*

Lend Me Your Comb---Kay Twomey—Fred Wise—Ben Weisman
 December 30, 1957 by Carl Perkins
 Sun 287 b/w *Glad All Over*

Little Queenie---Chuck Berry
 March 9, 1959 by Chuck Berry
 Chess 1722 b/w *Almost Grown*

Long Tall Sally---Enotris Johnson—Richard Penniman—Robert Blackwell
   March 12, 1956 by Little Richard
   Specialty 572 b/w *Slippin' And Slidin'*

Matchbox---Carl Perkins
   February 11, 1957 by Carl Perkins
   Sun 261 b/w *Your True Love*

Mr. Moonlight---Roy Lee Johnson
   January 15, 1962 by Dr. Feel Good and The Interns
   Okeh 7144 b/w *Doctor Feel Good*

Money (That's What I Want)---Berry Gordy—Janie Bradford
   December 10, 1959 by Barret Strong
   Anna 1111 b/w *Oh I Apologize*

%*My Bonnie (Lies Over The Ocean)*---Charles Pratt
   Originally Appeared—1881 in the Book: *Student Songs of 1881*
   (No Author Credited)
   First Published—1882 by Pratt, under the names J. T. Woods and
   H. J. Fuller
   Rock Version—August 6, 1958 by Ray Charles
   Atlantic 1196 b/w *You Be My Baby*

No No Song---Hoyt Axton—David P. Jackson
   Given to Ringo—1974
   March 28, 1975 by Hoyt Axton
   A&M SP 4510 (LP) **Southbound**

Nothin' Shakin' (But The Leaves On The Trees)---Cirino Colacrai—Eddie
   Fontaine—Dianne Lampert—Jack Cleveland
   Original—June 16, 1958 by Eddie Fontaine
   Sunbeam 105 b/w *Oh Wonderful Night*
   Hit—July 28, 1958 by Eddie Fontaine
   Argo 5309 b/w *Don't Ya Know*

Red Sails In The Sunset---Jimmy Kennedy—Will Grosz
   Introduced in the US in 1935 by Ray Noble and his Orchestra
   Rock Version—March 19, 1957 by Joe Turner
   Atlantic 1131 b/w *After A While*

Reminiscing---King Curtis
   August 14, 1962 by Buddy Holly
   Coral 62329 b/w *Wait Till The Sun Shines Nellie*

+*Richard Corey*---Paul Simon
   Based on a Poem by Edward A. Robinson
   February 14, 1966 by Simon & Garfunkel
   Columbia CS 9269 (LP) **Sounds Of Silence**

Rock And Roll Music---Chuck Berry
  September 30, 1957 by Chuck Berry
  Chess 1671 b/w *Blue Feeling*

Roll Over Beethoven---Chuck Berry
  May 14, 1956 by Chuck Berry
  Chess 1626 b/w *Too Much Monkey Business*

%*The Saints (Go Marching In)*---P. D.
  A Traditional American Song in the Public Domain
  Hit Rock Version—*The Saints Rock 'n' Roll*
    March 21, 1956 by Bill Haley and the Comets
    Decca 29870 b/w *R-O-C-K*

Sheila---Tommy Roe
  May 28, 1962 by Tommy Roe
  ABC 10329 b/w *Save Your Kisses*

Shimmy Shake---Joe South—Billy Land
  May 13, 1959 by Billy Land
  Esoteric 100 b/w *Four Wheels*

Slow Down---Larry Williams
  February 24, 1958 by Larry Williams
  Specialty 626 b/w *Dizzy Miss Lizzie*

Sneaking Sally Through The Alley—Allen Toussaint
  December 14, 1970 by Lee Dorsey
  Polydor 24-4042 (LP) **Yes We Can**

%*Sweet Georgia Brown*---Ben Bernie—Maceo Pinkard—Kenneth Casey
  Introduced—Spring 1925 by Ben Bernie and Orchestra
  Rock Version—November 13, 1957 by The Coasters
    Atco 6104 b/w *What Is The Secret Of Your Success*

%*Take Out Some Insurance On Me, Baby*---Charles Singleton—Waldenese Hall
  April 13, 1959 by Jimmy Reed
  Vee Jay VJ 314 b/w *You Know I Love You*

Tango All Night—Steve Hague—Tom Seufert
  September 27, 1976 by La Seine
  Ariola 7643 b/w *Union Strong Arm Men*

A Taste Of Honey---Ric Marlow—Bobby Scott
  Originally—From 1960 Play: *A Taste Of Honey*, performed by
    Bobby Scott and Combo
  First Recording—June 4, 1962 by The Victor Feldman Quartet
    Infinity 020 b/w *Valerie*
  Hit—June 18, 1962 by Martin Denny
    Liberty 55470 b/w *The Brighter Side*
  First Vocal Version—September 17, 1962 by Lenny Welch
    Cadence 1428 b/w *The Old Cathedral*

**This Be Called A Song*---Eric Clapton
  Given to Ringo—1976

'Till There Was You---Meredith Willson
  Originally—From 1957 Play: *The Music Man*, sung by Robert Preston
    and Barbara Cook
  First Recording—January 13, 1958 by Robert Preston and Barbara Cook
    Capitol WAO 990 (LP) **The Music Man** (Original Broadway Cast)
  Hit—May 18, 1959 by Anita Bryant
    Carlton 512 b/w *Little George*

To Know Him Is To Love Him---Phil Spector
  September 15, 1958 by The Teddy Bears
  Dore 503 b/w *Don't You Worry My Little Pet*

†*True Love*---Cole Porter
  Originally—From the 1956 Film: *High Society*, performed by Bing
    Crosby and Grace Kelly
  First Recording—August 15, 1956 by Bing Crosby and Grace Kelly
    Capitol 3507 b/w *Well Did You Evah*

Twist And Shout---Bert Russell—Phil Medley
  May 7, 1962 by The Isley Brothers
  Wand 124 b/w *Spanish Twist*

Where Have You Been All My Life?---Barry Mann—Cynthia Weil
  May 7, 1962 by Arthur Alexander
  Dot 16357 b/w *Soldier Of Love (Lay Down Your Arms)*

%*Why (Can't You Love Me Again)*---Tony Sheridan—Bill Crompton
  Original Recording—1958 demo tape by Tony Sheridan and The Shadows

Words Of Love—Buddy Holly
  June 17, 1957 by Buddy Holly
  Coral 61852 b/w *Mailman Bring Me No More Blues*

**You Don't Know Me At All*---Dave Jordan
  Given to Ringo—1976

Your Feet's Too Big---Ada Benson—Fred Fisher
  Popularized—December 26, 1939 by Fats Waller
  Bluebird 10500 b/w *Suitcase Susie*

For all the songs listed above, we've indicated their release on the original labels. This is not meant to send people scurrying to collector's record stores searching for old Bluebird discs, nor to imply that the songs were never again issued. Rather, we wish to emphasize the context of the original recording so that, in choosing a repackage or compiliation set, proper attention can be paid to the right label and the right recording. Beware of re-recordings on different labels. For example, the albums released by Chuck Berry on Mercury and Little Richard on Vee Jay contain new but mediocre versions of their past hits.

Of course, a number of songs *are* hopelessly out of print, but a surprising number aren't. Atlantic (Ray Charles, the Coasters, the Drifters) has a golden-oldie series of 45s, not to mention several excellent compilation albums. Motown has released multi-record *Greatest Hits* packages for most of its major artists. RCA (finally) gathered the Elvis *Sun Sessions* onto one LP, and has an excellent oldies series, too. Warner Brothers has issued a two-disc *Best Of* Phil Spector. MCA has done the same for Buddy Holly. Chess did it three times in its three-volume set of Chuck Berry's *Golden Decade*. Even odds-and-ends sets like the three-volume *American Graffiti* collections often contain surprise reissues. And some labels aren't even gone—they've just dropped out of immediate view. Specialty (Little Richard, Larry Williams, Lloyd Price) is still alive and well in Hollywood, California; and Sun (Carl Perkins, Johnny Cash, Jerry Lee Lewis) is doing fine in Nashville, Tennessee. If all else fails, write directly to them!

SW-11525

WINGS AT THE SPEED OF SOUND

Wings At The Speed Of Sound   Capitol SW 11525 (LP)

PANDEMONIUM

AERIAL BALLET

All My Loving
Parlophone GEP 8891 (EP)

A Hard Day's Night (extracts)
Parlophone GEP 8924 (EP)

The Beatles No.1
Parlophone GEP 8883 (EP)

Beatles For Sale
Parlophone GEP 8931 (EP)

Bootlegs

Bootlegs generally fall into one of three categories: Recordings of Live Concerts, Studio Out-takes, or Recordings of Radio/Television/Film Appearances. As more and more material is issued from record company vaults, the number of available bootleg recordings which are of a more than passing interest rapidly declines. The release of **Wings Over America, The Beatles At the Hollywood Bowl** and **The Beatles Live At The Star Club** has all but eliminated any need (or desire!) to suffer through "fifth row--second balcony" recordings of old concerts. As Capitol/EMI runs out of ways to re-package existing Beatle material, the temptation to plunder the vaults for alternate takes and unreleased new songs will undoubtedly prove impossible to resist. Eventually, then, any studio out-takes worth hearing (and some not) will probably be released through normal channels. Radio, TV and film appearances, though, usually don't lend themselves as well to commercial record release, and these still remain a prime, accessible source of material for collectors and fans alike (just plug in your home tape recorder and they're yours!).

In this section, we have chronologically arranged by recording date (if possible) the events since January 1976 which produced bootleg material. For pre-1976 recordings, see the "Bootlegs" chapter of *All Together Now*. We must point out here, as we did then, that the arrangement by performing date, rather than by appearance on a particular bootleg disc, was done for two reasons. It avoids the repetition inherent in cataloguing the many bootleg records available. More importantly, the very term *bootleg record* is a misnomer. Save for a handful of examples, none of the bootleg recordings were ever envisaged in the form they currently appear in: albums. Most of the performances contained were, in their original form, singular events: a TV show, a concert, or a prospective record. Their inclusion and exclusion in the available bootleg albums are totally a result of the whims of the generally unknown people who pressed them. Particular bootleg records, though, *are* recommended elsewhere in this book (in the Questions and Answers Section "Was

Paul, In Fact, Dead . . . And More Reasonable Questions.'').

January 25, 1976—Houston Concert
In 1975 and 1976, Bob Dylan spearheaded a drive to call attention to what he saw as the unjust conviction of Rubin "Hurricane" Carter on a murder charge. Several stops on his "Rolling Thunder Revue" tour were special benefits for Carter's defense fund. The "Hurricane II" benefit at the Houston Astrodome saw Ringo Starr sitting in on drums with Howie Wyeth and Joe Vitale. Ringo had no solo numbers.

January 1976—Studio Out-take,
Bernie Taupin, Elton John's song writing partner, began work on his second solo album early in 1976. It was planned to coincide with the release of his book, *The One Who Writes The Words For Elton John*, in early spring. Ringo joined Bernie on the cut *Cryin' Time* for the album, and even contributed some artwork to the book. Though the book was released on schedule, by the fall Taupin had shelved the LP.

April 20, 1976—New York City Civic Center Concert
For years a fan of Monty Python's Flying Circus—George snuck in a plug for the group when he appeared on the *Dick Cavett* show in 1971—Harrison gleefully joined them on stage one night of their first American tour to sing *Lumberjack Song*. Though this was not the night recorded for the **Monty Python Live At The Civic Center** souvenir LP, George did produce a British single of *Lumberjack Song* in 1975, which was re-released in 1976 as part of a double-single package **Python On Song**. This is fairly easy to find on import.

June 1976—Studio Out-take
Ringo sat in on the sessions of a new LP by Michael Parks of *Long Lonesome Highway* fame. The LP has yet to be released.

June 28, 1976—"Goodnight America" TV Segment (ABC)
Geraldo Rivera, who helped organize the first One-To-One Concert with John Lennon back in 1972, welcomed Paul and Linda McCartney on their first American tour with Wings by having them on his late-night show. Besides the usual chit-chat, excerpts were shown from Wings' Seattle King Dome concert on June 10 before a crowd of 67,000. The only song aired in its entirety was *Yesterday*. Excerpts from this interview were broadcast the next morning on *Good Morning America*.

July 1976---Wings From The Wings (3 LPs) Idle Mind Productions IMP 1117/1118/1119

As long as bootleggers confined themselves to balcony recordings of 10-year-old Beatle concerts, nobody *really* cared that much about their activities. They were an annoyance, to be sure, but not as big a problem to the record industry as the counterfeit tapes of current hit albums, pirated anthologies of hit groups, and simple stolen merchandise. However, when an album from Paul's first American tour appeared within *weeks* of the last show, available for purchase a full six months before the "official" version would be out, the industry took notice. This was direct competition with current product (the bootleg boxed package contained all 30 songs performed by Wings, spread over 3 albums--which were pressed on red, white and blue vinyl to honor the Bicentennial). The crackdown on bootleg sales was stepped up, so that the familiar plain white album packages became more and more difficult to spot at swap meets, fan conventions and other public gatherings. "Busts" involving thousands of records took place. But, like most great American industries, bootleggers have learned to adapt. They've begun specializing in compact 7-inch discs, easier to store and display. (and they don't look like bootleg *albums*.) There has also been a return to more uncommercial material (who but a collector would *want* a copy of Paul's **Ram** promo, **Brung To Ewe By Hal Smith**?). Besides, there always seem to be more people supporting and patronizing, rather than pursuing, the bootleggers. Capitol Records had to rush its release of the Hollywood Bowl Concert recording after it was discovered that radio stations across the country were spotlighting it in "exclusive advance premieres," though really only playing tracks from the various Hollywood Bowl bootlegs.

Early Fall 1976---Studio Out-takes

Ringo's first solo effort for Atlantic repeated the now familiar Ringo formula of gathering super-star friends into the studio to help in the writing, vocals, backing and production of his album tracks. Left over from **Rotogravure** were *All Right*, written by Ringo, *It's Hard To Be Lovers* with Keith Allison, and *Party*, a Ringo/Harry Nilsson effort.

October/November 1976---Promotional Films

Three promotional films were made to coincide with the release of George's first album on Dark Horse. Two were directed by friend Eric Idle: *Crackerbox Palace*, with cameo appearances by members of Monty Python's Flying Circus, and *True Love*, featuring George in a turn-of-the-century handle-bar moustach, proposing to a woman in a canoe. Harrison himself directed *This Song*, a wild romp through the court system which had just ruled against him in the *My Sweet Lord* case. All the soundtracks were from the album recordings. *This Song* and *Crackerbox Palace* were shown on *NBC Saturday Night* on November 20.

November 18, 1976—Taping For "NBC Saturday Night" Segment (NBC)

George actually didn't appear *live* on the *Saturday Night* program, instead taping his segments the Thursday before the broadcast. This allowed Harrison and Paul Simon, the program's host that week, to run through their performing spotlight a couple of times, and to chat with the audience. They played several takes of *Here Comes The Sun* and *Homeward Bound*, the songs used on the actual broadcast, as well as versions of *Bye Bye Love* and *Rock Island Line*. In reply to Simon's "Any requests for George?" the crowd called out their favorites, and George responded with quick off-the-cuff snatches of *Don't Let Me Wait Too Long, Yesterday* and *Bridge Over Troubled Water*. Harrison also appeared in the sketch opening the program, in which he and *Saturday Night* producer Lorne Michaels have a mock-argument over the amount of money George, only one fourth of the Beatles, should receive for appearing on the program (*Saturday Night* had offered $3200 for an appearance by all four Beatles).

November 24, 1976—Last Waltz Concert

The Band staged their gala final concert, dubbed "The Last Waltz," at San Francisco's Winterland on Thanksgiving eve. Following a sit-down turkey dinner, the audience was treated to a parade of super-star friends, among them Bob Dylan, Joni Mitchell, Van Morrison, Eric Clapton and others, joining the Band in selections spanning the length of their career. Ringo, who has a habit of turning up at such Rock Events, joined the stage festivities for the *I Shall Be Released* finale, and stayed on to play in a 30-minute jam which followed, also featuring members of the Band, Dr. John, Eric Clapton, Ron Wood, Carl Radle, Neil Young and Steve Stills. The entire concert was filmed by Martin Scorsese for a possible feature film and souvenir album set.

No,
You're Wrong
Part II

John Lennon was furious! In the three weeks since the release of **Sgt. Pepper**, pompous pundits and confused kids had been tearing the album apart, searching for God, the Holy Grail and—just maybe— a few grains of hash which everybody's favorite gurus might have managed to sneak in right past customs (perhaps by licking the label. . .)! John didn't really care whether people worshipped the vinyl or cut it into little pieces. What *did* offend his artistic pride were all the comments being made about the "thinly veiled references" to drugs in *Lucy In The Sky With Diamonds* (L-S-D). Bloody hell! If he were doing a tribute to drugs, it certainly wouldn't consist of a few "thinly veiled references"—he'd tackle the subject head-on with honesty and humor. So in a burst of energy, he sat down and wrote the *LS Bumblebee*, a song filled with tongue-in-cheek, mind-expanding images. Before John could progress any further than a rough rehearsal tape, though, the Beatles were scheduled to make their appearance on a world-wide TV hookup. John had to devote his energies to the song for that appearance, *All You Need Is Love*. This song was then rush-released as a single. For the flip, the still-unfinished *Bumblebee* was by-passed in favor of the already completed *Baby You're A Rich Man*. Quite unfortunate (in retrospect) as *Bumblebee*'s mock drug imagery would have been a delightful foil to *All You Need Is Love*.

As the much-touted Summer of Love sighed to an end, much of the LSD controversy had died down, too. Besides, John was already involved in a more complex piece, which eventually became *I Am The Walrus*. Still, *Bumblebee* was too good a song to waste. Lennon then remembered two British humorists he had always admired and had finally met the previous year in a BBC TV production, called "Not Only. . .But Also": Peter Cook and Dudley Moore. He gave them the rehearsal tape, with the invitation to rework it and release the song themselves. Cook and Moore dubbed their own voices onto the track, added a few more special effects and polished up the entire piece. John was quite pleased to hear the final product, which the duo released as a single in Britain (Decca F 12551). It bombed. Then faded into obscurity. Now it's a collector's item on both sides of the Atlantic.

An unearthed gem for the unending files of Beatlemania? A great story for an article in the Sunday Supplements? No, a complete fabrication. A tale we made up on a rainy afternoon. In fact, Peter Cook and Dudley Moore, who *are* two very talented British humorists, released the *LS Bumblebee* in January of 1967– six months *before* **Sgt. Pepper** came out! They wrote the tune as a spoof of the whole psychedelic craze. It was months later that some poor fool heard the Cook and Moore record and, obviously unfamiliar with their voices, assumed it to be Lennon in a put-down of the LSD charge. Over the years it gained nearly universal acceptance as a true Beatle bootleg. But, recently, the true story got out, and fans have been able to call off the digging for the few copies of the disc still around.

Yet almost from the beginning, Beatle fans have combed the vinyl jungle in a never-ending quest for a "complete" Beatles collection. In many cases, the search unearthed gems which, aside from the "Beatle" connection, were just plain good records: David Bromberg's first album; Howlin' Wolf's **London Sessions**; the Bonzo Dog Band's **Urban Spaceman**, to name a few. Unfortunately, the dependence on word-of-mouth clues and the claims of record manufacturers opened a market for exploitation, sometimes subtle, sometimes blatant, sometimes even unintentional!

One of the most popular sections in *All Together Now* was "No, You're Wrong." In the past two years, we've run into several more tales which must be put to rest, lest they cause unnecessary consternation among collectors and fans alike:

FEBRUARY 1977 (US) Decca 31382
 by the Beatles
 My Bonnie (English Intro)/*My Bonnie* (German Intro)
JULY 1976 (US) SFF/SOK 21
 by The Beatles
 How Do You Do It/Revolution

FEBRUARY 1977 (US) Swan 4197
by The Beatles
How Do You Do It/Komm, Gib Mir Deine Hand
LATE 1976 (US) PRO 4Q1-2 (EP)
by The Beatles
THE BEATLES GET TOGETHER!
side one: Kenny Everett Interview featuring *Cottonfields/*
George Harrison and Bob Dylan sing *When Everybody Comes To Town* and *I'd Have You Anytime*
side two: The Beatles and The Rolling Stones sing *Loving Sacred Loving* and *Shapes of Orange*/Mick Jagger sings *Too Many Cooks*
LATE 1975 (US) Tollie EP-1 8091 (EP)
by The Beatles
THEIR BIGGEST HITS
Love Me Do/Twist And Shout/There's A Place/P.S. I Love You
With the interest in Beatle esoterica increasing as the years go by, it was inevitable that "fake" pressings of some of their rarer recordings would appear. There's nothing really wrong with this, as long as the buyer understands what he's getting. A fan, unwilling to shell out $50 for a "real" copy of the obscure LP **Songs, Pictures And Stories Of The Fabulous Beatles** might be more inclined to buy an obviously newly pressed "fake" copy. Any real fan would already have the songs on the album (perhaps on a number of records!), but the **Songs, Pictures And Stories** LP has some nice cover work and some cute *Seventeen*-like "John Loves (insert *your* photo here)" kitsch. How could you properly recreate the emotions of 1964 without that?

Among true Beatles *aficionados* it has been generally conceded that one of the rarest, if not *the* rarest, item you could have in a *complete* Beatles collection is a mint copy of the Beatles' very first record, *My Bonnie* with the Beatles backing singer Tony Sheridan. Recorded in Germany, the earliest issuances of this disc had a spoken introduction by Sheridan in German or English, depending on what country you bought it in. Getting your hands on a copy with the English introduction is hard enough these days, but gaining possession of one with the German lead-in requires either a *very* lucky day record hunting or a *very* good friend who lived in Germany in 1961. These "German" discs have been known to command a price of $500 apiece. In early 1977, some generous soul who possessed both versions printed up a number of discs with the English-intro'd *My Bonnie* on the A side and the German-intro'd *My Bonnie* on the flip. He even reprinted the familiar Decca logo under which it appeared in the US in 1962. It goes for the eminently reasonable price of $3.00.

Such a practice, while no doubt technically illegal, hurts no one and, in fact, helps quite a few people. The number of people who really want this record is so small, in the overall view, that any non-paid royalties will hardly be missed. Meanwhile, a number of rabid record collectors are temporarily satiated.

Along the same lines, some studio quality out-takes have been pressed and released as singles. One featured the Beatles singing *How Do You Do It*, made at one of their earliest recording sessions but never previously issued. In 1976, RKO stations across the country aired the *How Do You Do It* cut, but added a voice track that whispered "exclusive" over every instrumental break. The single, though, is a clean, uncluttered recording, and even backed with an excellent alternate version of *Revolution* (from a 1968 TV performance). Even though packaged in a classy picture sleeve, no attempt is made to make you think that this is a long-lost commercial release. It's a specially printed collector's item, clearly made for fans and record collectors.

However, when the seller flatly states, or covertly implies, that the record he's selling is an authentic rare gem, some harm can occur. Of course, there's no accounting for how gullible some people can be, and it's hard to draw a firm line between assistance and dishonesty.

Around the same time that the "new" Decca single began appearing, another newly printed disc arrived on the market. It coupled the Beatles' version of *How Do You Do It* with the obscure version of *I Want To Hold Your Hand* that the Beatles did in German (*Komm, Gib Mir Deine Hand*, included on the Capitol LP **Something New**). The 45 was printed with the familiar white Swan label, the actual label in the U.S. for *Sie Liebt Dich* (*She Loves You*), the only other German-language recording the Beatles made. Since many Beatle fans have never even seen an authentic *Sie Liebt Dich* single, those of the more impressionable sort might jump to the conclusion that *Komm, Gib Mir Deine Hand/How Do You Do It* was the companion release to *Sie Liebt Dich*. It is possible that whoever printed up this record used the Swan label as an "in-joke," or for lack of any other label. But there are those to whom such generous assumptions cannot be given.

Ticket To Ryde Ltd. and Beatles For Sale, U.S.A. printed up a "limited collectors edition series" of an EP entitled **The Beatles Get Together!** Half the contents are of real value: British DJ Kenny Everett conducting a wildly off-beat interview with the Beatles broadcast in early 1968, and a really historic unreleased session produced by John Lennon and Mick Jagger singing *Too Many Cooks*, backed by an all-star lineup. Filling out space on side one is what seems to be George Harrison and Bob Dylan mumbling in the middle of an electrical storm. The real problem with this record is the blatant mislabeling of two cuts, said to be the Rolling Stones playing with the

Beatles (*Loving Sacred Loving* and *Shapes of Orange*). Not only does it not sound like any of the Beatles and Rolling Stones, these two cuts, as any dedicated Stones fan could tell you, are two sides of a single (*Loving Scared Loving* and *Shades of Orange*) by a group called The End, produced by Bill Wyman. The EP's sleeve contains the ultimate come-on to the collector mentality: down in the right hand corner, in the style of the Beatles' *White Album*, is a "specially" stamped number telling which of the "limited" 100 copies you have purchased. Rumor has it that a convention will soon be held of all those who purchased issue number nineteen.

This is mere nit-picking compared to the "service" performed in 1975 when (surprise!) an EP containing four Beatles songs (the two Beatle singles on Tollie Records) miraculously appeared. It had the authentic Tollie label and a very convincing picture sleeve. This was news to regular Beatle collectors, who thought they were aware of all Beatle material released in the US at that time. The disc was a fake, it soon became clear. Unlike the *My Bonnie* and *How Do You Do It* singles, however, this record was passed off as a genuine rare item, sometimes commanding a price of $100 or more. Unfortunately, the Beatles discography printed by Ticket To Ryde Ltd. in 1975 didn't help matters by mistakenly listing the EP as an actual release, even denoting label variations. Word eventually got around, though, before too many people were stung, and the EP has since become infamous, serving as a warning to collectors and fans of just how easy it is to manufacture authentic looking, high priced fakes.

MAR 20, 1970 (UK) Major Minor 691
    by Karen Young
    Que Sera, Sera/(one tin soldier)

Along the more mundane line of misconceptions comes this mildly successful single. In mid-1969 Paul McCartney worked out an arrangement of Doris Day's *Que Sera, Sera* for Apple protege Mary Hopkin to record. At first, however, it only came out on the Continent and, lest Britain be deprived of such brilliance, Karen Young released her own recording of the tune with McCartney's arrangement, which she properly credited. Due to the fact that Mary Hopkin's version wasn't released in the U.S. until June of 1970, some people had assumed that McCartney had something to do with the actual recording of Young's version. T'aint so.

MAY 11, 1971 (US) Warner Brothers WS 1914 (LP)
SEP 10, 1971 (UK) Warner Brothers K 46091 (LP)
    by Jackie Lomax
    HOME IS IN MY HEAD
        Rhythm Guitar:Rickie Redstreak
        Slide & Second Guitar:Frank Furter

Pseudonyms can often reek havoc on the process of logic. Recording contracts being what they are, well known musicians are often forced to hide behind the cloak of an alias (recall Blind Boy Grunt a.k.a. Bob Dylan?). In the late 60's, members of the Beatles began turning up as guest stars on their friends' albums, using pseudonyms. Some were mildly confusing (L'Angelo Mysterioso) while others (George Harrysong) hardly taxed the brain of even the densest DJ. The problem is, like finding bugs in your bed, once one is discovered, they seem to be everywhere. Take Jackie Lomax. One of the original Apple artists. George Harrison produces his recordings. Paul and Ringo appear on his records. Lomax eventually leaves Apple and signs with Warner Brothers, but is still friends with the Beatles. So when Lomax's first Warner Brothers album comes out in 1971, the Beatle fan "in the know" slyly arched his eyebrow at such spurious *non de plumes* as Rickie Redstreak and Frank Furter. Paul McCartney and George Harrison, right? Wrong! Jackie Lomax and Jackie Lomax! Says who? Jackie Lomax! Why? Obtuse immigration laws allowed him to sing on records recorded in the US but not to play instruments.

AUG 3, 1976 (US) Capitol ST 11542 (LP)
APR 8, 1977 (UK) Capitol EST-11542 (LP)
  by Klaatu
  KLAATU
    Calling Occupants Of Interplanetary Craft/California Jam/ Anus Of Uranus/Sub Rosa Subway/True Life Hero/Doctor Marvello/ Sir Bodsworth Rugglesby III/Little Mevtrino
MAR 21, 1977 (US) Capitol 4412
  by Klaatu
  Sub Rosa Subway/Anus of Uranus
    Oh Jesus, not again! First there was the Paul Is Dead Rumor. Then the Masked Marauders Hoax. Now the Klaatu Konspiracy. Sometimes it seems that these things are thought up by out-of-work press agents just so nine-year-old kids will bug Beatles authors for years thereafter ("but really, if you play **Sgt. Pepper** at 16. . ."). Really! People don't drag out Roy Wood albums and claim Elvis was playing maracas on the session ("Well, he was in town that week!"). No, it's much better for a group to come straight out like that group of already forgotten English rock 'n' rollers who, in 1976, stunned the record company executives at a closed circuit broadcast by bluntly stating that since nobody was using it, from now on they would use the name "The Beatles." Great. Maybe someone will change his name to Richard Nixon and ask David Frost to interview him.
    What? Klaatu? Oh yes, Klaatu. No, Klaatu is/am: John Woloschuk, L. M. Carpenter, Chip Dale, Terry Draper, David Long and Dino Tome. Yes, they were on Capitol (just like the Beatles).

Yes, Ringo borrowed from the same old science fiction movie, *The Day The Earth Stood Still*, for the motto for his **Goodnight Vienna** LP ("Klaatu Barada Nikto"). Yes, the writing, production and publishing credits are appropriately vague: produced by. . .Klaatu, written by. . .Klaatu, published by. . .Klaatunes. Didn't you wonder why it took six months before some East Coast DJ first broached the possibility of Klaatu being the Beatles? Klaatu supposedly sounds like the Beatles circa 1967. They do, to an extent. Well, everybody's happy now, right? Klaatu's manager says they're not the Beatles, and yet people keep buying the album. After all, Fabian did it for three years. Now don't ask about it anymore, OK?

Friends, Relatives, And Total Strangers

MIKE MCGEAR

For over ten years, Paul's younger brother, Michael, has pursued his own career in music, humor and poetry. When he began performing in the early sixties, Mike decided to change his surname from McCartney to McGear, removing the obvious "Paul McCartney's brother" stigma. For fans of the Beatles, though, following Mike McGear's career is not simply a case of collecting odd records by a Beatle relative, as with the discs released by John's dad and George's sister. Mike has been an important part of one particular branch of British humor, one which combines poetry, art, music and satire. It began for Mike with *The Liverpool One Fat Lady All Electric Show.*

Mike had planned to enter a British art school (like Paul's friend John Lennon), but a change in requirement standards left him standing on the outside. Instead, he spent several years as a tailor, a Catholic Bible salesman, and a ladies' hairdresser. In the early summer of 1962, he visited (and eventually joined) the Merseyside Art Festival, organized by John Gorman and poet Roger McGough. Following the festival, eight of the participants organized a number of poetry readings, which soon became a regular part of the Liverpool scene. Comedy sketches and duologues were added to supplement the solo poetry readings. This was *The Liverpool One Fat Lady All Electric Show*, an unwieldy moniker soon changed to the shorter *Scaffold*. In December 1963, a British TV scout spotted them and scheduled an audition. Three members stood out, and they became the final amalgam of *Scaffold*: Mike McGear, Roger McGough and John Gorman. They were signed to provide humorous sketches for the late-night British TV show *Gazette*, a forerunner of the *Eamonn Andrews* show. In 1964, they turned professional, appearing in dozens of clubs, theatres, universities, political meetings, and festivals.

It wasn't until 1966, however, that they cut their first disc, beginning a five year association with Parlophone records. Though the Beatles' George Martin produced this first record, *2 Days Monday/3 Blind Jellyfish*, this was not the start of super-star packaging and promotion for Scaffold; their failure to satisfy the rock-starved kids while on the circuit with groups like the Yardbirds underscored the wisdom of such a decision. They worked better in the smaller venues, to an audience more willing to give satire, poetry, humor *and* music a try. Scaffold continued to cut singles which, for the most part, were more in the line of novelty items; *Goodbat Nightman*, for example, was a send-up of the popular *Batman* TV show. Then, surprisingly, they clicked with a top ten hit in late 1967, *Thank U Very Much*. Mike McGear wrote it while talking on the phone to Paul, thanking him for the gift of a Nikon camera. Paul dropped by the studios while Scaffold was cutting the disc, gave a few helpful suggestions, and then watched it zip up the charts. (Reputedly, it was also Prime Minister Wilson's favorite record—the inclusion of a "thank you" to the Queen undoubtedly helped explain his soft spot for the tune).

Paul, however, took a more active role in a "solo" album project by Roger McGough and Mike McGear in 1968. A few super-stars, including Jimi Hendrix, joined the duo for the recording, but it still remained firmly in the hands of Mike and Roger. Mike got his chance to sing a few rock numbers (Scaffold wasn't really equipped for searing guitar solos), while Roger was given enough room to present his extended (twelve minutes) poetic tale of the development and dissolution of a love affair, "Summer With Monika". The album garnered rave reviews on its release, and was followed up just two months later with the first Scaffold album. Actually a live concert recording, this LP pretty well captured Scaffold's stage act—there's poetry (including a duologue), music, sketches and satire. Dave Mason provided the guitar accompaniment.

In the fall, American fans got their first real taste of Scaffold with the release of the album **Thank U Very Much**. It was the traditional American presentation of a new British act: the minor American hit (and title cut), all their other old singles, plus a few new items including one track which was never subsequently released in Britain (*Knees Up Mother Brown*). In Britain, meanwhile, the group released what was to be their biggest record yet, *Lily The Pink*. Again, there was the aura of super-stars about it (Jack Bruce played bass, Graham Nash sang the bit about Jennifer Eccles), but it was still all Scaffold's tune (basically, a new arrangement of a traditional bar song). The record topped the British charts by the end of the year, and gave the group its first real commercial (not just artistic) success.

A new album in Britain, L.P., combined both studio tracks on one side and a "live" (in the EMI studios) humor and poetry performance on the other. Musically, they broke out of the novelty-song/bar-room-singalong syndrome. The "live" side, which lasted over half an hour, was, in several ways, better than the live performance on the previous LP. Transitions were tighter, there was less filler, and both the poetry and humor included more topical subjects such as Russian dissidents, American race riots and the Viet-nam war (though even the light and happy *Thank U Very Much* had dropped in a reference to napalm). They pulled an excellent song from the album, *Charity Bubbles*, and recut it as the follow-up single. A repeat of the success of *Lily The Pink* failed to materialize, and the group started feeling the pressure—among themselves—to produce another hit. They churned out several forgettable singles over the next two years and then they just needed a rest. And they took it. From each other. From recording. Parlophone didn't renew their contract.

Instead, in March of 1971, Mike decided to record a solo album. He asked friends Zoot Money (piano), Andy Roberts (guitars), Dave Richards (bass), Gerry Conway (drums), Norman Yardley (gob iron), and John Megginson (piano) to join him in the project. Roger McGough co-authored about half the songs, and other musicians sat in from time to time (Brian Auger on organ, for instance). The project took about a year to complete, and was released in April of 1972 on Island records in Britain. Island soon became the home of another combination of talent, GRIMMS: John Gorman, Andy Roberts, Neil Innes, Roger McGough, Mike McGear and Viv Stanshall—the initials of all their surnames spelled the group's name—joined by Zoot Money and Gerry Conway. They joined forces to try to overcome one of the chief limitations on a group like Scaffold: the size of an audience they could approach. Three performers versus Madison Square Garden, for instance, might be hopeless. Such hopeless odds, in fact, had all-but-destroyed another British humor band years earlier on their American tours, the Bonzo Dog Band. A fully equipped troupe of eight such as Grimms, however, could tackle a larger arena while still allowing for the lusty insanity inherent in all of its members. Grimms cut two LPs for Island in 1973, **Grimms** and **Rockin' Duck**, the second LP finally being released in America in 1976 on Island's Antilles record label. However, such a large cast resulted in sub-groups carrying on within the group. Neil Innes, for instance, began developing some standard skits which would see him through the next three years. Mike McGear, Roger McGough and John Gorman even broke from the group long enough to cut a Scaffold "solo" album of sorts, **Fresh Liver**, though various members of Grimms, as well as the Average White Band, guested on the LP.

On the surface, then, it seemed that in Grimms was an ideal, if volatile, situation: a large group that allowed individual pursuits but which could use its strength (in numbers) to expand the horizons of all the members. As 1973 drew to an end, though, Mike McGear was disturbed by what he saw as the growing tendency of Grimms to aim itself toward *smaller*, less awesome projects and performing spots. Perhaps the members just couldn't overcome their affection for arty, intimate performing arenas as easily as they thought. Clearly, there was problem in direction and management. So Mike, a married man with family responsibilities, left the group and decided to pursue his talents in writing children's books. Not as glamorous, but not as unpredictable, either.

Speaking to Paul, Mike discovered that his brother, too, had lost a group (in his case, two Wings had just taken flight). At Paul's suggestion, the two agreed to undertake a project together. Probably a single. But it soon mushroomed. First, it became a Scaffold reunion with the May release of the old Dominic Behan song *Liverpool Lou* as a single on Warner Brothers. The disc, produced by Paul, hit top ten in Britain, as critics and fans alike welcomed the return of Scaffold. It was followed four months later by the *McGear album, one of the *best* collaboration projects Paul has ever produced. Ten new McCartney compositions and co-compostitions came out of the *McGear sessions. Paul himself, with Wings, released no album that year, so all his energies and inspiration seemed poured into his brother's LP. Yet, despite the *obvious* presence of Paul (and Wings) throughout the LP, it never took off. Three singles were released in Britain, one in America. It was cut-out in 1976, and now ranks as one of the great, generally undiscovered, gems of rock.

Scaffold, however, was back together again. They closed the year with a special Christmas single for Warners, *Mummy Won't Be Home For Christmas*, and put the finishing touches on their upcoming LP. Released in February 1975, **Sold Out** marked a shift in Scaffold's approach to an album. Instead of trying to include "some live, some poetry, some songs, some skits, etc.," **Sold Out** concentrated almost exclusively on music and clever musical bits. *Ramsbottom* parodied the old *Chicago* song: *Pack of Cards* mocked the pretentious *Deck of Cards*; and *Cokey Cokey, Leaving of Liverpool* and *Mingulay Boating Song* were old English favorites. And it all worked! Old friends like John Megginson, Zoot Money, Gerry Conway and Andy Roberts again backed the group, joined by new friends like 10cc's Lol Cream. Perhaps buoyed by the success of *Liverpool Lou*, included on the LP, they tackled their new material with vigor. Or perhaps they just *Sold Out* and wanted a *hit* album. In either case, the Scaffold reunion LP had to be judged a success. However, since *Liverpool Lou* hadn't hit in the US, the album wasn't released in America.

Nineteen-seventy-five saw one final effort by Warner Brothers to break Mike McGear as a solo artist. He was sent on an extensive

English interview/personal appearance tour to promote a silly throw-away tune, *Dance The Do* (one last song written and produced by Paul McCartney). *Dance The Do* promotions were held all over England. Nothing much happened. After releasing several more tracks from **McGear*, all with equal success, Warners and Mike and Scaffold parted company.

Then, Grimms resurfaced and signed a deal with DJM records, though this time Mike McGear wasn't included as a part of the group (Roger McGough and John Gorman, however, were). They released a single in the summer of 1975, *Backbreaker*, and an album, **Sleepers** in 1976. It's still all one big family, though. Another single, *The Womble Bashers of Walthamstow*, pulled from the **Sleepers** LP in 1976 found intself in competition with another song released the same day, *The Womble Bashers* by the Bashers (really just Grimms on another label, aided and abetted by Mike McGear). Solo efforts apart from Grimms, then, abound. Neil Innes. Andy Roberts. In 1975 Roger McGough and Brian Patten released an album of poetry for Argo, **British Poets of Our Time**. Even John Gorman *finally* released his first solo effort, **Go Man Gorman**, in April of 1977.

For the most part, though, some stability settled on Mike Mc-Gear's career beginning in 1976. Scaffold was back on the road as Scaffold, once again playing small and medium-sized halls. Mike cut a solo record for EMI called *Doing Nothing All Day* (produced by Peter Winfield), before Scaffold settled at Bronze records, now distributed by EMI. Their first Bronze single, *Wouldn't It Be Funny If You Didn't Have A Nose/Mr. Noselighter*, was a tribute to/promotion for Roger McGough's new book, *Mr. Noselighter*. By early 1977, both a new Scaffold LP and a Mike McGear solo effort were in the works.

The Scaffold/Grimms combination often shares the same stage. Recently (April 1, 1977) they joined an all-star cast of British humorists at London's Royal Albert Hall in a special benefit for the British Institute for the Achievement of Human Potential and the Mind.

MAY 6, 1966 (UK) Parlophone R 5443
by Scaffold Prod: George Martin
A: *2 Days Monday* --John Gorman—Mike McGear—Roger McGough—
    2:23
B: *3 Blind Jellyfish*—John Gorman—Mike McGear—Roger McGough—
    1:58

DEC 2, 1966 (UK) Parlophone R 5548
by Scaffold Prod: John Burgess
A: *Goodbat Nightman*—Mike McGear—Roger McGough—*2:09*
B: *Long Strong Black Pudding*—John Gorman—Mike McGear—Roger
    McGough—*2:12*

NOV 4, 1967 (UK) Parlophone R 5643
JAN 8, 1968 (US) Bell 701
by Scaffold Prod: Tony Palmer
A: *Thank U Very Much*—Mike McGear—*2:30*
B: *Ide B The First*—Mike McGear—Roger McGough—*2:30*

MAR 15, 1968 (UK) Parlophone R 5679
MAY 27, 1968 (US) Bell 724
by Scaffold Prod: Norrie Paramor
A: *Do You Remember?*—Mike McGear—Roger McGough—*2:48*
*B: *Carry On Krow*—Traditional arr. John Gorman—*1:53*

MAY 17, 1968 (UK) Parlophone PCS 7047 (LP)
by Mike McGear and Roger McGough
MCGOUGH AND MCGEAR Prod: Paul McCartney, Mike McGear,
Roger McGough, and Friends as "All of Us"
side one
  So Much—Mike McGear—Roger McGough—*4:30*
  Little Bit Of Heaven—Roger McGough—*1:47*
  Basement Flat--Mike McGear—Roger McGough—*2:30*
  From "Frink, A Life In The Day Of" and "Summer With Monika"—
    Roger McGough—*12:00*
    Prologue—Roger McGough—Andy Roberts
    Introducing: Moanin'—Roger McGough—Timmons
    Anji—Roger McGough—Graham
    Epilogue—Roger McGough—Andy Roberts
side two
  Come Close And Sleep Now—Roger McGough—*2:03*
  Yellow Book—Mike McGear—Roger McGough—*2:07*
  House In My Head--Mike McGear—Roger McGough—*3:26*
  Mr. Tickle—Mike McGear—*3:18*
  Living Room—Mike McGear—*2:36*
  Do You Remember?—Mike McGear—Roger McGough—*3:08*
  Please Don't Run Too Fast--Mike McGear—*1:20*
  Ex Art Student—Mike McGear—Roger McGough—*6:31*

JUN 14, 1968 (UK) Parlophone R 5703
by Scaffold Prod: Norrie Paramor
A: *1–2–3*—Mike McGear—*3:27*
B: *Today*—Mike McGear—*2:40*

106

JUL 5, 1968 (UK) Parlophone PCS 7051 (LP)
Recorded Live at the Queen Elizabeth Hall
by Scaffold
THE SCAFFOLD Prod: Norrie Paramor assisted by Tim Rice
side one: Act One
  Ten Whiskey Bottles—John Gorman—*4:11*
  Virginity—Roger McGough—*2:40*
  Son Of Lent—Roger McGough—*3:30*
  Love Story—Roger McGough—*6:35*
  Old Folks—Roger McGough—*4:35*
  2 Days Monday—John Gorman—Mike McGear—Roger McGough—*3:03*
side two: Act Two
  Father John—John Gorman—*9:08*
  This Must Be Love—Roger McGough—*3:33*
  Poetry
    Two Early Morning Poems—Roger McGough—*0:38*
    Lollipopman—Roger McGough—*0:10*
    Poem For National LSD Week—Roger McGough—*0:10*
    My Cat And I—Roger McGough—*0:35*
    The Act Of Love—Roger McGough—*0:44*
    Let Me Die A Young Man's Death—Roger McGough—*1:09*
  Dear Diary—Mike McGear—*2:05*
  Thank U Very Much—Mike McGear—*2:05*

SEP 2, 1968 (US) Bell 6018 (LP)
by Scaffold
THANK U VERY MUCH Prod: Norrie Paramor except †John Burgess,
%George Martin and $Tony Palmer
side one
  †LONG STRONG BLACK PUDDING—John Gorman—Mike McGear—
    Roger McGough—*2:12*
  †GOODBAT NIGHTMAN—Mike McGear—Roger McGough—*2:09*
  %2 DAYS MONDAY—John Gorman—Mike McGear—Roger McGough—
    2:23
  %3 BLIND JELLYFISH—John Gorman—Mike McGear—Roger McGough—
    1:58
  $THANK U VERY MUCH—Mike McGear—*2:30*
  $IDE B THE FIRST—Mike McGear—Roger McGough—*2:30*
side two
  DO YOU REMEMBER?—Mike McGear—Roger McGough—*2:48*
  Knees Up Mother Brown (Knees Down Mother Brown)—Weston Lee—
    Roger McGough—*2:16*
  1–2–3—Mike McGear—*3:27*
  TODAY—Mike McGear—*2:40*
  Please Sorry—Mike McGear—*2:30*
  Jelly Covered Cloud—John Gorman—*3:40*

OCT 18, 1968 (UK) Parlophone R 5734
DEC 16, 1968 (US) Bell 747
by Scaffold Prod: Norrie Paramor
A: *Lily The Pink*—Traditional arr. John Gorman—Mike McGear—
      Roger McGough—*4:15*
B: *Buttons Of Your Mind*—Mike McGear—Roger McGough—*3:24*

107

MAY 23, 1969 (UK) Parlophone PCS 7077 (LP)
Side two recorded live: January 12, 1969 at EMI Studios
by Scaffold
L.P. Prod: Norrie Paramor
side one: Music
  1–2–3—Mike McGear—*3:27*
  Oh! To Be A Child—Mike McGear—Roger McGough—*1:56*
  Stop Blowing Those Charity Bubbles—Mike McGear—*2:10*
  I Can't Make You Mine—Mike McGear—Roger McGough—*2:39*
  TODAY—Mike McGear—Roger McGough—*2:40*
  JELLY COVERED CLOUD—John Gorman—*3:40*
  LILY THE PINK—Traditional arr. John Gorman—Mike McGear—
    Roger McGough—*4:15*
side two: Humor & Poetry—*34:25*
  Fancy Goods—Roger McGough—*2:01*
  The Little Plastic Mac—Roger McGough—*2:14*
  Buchs—Roger McGough—*3:55*
  10:15 Thursday Morning—Roger McGough—Andy Roberts—*2:30*
  Father John No. 2—John Gorman—*5:42*
  Tim—Roger McGough—*1:03*
  Birds—Roger McGough—Andy Roberts—*2:17*
  Poems
    Russian Bear—Roger McGough—*2:23*
    Discretion—Roger McGough—Andy Roberts—*2:00*
    My Busseductress—Roger McGough—*2:04*
    Naughty Girl—Roger McGough—*1:44*
  Boxes—John Gorman—Roger McGough—*5:20*

JUN 27, 1969 (UK) Parlophone R 5784
by Scaffold Prod: Norrie Paramor and Tim Rice
A: Charity Bubbles—Mike McGear—Roger McGough—*2:34*
*B: *Goose*—Mike McGear—Roger McGough—*2:34*

OCT 17, 1969 (UK) Parlophone R 5812
by Scaffold Prod: Norrie Paramor
*A: *Gin Gan Goolie*—Mike McGear—Roger McGough—*2:43*
*B: *Liver–Birds*—John Gorman—Mike McGear—Roger McGough—*2:27*

JUN 5, 1970 (UK) Parlophone R 5847
by Scaffold Prod: Brian Gasciogne and Howard Blake (A side); Norrie
  Paramor (B side)
*A: *All The Way Up*—Howard Blake—*3:23*
B: PLEASE SORRY—Mike McGear—*2:30*

OCT 23, 1970 (UK) Parlophone R 5866
by Scaffold Prod: Simon Napier and Ray Singer
*A: *Busdreams*—Mike McGear—Roger McGough—*2:02*
*B: *If I Could Start All Over Again*—John Gorman—*1:58*

NOV 6, 1970 (UK) EMI Star Line SRS 5042 (LP)
by Various Artists
**REACH FOR THE STARS – NATIONAL KIDNEY RESEARCH FUND
BENEFIT LP**
side two
  cut six: *CHARITY BUBBLES*—Mike McGear–Roger McGough–*2:34*
    by Scaffold Prod: Norrie Paramor and Tim Rice

OCT 1, 1971 (UK) Parlophone R 5922
by Scaffold Prod: Norrie Paramor
*A: *Do The Albert*--Mike McGear–Roger McGough---*2:59*
*B: *Commercial Break*---Mike McGear–Roger McGough—*3:00*

APR 7, 1972 (UK) Island WIP 6131
by Mike McGear Prod: Mike McGear
A: *Woman*---Mike McGear–Roger McGough--*3:02*
*B: *Kill*--Mike McGear--*1:57*

APR 21, 1972 (UK) Island ILPS 9191 (LP)
by Mike McGear
WOMAN Prod: Mike McGear
side one
  Woman—Mike McGear–Roger McGough–*3:02*
  Witness—Mike McGear–Roger McGough–*4:11*
  Jolly Good Show—Mike McGear–Roger McGough–*3:06*
  Benna—Mike McGear–*0:15*
  Roamin A Road—Mike McGear–*2:21*
  Benna—Mike McGear–*0:09*
  Sister—Mike McGear–*3:11*
  Wishin—Mike McGear–Roger McGough–*3:21*
side two
  Young Young Man (Five Years Ago)—Mike McGear–Roger McGough–
    0:59
  Young Man (Five Years Later)—Mike McGear–Roger McGough–*2:47*
  Edward Heath—Mike McGear–*0:55*
  Bored As Butterscotch—Mike McGear–Roger McGough–Friend–*2:49*
  Uptowndowntown—Mike McGear–*2:25*
  Blackbeauty—Mike McGear–*0:55*
  Tiger—Mike McGear–Roger McGough–*5:14*
  Strawberry Jam (fades)—Mike McGear–*2:09*

FEB 9, 1973 (UK) Island HELP 11 (LP)
by Grimms
GRIMMS Prod: Roger McGough and Neil Innes
side one: *25:49*
  Interruption At The Opera House (Part One)--Brian Patten–*1:37*
  Three Times Corner—Zoot Money–*4:51*
  Sex Maniac—Roger McGough–*2:51*
  Galactic Love Poem—Adrian Henri–*1:00*
  Chairman Shankly—Adrian Henri–*2:33*
  Italian Job—Traditional arr. John Gorman—Mike McGear—Roger
    McGough–*2:07*
  Albatross Ramble—Brian Patten–*3:54*
  Humanoid Boogie--Neil Innes–*6:01*

side two: *22:36*
  Short Blues—Neil Innes—*1:00*
  Summer With The Monarch—Roger McGough—*2:30*
  Twyfords Vitromant—Neil Innes—*2:47*
  Following You—Zoot Money—*4:22*
  Newly Pressed Suit—Roger McGough—*0:48*
  11th Hour—Roger McGough—*1:57*
  Con. Gov. Fig.—Roger McGough—*0:08*
  Brown Paper Carrier Bag—Roger McGough—*0:56*
  Jellied Eels—Mike McGear—*4:30*
  Interruption At The Opera House (Part Two)—Brian Patten—*1:03*

MAY 25, 1973 (UK) Island ILPS 9234 (LP)
by Scaffold
FRESH LIVER Prod: Tim Rice and Roger Watson
side one
  Knickers—John Gorman—Mike McGear—Roger McGough—*0:16*
  Devon's Dead—Mike McGear—Roger McGough—*3:45*
  Plenty Of Time—Mike McGear—Roger McGough—*3:35*
  Fagorf—John Gorman—John Megginson—*3:40*
  Fax 'n' Figgers—Mike McGear—Roger McGough—*4:59*
  Nuclear Band—Mike McGear—Roger McGough—*3:55*
  W.P.C. Hodges—John Gorman—Mike McGear—Roger McGough—*0:14*
  Knickers—John Gorman—Mike McGear—Roger McGough—*0:14*
side two
  Aren't We All?—Roger McGough—John Megginson—*2:30*
  Twist—Roger McGough—*2:58*
  Psychiatrist—Roger McGough—*2:00*
  Deep North—Roger McGough—*1:30*
  Fish—Roger McGough—Andy Roberts—*2:14*
  Fishfriars—Roger McGough—*4:15*
  S.S.—Roger McGough—*3:27*
  I Remember—Neil Innes—Roger McGough—*2:38*

OCT 5, 1973 (UK) Island ILPS 9248 (LP)
MAR 30, 1976 (US) Antilles AN 7012 (LP)
by Grimms
ROCKIN' DUCK Prod: Grimms
side one
  Rockin' Duck—Neil Innes—*1:50*
  Songs Of The Stars—Andy Roberts—*3:15*
  The Right Mask—Brian Patten—*1:40*
  Policeman's Lot—John Gorman—*3:20*
  Question Of Habit—Roger McGough—*1:30*
  Take It While You Can—Mike McGear—Roger McGough—*3:00*
  Poetic Licence—Roger McGough—Brian Patten—*0:35*
  The Masked Poet—John Gorman—*0:30*
side two
  Hiss And Boo—John Gorman—*1:45*
  Gruesome—Roger McGough—Andy Roberts—*1:40*
  FX—Roger McGough—*3:15*
  Blab Blab Blab/EEC—Neil Innes—Roger McGough—*2:20*
  Backwards Thro' Space—Roger McGough—*0:55*
  OO–Chuck-A–Mao-Mao—Neil Innes—*3:40*
  End Of The Record—Roger McGough—*1:10*

NOV 2, 1973 (UK) EMI 2085
by Scaffold Prod: Norrie Paramor except † Tony Palmer
side one
  LILY THE PINK—Traditional arr. John Gorman—Mike McGear—Roger
    McGough—*4:15*
side two
  †THANK U VERY MUCH—Mike McGear—*2:30*
  DO YOU REMEMBER?—Mike McGear—Roger McGough—*2:48*

MAY 24, 1974 (UK) Warner Brothers K 16400
JUL 29, 1974 (US) Warner Brothers 8001
by Scaffold Prod: Paul McCartney
A: *Liverpool Lou*—Dominic Behan—*2:58*
*B: *Ten Years After On Strawberry Jam*—McCartney—*2:52*

SEP 6, 1974 (UK) Warner Brothers K 16446
OCT 28, 1974 (US) Warner Brothers 8037
by Mike McGear Prod: Paul McCartney
A: *Leave It*—McCartney—*3:44*
*B: *Sweet Baby*—McCartney—Mike McGear—*3:39*

SEP 27, 1974 (UK) Warner Brothers K 56051 (LP)
OCT 14, 1974 (US) Warner Brothers BS 2825 (LP)
by Mike McGear
MCGEAR Prod: Paul McCartney
side one
  Sea Breezes—Bryan Ferry—*4:52*
  What Do We Really Know?—McCartney—*3:28*
  Norton—McCartney—Mike McGear—*2:35*
  Leave It—McCartney—*3:44*
  Have You Got Problems?—McCartney—Mike McGear—*6:16*
side two
  The Casket—McCartney—Roger McGough—*4:19*
  Rainbow Lady—McCartney—Mike McGear—*3:26*
  Simply Love You—McCartney—Mike McGear—*2:47*
  Givin' Grease A Ride—McCartney—Mike McGear—*5:35*
  The Man Who Found God On The Moon—McCartney—Mike McGear—
    6:26

DEC 7, 1974 (UK) Warner Brothers K 16488
by Scaffold Prod: Mike McGear and John Megginson
A: *Mummy Won't Be Home For Christmas*—Mike McGear—Roger
    McGough—*4:09*
*B: *The Wind Is Blowing*—John Gorman—*2:57*

FEB 7, 1975 (UK) Warner Brothers K 16520
by Mike McGear Prod: Paul McCartney
A: *SEA BREEZES*—Bryan Ferry—*4:52*
A: *GIVIN' GREASE A RIDE*—McCartney—Mike McGear—*5:35*

111

FEB 7, 1975 (UK) Warner Brothers K 56067 (LP)
by Scaffold
SOLD OUT Prod: Mike McGear and John Megginson except †Paul
  McCartney
side one
 †*LIVERPOOL LOU*--Dominic Behan—*2:58*
  Potato Clock—Mike McGear—Roger McGough—*2:40*
  Mingulay Boating Song—Traditional arr. Scaffold—*2:16*
  Ramsbottom (Chicago That Toddling Town)—Fred Fisher (Parody
   lyrics added by Scaffold)—*1:35*
  Beilins Boneyard—Roger McGough—*2:30*
  Liverpool Girls—Roger McGough—Traditional arr. Scaffold—*2:30*
  Cokey Cokey—Jimmy Kennedy—*2:32*
side two
  Pack Of Cards—Mike McGear—Roger McGough—*5:44*
  MUMMY WON'T BE HOME FOR CHRISTMAS—Mike McGear—
   Roger McGough—*4:09*
  Leaving Of Liverpool—Traditional arr. Scaffold—*3:16*
  Julery Shop Leslie—Harvey—*3:29*
  Lord Of The Dance--Carter—*2:32*

FEB 14, 1975 (US MAIL ORDER) Warner Brothers PRO 596 (2 LPs)
by Various Artists
THE FORCE
side three
  cut six: *NORTON*—McCartney—Mike McGear—*2:35*
   by Mike McGear Prod: Paul McCartney

MAR 1, 1975 (UK) Warner Brothers K 16521
by Scaffold Prod: Mike McGear and John Megginson
A: LEAVING OF LIVERPOOL—Traditional arr. Scaffold—*3:16*
B: PACK OF CARDS—Mike McGear—Roger McGough—*5:44*

JUL 4, 1975 (UK) Warner Brothers K 16573
by Mike McGear Prod: Paul McCartney
*A: Dance The Do--McCartney—Mike McGear—*2:59*
B: NORTON—McCartney—Mike McGear—*2:35*

NOV 14, 1975 (UK) Warner Brothers K 16658
Reissued: January 30, 1976
by Mike McGear Prod: Paul McCartney
A: SIMPLY LOVE YOU—McCartney—Mike McGear—*2:47*
B: WHAT DO WE REALLY KNOW?—McCartney—*3:28*

JUN 11, 1976 (UK) Virgin VS 154
by The Bashers Prod: Mike McGear
*A: The Womble Bashers—Mike McGear—Roger McGough—*2:58*
*B: Womble Bashers Wock—Mike McGear—Roger McGough—*2:58*

JUN 18, 1976 (UK) EMI 2485
by Mike McGear Prod: Peter Winfield
*A: Doing Nothing All Day—Unknown—*2:16*
*B: A to Z—Mike McGear—*3:10*

OCT 29, 1976 (UK) Bronze BRO 33
by Scaffold Prod: Mike McGear
*A: *Wouldn't It Be Funny If You Didn't Have A Nose*—Mike McGear—
    Roger McGough—*3:11*
*B: *Mr. Noselighter*—Mike McGear—Roger McGough—*3:17*

MARCH 1977 (US) Antilles AX 7000 (LP)
by Various Artists
THE GREATER ANTILLES SAMPLER
side one
  cut four: *TAKE IT WHILE YOU CAN*—Mike McGear—Roger
  McGough—*3:00*
    by Grimms Prod: Grimms

MAR 18, 1977 (UK) Music For Pleasure MFP 50317 (LP)
by Various Artists
ORIGINAL ARTISTS HITS OF THE 60'S
side one
  cut one:*THANK U VERY MUCH*—Mike McGear—*2:30*
    by Scaffold Prod: Tony Palmer

APR 22, 1977 (UK) Bronze BRO 39
by Scaffold Prod: Mike McGear and John Megginson
*A: *How D'You Do*—Traditional arr. Mike McGear—Roger McGough—
    2:45
*B: *Paper Underpants*—John Gorman—Mike McGear—Roger McGough—
    3:10

Other Relatively Friendly Strangers

Apart from Brother Michael, several friends of the Beatles (and some total strangers) have released discs which eventually catch the attention of many Beatle fans. The "Pandemonium Shadow Show" section of *All Together Now* chronicled a number of these. There are a few others worth noting, some even worth buying:

SEP   2, 1972 (US) Banana/Blue Thumb BTS 38 (LP)
by The National Lampoon
RADIO DINNER
side one
   cut four: *Magical Misery Tour*---Christopher Cerf---arr. Christopher
   Guest---*4:08*
side two
   cut five: *Concert In Bangla Desh*---Michael O'Donoghue—Tony
   Hendra---*3:26*
First of all, this is a very funny album. You should buy it anyway. Aside from that, the image of the Beatles seems to float through this entire LP, popping up here, there, and everywhere. The two main contributions are the brilliant *Magical Misery Tour*, a fabulously barbed parody of Lennon's *Rolling Stone* interview, and *Concert In Bangla Desh*, a parody on George's charity concert, which doesn't really go anywhere. On *Magical Misery Tour*, Tony Hendra and Melissa Manchester play John and Yoko, respectively, backed by Jim Payne on drums, John "Cooker" Lo Presti on bass, and Melissa on piano. Tony Hendra and Christopher Guest play the "sit-down tragedy team" on *Concert In Bangla Desh*.

DECEMBER 1975 (US) Epic PE 33956 (LP)
by The National Lampoon
GOODBYE POP
 A History Of The Beatles---*1:52*
The years since the first National Lampoon LP have seen many radio stations attempt so-called definitive histories of rock 'n' roll. Most were a complete waste of time. In the final word on this topic, the Lampoon folks told the history of the Beatles in the ultimate condensation by a (fictitious) radio-pop historian. For nearly two minutes, some poor soul mumbles on about Tony Sheridan and George Harrison being dead. . .and. . . What else is there?

OCT 5, 1976 (US) Passport PPSD 98018 (LP)
by Eric Idle and Neil Innes
THE RUTLAND WEEKEND TELEVISION SONG BOOK
I Must Be In Love—Neil Innes—*2:39*

NBC's *Saturday Night Live*, in a great running parody of the never-ending "Bring Back The Beatles" efforts ("Now if we all offer our first born. . .") has a standing offer of $3200 (upped from $3000) for the Beatles to reunite on the show. The first time Eric Idle—member of Monty Python and friend of George Harrison—hosted *Saturday Night* (October 2, 1976), he "made up" for not bringing the Beatles by presenting the next best thing—The Ruttles, English studio musicians led by ex-Bonzo Dog Band-er Neil Innes, all wearing mop-top wigs. The song they performed, *I Must Be In Love*, was a classic Neil Innes parody, so close to the original that many might miss the point. Though the Ruttles—Dirk, Kevin, Stig and Nasty—have yet to commence a world tour, Nasty (Innes) did join Eric Idle on his second appearance as host for *Saturday Night* (April 23, 1977) performing the Lennonesque tune, *Cheese & Onions*.

SEP 26, 1975 (UK) Polydor 2383 361 (LP)
DEC 9, 1975 (US) Polydor PD 6517 (LP)
by Barclay James Harvest
TIME HONOURED GHOSTS
Titles

In the late 1950's, some rock 'n' roll singers figured the easiest way to get a hit was to "compose" a song consisting of as many references to other hit songs as possible. This reached its ultimate extension in the Dickie Goodman *Flying Saucers* records, which used actual excerpts from the hit records. At least Goodman was deliberately being funny. Now we have Barclay James Harvest, an otherwise OK group, who received a mysterious inspiration from above to string together into one song as many Beatle song titles as possible. Harry Nilsson did this in 1967 with *You Can't Do That*, but Harry was just having fun while devising a catchy song. Barclay James Harvest, however, wrap their attempt in the hoary cloak of "deep significance." The non-related song titles are strung together incantation-like in yet another of the unfortunate attempts to lift the four mortal Beatles into a more divine stratosphere.

JAN 19, 1976 (US) RCA APL 1-1031 (LP)
FEB 27, 1976 (UK) RCA RS 1015 (LP)
by Harry Nilsson
SANDMAN

JUN 28, 1976 (US) RCA APL 1-1119 (LP)
AUG 20, 1976 (UK) RCA RS 1062 (LP)
by Harry Nilsson
THAT'S THE WAY IT IS
JUL 19, 1977 (US) RCA AFL 1-2276 (LP)
JUL 23, 1977 (UK) RCA PL 12276 (LP)
by Harry Nilsson
KNNILLSSONN

Old Harry's been having his problems lately. He started in 1976 with the star-studded but disasterous **Sandman** LP. The follow-up, **That's The Way It Is**, while a noticeable improvement, still fell far short of his best works. Ringo is given general "thanks" credit on both of these albums, and some think he may have even played drums on a few cuts. He might have. In any case, Harry gave his super-star friends a rest and recorded his 1977 **Knnillssonn** album backed only by strings and studio session men.

FEB 19, 1963 (US) Laurie 3152
APR 12, 1963 (UK) Stateside SS 172
by The Chiffons
 He's So Fine/(oh my lover)

APR 16, 1969 (US) Pavillion 20001
MAY 16, 1969 (UK) Buddah 201 048
by The Edwin Hawkins Singers
 Oh Happy Day/(jesus, lover of my soul)

In yet another of the endless court suits involving the Beatles, George Harrison was pulled into court for supposedly plagarizing the basic riff from the 1963 hit *He's So Fine* in his 1970 hit *My Sweet Lord*. Harrison insisted that if anything the song was modeled after the Edwin Hawkins Singers' version of the spiritual classic *Oh Happy Day*.

NOV 5, 1976 (US) EMI 2560
FEB 8, 1977 (US) EMI 4381
by Jimmy McCulloch & White Line
A: Too Many Miles---Jimmy McCulloch---Colin Allen---*4:16*
B: Call My Name---Dave Clair---*4:03*

Before leaving Wings, guitarist Jimmy McCulloch launched a brief "solo" career, while still remaining a part of Paul's group. He formed his own "group," White Line (including his brother) and released a single in late 1976. Following his departure from Wings in 1977, McCulloch (previously a stand-out performer in Thunderclap Newman and Stone the Crows) joined the veterans of the newly-formed Small Faces, who had just inaugurated a British comeback tour to coincide with their first new album release.

APR 29, 1977 (UK) EMI EMC 3175 (LP)
MAY 17, 1977 (US) Capitol ST 11642 (LP)
by Percy "Thrills" Thrillington
THRILLINGTON
Too Many People/3 Legs/Ram On/Dear Boy/Uncle Albert/Admiral Halsey/Smile Away/Heart Of The Country/Monkberry Moon Delight/Eat At Home/Long Haired Lady/Back Seat Of My Car
In late 1972, McCartney productions announced the signing of Irish bandleader Percy 'Thrills' Thrillington ("that's for real," the press release pointed out) to record an instrumental version of Paul's 1971 hit album, **Ram**. Thrillington's project was delayed slightly (five years!), but the album was finally released in 1977. Unfortunately, many of the tunes weren't that great anyway; without vocals they're even worse. File with George Martin and David Hentschel.

AUG 24, 1964 (US) Liberty LST 7388 (LP)
FEB 19, 1965 (UK) Liberty LBY 1218 (LP)
by The Chipmunks
THE CHIPMUNKS SING THE BEATLES HITS Prod: Ross Bagdasarian
All My Loving/Do You Want To Know A Secret/She Loves You/From Me To You/Love Me Do/Twist And Shout/A Hard Day's Night/P.S. I Love You/I Saw Her Standing There/Can't Buy Me Love/Please Please Me/I Want To Hold Your Hand
During the height of the British Invasion in 1964, the reputations of established American groups were put on the line. They had to compete head-on with the British rockers, and many fell by the rock wayside. Never one to shirk a challenge, producer Ross Bagdasarian (David Seville) took the Chipmunks, who had built a successful career on covering old standards, into the studio and recorded an entire album of Beatle hits, with Theodore and Dave on guitars, Simon on drums, and Alvin on harmonica and guitar. The Chipmunk vocal harmonies meshed perfectly with the style of those early Beatle tunes. It was probably on the strength of this album, released in Britain the next year, that Paul McCartney decided to include the Chipmunk-type vocals in a cut (*Take Your Time*) on **Holly Days**, the 1977 Denny Laine—Paul McCartney album tribute to Buddy Holly. The original Chipmunk album, though, remains a top item for collectors.

Was Paul, In Fact, Dead . . . And Other Reasonable Questions

After getting as ensconced in the story of the Beatles as was necessary for this sort of book, it is very easy, at times, to forget (or even ignore) questions which to the average fan seem extremely perplexing. Throughout the country, at Beatle fan conventions, many of the same questions are asked over and over again. As a sort of public service (we're very public spirited!) we've set up the following Socratic Dialogue:

Q: Is Paul Dead?

A: Yes . . . ha! Just kidding. "But seriously folks . . ." Voted the most tiresome, overasked question of the decade, this whole "mystery" seems unwilling to completely die out even after eight years. Being *extremely* tired of the entire matter, we'll try to clear it up as quickly as possible.

In late 1969 around the time of **Abbey Road**'s release (and as the Beatles were breaking up) a rumor, apparently starting in a mid-west radio station, that Paul McCartney was dead swept the country. Not just suddenly dead, but dead for up to three years. The Beatles had stopped touring in August of 1966 and had been relatively inaccessible ever since. The idea of Paul being dead seemed oddly appealing. It allowed for a much more "acceptable" explanation for the disintegration of one of the central forces of the 1960's, much like the real, tangible desire many people feel for a link between the Kennedy and King assassinations. Many people find the random nature of life unacceptable, rejecting the fact that many things said and done by people in the public eye mean either nothing or nothing understandable outside of a small circle of friends (i.e., an inside joke). Infusing diverse objects like a random photograph or a doggerel song with "hidden" inner meanings bestows superhuman attributes to the artist/idol, while at the same time allowing the average fan to feel a personal kinship by being able to "figure it

119

out."

Within a month of the rumor's start, an elaborate concordance had been unearthed by various amateur archeologists, beginning with the **Sgt. Pepper** album in 1967, the first album released after the Beatles stopped touring. The detailed cover of **Sgt. Pepper** showed a gathering around a grave with flowers in the shape of a guitar (was it Paul they were burying?). The character behind Paul has his palm outstretched above McCartney's head, said to be the traditional Norse symbol of death. The inside pictures showed Paul with a shoulder patch which apparently said "O.P.D.", a common abbreviation for "Officially Pronounced Dead". The back cover picture of the four Beatles has John, George and Ringo facing the camera, but Paul (mysteriously) showing only his back, and (wait! there's more!) George is pointing to a phrase, "Wednesday Morning at Five O'Clock" on the lyrics laid over the Beatles' picture (this supposedly referred to the time of day Paul was involved in a fatal or crippling car crash). This car crash was the most commonly accepted cause of Paul's disappearance. To replace him, the story goes, the Beatles took in the winner of the Paul McCartney look-alike contest (perhaps the mysterious Billy Shears referred to in the title song).

The November 1967 album **Magical Mystery Tour** was chockablock full of prospective clues. If you held the album cover up to a mirror, a phone number is said to be visible in the design of the word *Beatles*. If an intrepid American were to call this number, with the correct London prefix and at the right time, the one-and-only Billy Shears (himself) would give explicit directions toward Pepperland, the paradise-on-earth depicted in the movie *Yellow Submarine*. This may all sound absurd now, but at the time it was gospel. A caller to an all-night radio show on the topic fervently explained that three of his friends had recently called the number and vanished! What was in Pepperland was never quite clear. Perhaps it was Paul McCartney living out a tortured existence as a crippled vegetable. (Who knows, maybe along with Jack Kennedy and Marilyn Monroe.) Inside the **Magical Mystery Tour** album were numerous stills from the Beatles' film of the same name (*never* seen in the U.S. at that time, please note). One photo showed all four in white tuxedos. All but Paul had red carnations on their lapels; Paul's was black, signifying *death*! At the very end of the fade of "Strawberry Fields Forever," a previous single tacked onto the American album, John mumbles a line said to be "I buried Paul" which John later claimed was "Cranberry Sauce," which also sounds like "I'm very bored" (an apt statement in regards to such nit-picking). Featured extensively on the album is the image and notion of the walrus, signifying. . .well, that never was made clear.

120

The November 1968 double *White Album* had John "confirm-ing" that Paul *was* the walrus, later recanted in *God*. Much more confusing was the track labeled *Revolution No. 9*–an eight-minute melange of sound effects and tape loops mainly devised by John. It was radically different from anything the Beatles had put on rec-ord before. Actually just part of a newly developing interest John was showing in esoterica in general (see his & Yoko's **Two Virgins** album), *Revolution No. 9* was poured over, played backwards, separated and analyzed. The fact that the beginning of EMI test tape number nine, unfortunately sounding like John, was repeated over and over and seemed to say "Turn Me On Deadman" when played backwards was the final nail in the coffin (sorry) for many people. *Revolution No. 9* was seen as a story in sound of Paul's car crash, incineration and death. Inasmuch as Lennon threw in so many spur-of-the-moment ideas, *Revolution No. 9* was the perfect choice into which one could read anything he chose.

Finally (thank goodness) came **Abbey Road**, with its famous cover. The four Beatles were said to be symbolizing a funeral proces-sion: John, resplendent in white, would be the preacher. George, in work shirt and blue jeans, would be the gravedigger. Ringo, in black, would be in mourning. And Paul, seemingly out of step with the others, would be dead (he alone was barefoot). True enthusiasts, un-aware of the British license plate system, interpreted the Volkswagon plate "281F" as a reference to how old Paul would be "if he had lived."

Such clues (and *many many* others of the more obscure variety) were batted about and put to unbelieving English executives and friends by scoop-hungry American DJs. Some enterprising soul even collected the main clues, put a back beat behind it, and released a record on MGM called *The Ballad Of Paul*. Paul, as it turned out, happened to be incommunicado on his new Scottish farm. With the 1970 release of his first solo album, and the birth of his first child, the rumors died down.

Aside from marking the first "Bring Back The Beatles" hysteria, the whole "Paul Is Dead" affair was the ultimate limit of insane fandom. Granted, most Beatle songs say *something*, but much, if not all, of the surrounding ephemera (i.e., cover work and photos) are, and always have been, spurious momentary decisions containing nothing more intense than an occasional private joke. To a genera-tion getting ready to proclaim the Beatles as prophets (a role they never asked for), such light-heartedness was the ultimate, unac-ceptable crime.

Nonetheless, old rumors never die. . .say, where is Judge Crater?

Q: What are those Christmas discs the Beatles released all about?

A: From 1963 to 1972, the Beatles had an official fan club which published a newsletter and issued photos. As a special treat to club members, the Beatles recorded a special Christmas message in 1963 (sent free to all British members). The thin plastic disc, like those sometimes found in magazines, was five minutes of the fab four wishing one-and-all a Merry New Year and a Happy Christmas, expressing thanks for the gifts and support, and doing unique arrangements of a few Christmas carols. The disc was enthusiastically received and became a yearly tradition. By Christmas 1964 the Beatles, now also a smash in America, had a U.S. branch of the fan club. While British club members were receiving a new, 1964 disc, American members got the year-old 1963 premiere disc. Thereafter, though, they both received the same thing.

By 1966, the recordings began deviating from the traditional *thank-you*'s, and adopting a more creative, zany outlook. The Christmas messages began taking on the form of mini-comedy skits, using sound effects and play-on-words, akin to what the four-man Firesign Theatre was beginning to do on Los Angeles radio. The 1966 and 1967 recordings are gems of their sort. The Beatles show a side rarely seen, except maybe in diluted form in their movies, that of more-than-adequate comedy actors, strongly based in English-Goon Show-Peter Sellers style. By 1968 and 1969, however, with the group coming apart, the desire was not there to spend time on producing a complicated skit. Instead, the last two years are mostly edited-together messages and ditties from the four separate Beatles (both are even edited by outside friends). The 1968 message contains a forgettable team-up of George Harrison and Tiny Tim. By Christmas 1970, the Beatles fan club, with the group broken up, had no new recording for its members. Instead, it placed all seven recordings on one "real" album on the Apple label. The American version even had a very nice "growth of the Beatles" photo montage on the cover. This LP, also, was only sent to club members. In 1971, with again nothing new to present, the club offered each member the opportunity to purchase two extra copies if they wished. In 1972, the club went out of existence, leaving **The Beatles Christmas Album** as one of the rarer Beatle recordings around. To alleviate this, the friendly bootleggers soon began pressing discs containing all seven messages. Such albums are relatively easy to find and well worth the money. Along with *You Know My Name (Look Up My Number)*, the flip of the *Let It Be* single, the Christmas messages capture forever the great sense of humor of the four Beatles.

Q: **Are there any Beatle songs in which different takes were released?**

A: Yes, eight that we know of. Why? Good question. Ask George Martin. Five of the eight came from the Beatles' early recording era. At the Beatles' first recording session in May of 1961, when they were an instrumental backing group for singer Tony Sheridan, they recorded (among other things) that old favorite *Sweet Georgia Brown*. In 1964, when the Beatles were world-famous, these old German recordings were reissued. Tony Sheridan, still an aspiring singer, re-recorded the vocal track to *Sweet Georgia Brown* to add up-to-date references to the Beatles, their hairstyles and their fans. It is this re-recorded version which is the only one currently available; on the American Atco album **Ain't She Sweet** an additional lead electric guitar was also dubbed in on this track. Only the original 1962 German EP release of *Sweet Georgia Brown* has the original Sheridan vocal.

The Beatles' first recording session on their own (September 11, 1962) produced their first single *Love Me Do/P.S. I Love You*. Ringo had been with the group only a month at this time, and producer George Martin was unsure of his ability. Consequently, he had session drummer Andy White there as stand-by. Apparently 17 takes were required before all were happy with *Love Me Do*. During these 17 tries, Ringo and Andy White switched off on drums, with Ringo relegated to the tambourine. When the record was released in October, a version with Ringo on drums was the A-side, done perhaps to assure Ringo of his solid position in the group. In February of 1963, this same version of *Love Me Do* was issued in North America on Capitol of Canada. One year later, when the Beatles were American stars, this Canadian single would hit the American charts until a more accessible American pressing replaced it. In late March 1963, as the Beatles were piecing together their first LP (**Please Please Me**), they added on their two previous singles. Another take of *Love Me Do*, one with Andy White playing drums, was put on the album. It is this version which appeared on all subsequent European and American Beatle records; in fact, the British single version was changed soon thereafter to be in line with the LP. The Capitol of Canada single is the "easiest" way to get hold of the original recording, but even that is hard to find. The simplest way to tell the difference between the two versions is to notice the lack (in the original) of the easily heard tambourine of the popular version.

The other single put on the **Please Please Me** LP was the title track, *Please Please Me*. Released in January 1963 in Britain, and in February on Vee Jay in America, the original "hit" version was also substituted on the album by a nearly-identical alternate take. On the last chorus John and Paul, singing together, begin to sing different lines. John, on the next line, gives a chuckle at the mix-up. Other than that, they are nearly identical. All of the versions of *Please Please Me* on singles and EPs in Britain, and all versions on Vee Jay in America, have the original "correct" take. All the Capitol and Parlophone albums have the second version.

The LP **With The Beatles**, mostly identical with the **Beatles' Second Album** in the U.S., contains the Beatles' version of the old Motown hit *Money*. When an EP was pulled from the album in Britain, a different take of *Money* was substituted. It can be recognized by the "quieter" introduction and John's different vocals near the fade-out of the song.

For reasons which now seem totally incomprehensible, an "extra" verse was included on *I'll Cry Instead* on the American **A Hard Day's Night** soundtrack (United Artists) and Capitol's single, while all other issuances have that verse missing.

Near the end of the Beatles' recording career, a few more discrepancies popped up. The song *It's All Too Much* contains a verse in the *Yellow Submarine* soundtrack not present on the soundtrack album. The songs *Get Back* and *Let It Be*, both originally issued as singles, wound up on the **Let It Be** album, but with alternate takes substituted. The two single versions appear on the "best of" 1967-1970 double album. In an apparent slip, the version of *Get Back* included on the **Rock And Roll Music** compendium LP is actually the **Let It Be** album version, though the liner notes say it's the single.

The final example is *Across The Universe*, a song the Beatles had kicked around for a year or two before finally including it on the **Let It Be** album. An earlier, totally different arrangement of the song was issued in Britain in 1969 on a charity album for the World Wildlife Fund called **No One's Gonna Change Our World**. The earlier version opens with the sounds of birds flapping their wings, and includes the backing vocal talents of two girls, Lizzie Bravo and Gayleen Pease, who were literally pulled off the street at the time of the recording.

Aside from these, there are numerous differences to be found in the different "mixes" of Beatle songs found on various domestic and foreign pressings. Some seem deliberate additions or subtractions made at the last moment: an added harmonica riff on *Thank You Girl*, the deleted hi-hat count-down for *All My Loving*, the deleted trumpet ending on *Penny Lane*, the few extra beats on

I Am The Walrus, and the like. More obvious and more confusing is the generally inferior quality of the stereo mixes on many American Capitol releases. For this reason, many Beatle fans consider the money spent buying the stereo British albums well worth it.

Q: Did you guys make any mistakes in "All Together Now?"

A: You bet! The ones we're going to tell you about are a few important omissions.

The obscure Ringo Starr co-composition, *Rock and Roller*, released in Britain by co-author Billy Lawrie, was, in fact, put on an album in the UK called **Ship Imgination** (RCA SF 8395).

Jotta Herre, a Dutch group of impeccable morals, were incorrectly credited as the original recorders of Paul's song *Penina*. Our original assumption, listed in the first hardcover issue, was correct. Internationally obscure artist Carlos Mendes deserves that credit. Paul, vacationing in Portugal, wrote the song about a local hotel, and seemingly "gave" it to Mendes. When Mendes' version was issued (July 18, 1969 on European Parlophone QMSP 16459, backed with *Wings Of Revenge*), McCartney's publishing company, Northern Songs, were a bit miffed in that Paul thought so much of the song he forgot to tell them about it. Paul can be heard playing around with the tune on one of the many *Let It Be* era bootlegs.

The late Mal Evans, for years the Beatles' road manager and "go-fer," revealed in one of his last interviews that he, in fact, co-wrote both *Fixing A Hole* and the title cut to **Sgt. Pepper's Lonely Hearts Club Band**. To keep the Lennon/McCartney songwriting credit intact, Mal's name was left off the record but, apparently, he was paid royalties anyway.

In the realm of total oversight, we were too thick to see through the obfuscating pseudonym ("English Ritchie") used by Ringo on one of Steve Stills' innumerable albums, his first on Columbia, **Stills** (Columbia PC 33575 released on June 17, 1975 in America). Ringo played drums on the cut *As I Come Of Age*, recorded back in 1971 at London's Island Studios. David Crosby and Graham Nash also joined Stills on vocals.

We also failed to detect a super-star aura surrounding the 1972 release of Rudy Romero's album **To The World**, on the short-lived Tumbleweed label (TWS 108). George Harrison played Guitar on three tracks (*Lovely Lady, Nothin' Gonna Get You Down* and *Doing The Right Thing*) and sang backing vocals on one other (*If I Find The Time*). Todd Rundgren and Phil Upchurch, as well as Attitudes' producer Lee Kiefer, also appeared on the record.

After vigorous lobbying by various interests, we have finally been convinced that George Harrison probably plays guitar on the live **Delaney And Bonnie On Tour** LP, recorded December 7, 1969 at Croydon's Fairfield Hall in Britain, and released in America on April 7, 1970 (Atco 33-326).

Q: In "All Together Now" you stated that the Hamburg Star Club tapes were recorded in December of 1962. Yet when they were finally released in 1977, some people, even a few who were around back then, said the tapes were recorded earlier. How do you know you're right?

A: We've discovered that very often the worst source of information is someone who was there at the time! It's too easy to confuse memory and fact, especially for events occurring fifteen years ago. So, even while drawing from first person interviews, articles and books, we've always made it a point to check several sources, some of which, at first glance, seem to have little to do with the events in question. Our information on the Hamburg tapes was drawn from a wide range of these sources, and it allowed us to identify the recordings in great detail, even though neither of us was anywhere near Germany in 1962!

First, there's the matter of the songs themselves. On the two record set, several are incorrectly identified. One song is identified as *Talkin' 'bout You*, written by Ray Charles. Charles did write and record a song by that name in the late 50's, but it's not the song the Beatles performed at the Star Club. They sang *I'm Talking About You*, a Chuck Berry tune released in 1961. The slurred vocal on the Berry tune makes confusion of the two songs easy enough, especially to someone who's never heard either one; this undoubtedly happened here. Several other songs on the record are simply credited to the wrong authors (*Lend Me Your Comb, Nothin' Shakin', Red Sails In the Sunset*). One (*Where Have You Been All My Life*) lists no author at all!

To arrive at the actual recording date of the Hamburg tapes (December 1962), it became necessary to find sources which would *clearly* identify the exact time period of the performance. Our research indicated that the Beatles appeared at the Star Club three times in 1962: from about April 23-June 4 (to open the club); November 1-14; and December 18-January 1. A careful listen to the tapes turned up several references by the group to Christmas and the Christmas season. Allan Williams (the Beatles' first manager and the man who spearheaded the drive to release the tapes to the public) described the recording as taking place at Christmas (in his book *The Man Who Gave The Beatles Away*), though he mistakently dated the event at Christmas *1961*—four months before the Star Club ever opened its doors!

126

Nonetheless, many people contended that the recordings were made during the April/June Star Club stint. To eliminate that possibility, we turned to the songs performed by the Beatles on the Star Club tape. Nearly all were cover versions of tunes written by other artists. The original versions of three of them (*Twist And Shout, Sheila, Where Have You Been All My Life?*) weren't even released until May of 1962. It was *possible*, but highly unlikely, that the Beatles (in Hamburg) would have been able to acquire copies of these records instantly upon their release in America — and immediately incorporate them into their stage show. However, it was totally *impossible* for the group to have performed two songs at all: Frank Ifield's version of *I Remember You* and Buddy Holly's *Reminiscing*. Ifield released his own recording of the old war film hit (from the flick *The Fleet's In*) in Britain on June 29, 1962 (Columbia DB 4856), nearly a month after the Beatles returned from the April/June appearance in Hamburg. By mid-July it topped the British charts. The Beatles' version on the Star Club tapes was a straight mock-up of that hit — complete with exaggerated harmonica work by John. Buddy Holly's *Reminiscing* was recorded back in 1958, but remained unreleased, locked in the company vaults until 1962, when Norman Petty acquired the rights to issue old Holly material. His first release in both Britain and America was, indeed, *Reminiscing*, issued on August 14, 1962 in the US (Coral 62329) and September 7, 1962 in Britain (Coral Q 72455). This was a full *two months* after the group returned from its April/June Star Club stint.

So, the Star Club tapes were recorded in December of 1962: after Ringo had joined the group (he wasn't just sitting in), after the Beatles had signed with EMI; in fact, after thay had recorded their second Parlophone single!

Q: Why doesn't "All Together Now" look like other discographies?

A: We're not like other discographers. We took the point of view of most Beatle fans, that is, of a record consumer, whose basic Beatle library is composed of records. ("And by records ye shall know them!" the Bible might say.) Most discographers go recording-session-by-recording-session. While this method has its advantages, we felt it loses a feeling for how the group was presented to the public, and the context in which the records appeared. We tried to keep the main benefits of the traditional system by instituting our unique (and sometimes complicated) theory of reissues, and by including recording dates when possible.

In a purely editorial decision, we unilaterally decided to ignore such secondary issues as matrix numbers, alternate mixes, and label variations. Some people find these topics extremely interesting. We don't.

When you get down to basics, the Beatles are music. Not typeface on a record, company logos, or fancy packaging. Their legacy, *all* that is really left to us, is their records. People collect records; they don't collect recording sessions.

Q: Don't you think there are any other Beatle out-takes flying around?

A: Without a doubt. We only listed the out-takes generally known to exist by those outside EMI, only a few of which have ever gotten onto bootleg tapes. There must certainly be somewhere innumerable hours of rehearsal and practice tapes, though the number of "new songs" would probably be very limited. It gets back to the old question of: How many versions of *Get Back* do you really want to hear? In the past few years, with the four Beatles recording separately, the amount of out-take material has, of course, increased. Paul had two songs left over from his mid-1974 recording session, *Hey Diddle* and *Proud Mum*. Unused from the **Venus and Mars** sessions were *Karate Chaos, Lunchbox and Odd Sox,* and *Sea Dance*. John has a song called *Incantation*, co-written with Roy Cicala, left over from the **Walls And Bridges** era. Hopefully someday soon we will get to hear the one and only John Lennon and Phil Spector co-composition, *Here We Go Again*, from their team-up for the **Rock 'n' Roll** LP sessions. Apart from the two songs written for Cilla Black in 1972, *You've Got To Stay With Me* and *When Every Song Is Sung* (retitled *I'll Still Love You* on Ringo's **Rotogravure** album), George has an instrumental lying around, *Sound Stage of Mind*, which he played during his American tour.

Ringo, not the most prolific writer in the world, does have a few songs "in the can" now. One is left-over from his co-writing work with Billy Lawrie, *Where Are You Going?*, while three were left over from the **Rotgravure** sessions: *All Right, It's Hard To Be Lovers*, with Keith Allison, and *Party*, with Harry Nilsson.

Not to be confused with out-takes, however, are working titles of songs which were later released. Among the more famous of these in regards to Beatle songs: *Scrambled Egg (Yesterday), Auntie Gin's Theme (I've Just Seen A Face), That's A Nice Hat—CAP (It's Only Love), The Void (Tomorrow Never Knows), Daisy Hawkins (Eleanor Rigby), Badfinger Boogie (With A Little Help From My Friends), This Is Some Friendly (Don't Pass Me By)* and *Los Paranois (Sun King)*.

128

Q: If you want to buy some bootleg records, what are the best ones to look for?

A: The worst ones to look for are the live ones. All, repeat, all live Beatle LPs are lousy. The only one close to acceptable is a tape of their July 1966 Tokyo Concert. With Capitol releasing the **Live At The Hollywood Bowl** LP, from 1964 and 1965, the market has hopefully dried up on live Beatle LPs. The same goes for Paul, whose three-LP **Wings Over America** set renders useless the varied live Wings LPs going back to 1972.

There are innumerable bootleg LPs containing out-takes and radio/TV performances during the Beatles' career. Some have a few good cuts on them (*Soldier Of Love, I Got A Woman* and *Some Other Guy*) but, with bootleg packaging as haphazard as it is, you spend your money and you take your chances. The now available double LP of the Beatles in Hamburg, recorded in 1962, is a much more accessible way to get a good example of this sort of thing. Many of the previously unavailable Beatle favorites are included on it. One bootlegged cut to keep a sharp eye out for, though, is a fabulous version of the Isley Brothers' *Shout* performed live on the British TV show *Around The Beatles* (May 1964). It's great. Beware of a Murray the K interview record which contains a short snippet of the song. Insist on the full, unexpurgated version.

As for bootleg albums, the most interesting is one alternately called **As Sweet As You Are** or **Yellow Matter Custard**. Recorded in 1962 before their first LP, this has the Beatles doing fourteen songs, all written by other people, only one of which they ever released. It's a great insight into the musical influences which made the Beatles. And though hampered by a low-fidelity recording, it's actually an album you would pull out to play for pleasure (a *rarity* among bootlegs).

Another early recording worth picking up is the Beatles' version of *How Do You Do It* (a hit for Gerry and the Pacemakers in 1963). This studio session out-take was issued as a single in 1976, backed with a rousing version of *Revolution* (from a 1968 television appearance).

Of a more historical interest are tapes of the Beatles first two appearances on the *Ed Sullivan* show in 1964. Called various things, including *Beatlegged Live*, this can be a welcome companion piece to your memories, if you happen to have seen the original.

As previously mentioned, a bootleg containing all the Beatle Christmas messages (1963-1969), not only interesting but actually funny, is readily available.

The "first" Beatle bootleg was the *Let It Be/Get Back* bootleg. Originally intended as an actual release, it was held up at the last minute and replaced by the Phil Spector-produced **Let It Be** album. The original un-Spectorized version is useful as a comparison with the final product, and contains an early version of Paul's *Teddy Boy*; but if you don't like **Let It Be**, this isn't going to change your mind.

For the same era, but of higher quality and greater interest, is the double LP set commonly called **Sweet Apple Trax**. This traces the progress (or lack of) on songs that wound up on both **Let It Be** and **Abbey Road**. *Get Back* is thoroughly traced from its start as *Commonwealth Song*, a political diatribe on British racism, to a finished product resembling the version we all know. Other highlights are a complete version of the unreleased Lennon/McCartney/Harrison/Starkey song *Suzy Parker*, a short working version of Paul's *Penina*, and some half-hearted workouts of old rock 'n' roll standards. Sound is of nearly studio quality.

Of more than passing interest is an LP called **Telecasts**, containing the highlights of John & Yoko's lightning tour of American talk shows in the spring of 1972. Both talk and music are included, and the recording features the "historic team-up" of John Lennon and Chuck Berry.

Finally, for those of you who can't afford buying prints of all their movies, the soundtracks to all five Beatle films (*A Hard Day's Night, Help, Magical Mystery Tour, Yellow Submarine* and *Let It Be*) can provide entertainment on lonely weekends.

Above all, be cautious when buying bootlegs. The only money-back guarantee a bootlegger offers is: "If you don't like it, you don't have to play it."

Oh yes, they're all illegal.

Q: Assuming I'm a middle-level Beatle fan with plenty of old scratchy mono American LPs I don't want to play on my new stereo system, what's the quickest, cheapest way I can get all of the Beatles' songs?

A: Capitol records will love us for this, but it's worth the extra bucks to buy as many of the British Beatle albums as you can. The quality, especially the 1963-1966 era stuff, is noticeably better than the American equivalents, and with the American record industry's recent price hike, the price differential is close to nil. These English LPs are now readily available as imports in most major record stores.

The eight British albums which are a complete necessity are: **Please Please Me, With The Beatles, A Hard Day's Night, Beatles For Sale, Help, A Collection of Beatles' Oldies, Rubber Soul** and **Revolver**. Eight other albums are available in identical form in Britain and America: **Sgt. Pepper, Magical Mystery Tour, The Beatles** (*The*

White Album), **Yellow Submarine, Abbey Road, Let It Be, The Beatles with Tony Sheridan** and **The Beatles At the Hollywood Bowl.** For its American release, **The Beatles Live!** At the Star Club replaced four tracks appearing on the original British and German packages with four different songs from the "King-size" Taylor tapes. It's necessary, then, to purchase both the foreign and domestic sets. This leaves some 21 songs unaccounted for. Most can be taken care of by picking up two other American LPs, **The Beatles' Second Album** and **Hey Jude.**

And then there were 9. . .Now it gets a bit harder, but not much. Most of these 9 are available on other American LPs, but if you're out to cut costs, the best way is to pick up seven 45s. Five are identical in Britain and America: *She's A Woman* (flip of *I Feel Fine*), *Yes It is* (flip of *Ticket To Ride*), *I'm Down* (flip of *Help*), *Inner Light* (flip of *Lady Madonna*) and *You Know My Name* (flip of *Let It Be*). The song *This Boy*, on the American **Meet The Beatles** LP, was the flip side of *I Want To Hold Your Hand* in Britain. EMI had a big push on all their old Beatle singles in 1976, and these are still readily available from stores that sell import records.

Now a bit tougher. If you want the Beatles doing *She Loves You* and *I Want To Hold Your Hand* in German (*Sie Liebt Dich/ Komm, Gib Mir Deine Hand*), both are on a 45 put out by Odeon (Odeon C006 04204) in Germany, and still available.

That takes care of all the *songs* they released. In an earlier question, we discussed the eight alternate takes also released. A few of these are close to impossible to get now, but many can be snapped up quickly. One, the single version of *Let It Be*, is already taken care of by buying the flip side, *You Know My Name*. The single version of *Get Back* can be found anywhere. The version of *I'll Cry Instead* with the extra verse is still available on a Capitol single or, if you must, the United Artists soundtrack album. The second version of *Money* is only available on the British EP **All My Loving**, still available by import. The first ("no mistake") version of *Please Please Me* is most accessible as an Oldies 45 single, found in lesser-quality record shops and even department stores, though it also appears on the British import single and a British EP **The Beatles' Hits**. The first version of *Across The Universe* only appeared on the **No One's Gonna Change Our World** British charity LP, which is getting harder to find these days.

Is that enough for you? Hopefully. All that now separates you from a "complete" Beatles collection are two alternate versions of songs you should already have. Both are *very* hard to find and cannot be ordered anywhere. The original issue of *Love Me Do* is best found on an out-of-print Capitol of Canada 45 (if you're lucky, you might find it at a garage sale). The version of *Love Me Do* now found on the British single is *not* the first version. Only the original pressings had the first version, and your chances of finding that anywhere west of Greenland are slight.

Last and least is the version of *Sweet Georgia Brown* with Tony Sheridan's original vocals. As far as we know, this was only issued on an EP in Germany in 1962, which nobody bought then. Your chances of finding it now might be easily described as remote. We don't even have a copy.

Assuming you started from scratch and kept your eyes open (and not counting the last two out-of-print items), the above collection should cost about $160.00. Sounds like a lot, but think of it as an investment for the future.

Q: What about Beatle solo efforts?

A: We've assumed that any Beatle fan would naturally want to possess *every* group composition as a matter of course. The quality of the solo efforts, however, is more uneven and subject to each fan's individual taste. Besides, the solo tracks have not been repackaged nearly as often, so it's not that difficult or confusing to amass a complete collection for any individual Beatle. Still, some tracks on singles never made it onto albums, and it's worth pointing these out, as they might easily be overlooked.

Ringo's flip side gems include *Coochy Coochy* (flip of *Beaucoups of Blues*), *Blind Man* (flip of *Back Off Boogaloo*), *Down And Out* (flip of *Photograph*) and *Just A Dream* (found as the flip to both *Wings* and *Drowning In The Sea Of Love*). If you buy one more single, *It Don't Come Easy/Early 1970*, you won't have to buy Ringo's **Blast From Your Past** greatest hits LP.

George's single-only tracks include *Miss O'Dell* (flip of *Give Me Love*), *Deep Blue* (flip of *Bangla Desh*) and *I Don't Care Anymore* (flip of *Dark Horse*). George's greatest hits LP includes only one track not previously available on an album, the single *Bangla Desh*. Since you need that single for *Deep Blue* anyway, purchase of the LP is unnecessary.

John has only two tracks available only as singles, *Give Peace A Chance* (**Shaved Fish** included only a brief excerpt) and *Move Over Ms. L* (flip of *Stand By Me*). John's **Shaved Fish** is an excellent greatest hits album, well worth purchasing.

Paul is long overdue for a greatest hits LP. Some of his best songs are still available only as singles. These include *Another Day/Oh Woman Oh Why*, *Give Ireland Back To The Irish/(Instrumental Version)*, *Mary Had A Little Lamb/Little Woman Love*, *Hi Hi Hi/C Moon*, *The Mess* (flip of *My Love*), *I Lie Around/Live And Let Die* (unless you *want* to buy the soundtrack album for just the title cut),

Country Dreamer (flip of *Helen Wheels*), *Zoo Gang* (British flip of *Band On The Run*) and *Junior's Farm/Sally G*. After you sort through these singles tracks, it's very easy to scoop up the albums necessary to complete each solo collection.

Q: What about Beatle records released overseas? Some collectors consider these foreign discs essential to a complete Beatles collection; are they worth the price?

A: As a number of collectors reach the point at which they have a nearly complete American and British Beatle collection, they begin to turn their hungering eyes on that pulsating virgin territory — foreign discs. The whole fun of collecting *is* collecting, not having a complete collection;hence, the proclivity by some to get into the open-ended foreign market. This always struck us as slightly absurd and masochistic. There is no way any human being in this or any other lifetime will ever gather under one roof *all* international Beatle releases (not to mention solo records and other Apple artists). To hopefully "cut off at the pass" any such tendencies nurturing in the hinterlands, we'd like to present a list of the only foreign releases we find worthy of note.

The prime category is, naturally, different recordings. The Beatles recorded two songs in a foreign language (*She Loves You* and *I Want To Hold Your Hand*—in German); a number of Apple and Dark Horse artists did the same. Mary Hopkin (certainly of universal appeal) recorded and released four (French, German, Spanish and Italian) foreign language versions of her first hit *Those Were The Days*. All five contained the same musical back-up with only the vocal track replaced. In 1971 she recorded *Let My Name Be Sorrow* in Japanese. Japanese seemed to be a popular language around Apple. Yoko Ono (who should certainly know from whence she speaks on this topic) recorded, with Elephant's Memory, a special single *Jose Joi Banzaie (Parts 1 & 2)* released only in Japan around 1973. Splinter, Dark Horse artists, took the time to record *Lonely Man* in Japanese, though it didn't come out until 1976, a year after the song's original release. A month later, they released another single in Japan, containing two tracks (in English!) not otherwise available: *Love Is Not Enough* and *White Shoeleather*. (They did record another version of *Love Is Not Enough* for their **Two Man Band** album.)

Apart from these "new" recordings, the foreign market also contains a few rare discs which, for various reasons, have no equivalent in either Britain or America. Badfinger's first album (when they were still known as the Iveys) *planned* for general release only got out in Japan and some European countries. A number of songs would end up on the **Magic Christian Music** album, but six tracks were hereafter lost. Two of the dozen Japanese Beatle EPs are of some interest to Americans. AP-4118 contains the only known "stereo" mix of *Sie Liebt Dich* (*She Loves You* in German), while AP-4110 has a "true" stereo mix of *I'm Down*, which appears on the American **Rock And Roll Music** LP in inferior "fake" stereo.

Two foreign LPs might be considered in the "nice to have" category. **The Stars Sing Lennon--McCartney** is a fine source of a number of currently unavailable Lennon/McCartney songs "given" to other artists. It first appeared in Britain on the EMI Music for Pleasure budget label (mfp 5175), but is currently more accessible through the 1974 Dutch pressing (Delta Star DS 4015). Also attracting collector interest are the few Russian releases of Beatle albums. The first was Wings' **Band On The Run**. We can only imagine how the Kremlin will react to the White Album's *Back In The U.S.S.R.!*

Beyond this, you're on your own. The French, like the British, reserviced their Beatle singles in 1976, adding some new very nice colorful picture sleeves. But if you start collecting international picture sleeves, you'll die of heartbreak.

Q: Assuming I have any money left, and wanted to amass a reasonably complete Beatles' library, which books (other than this gem I'm holding in my hands) are worth reading (even buying)?

A: Hundreds, yes friends, hundreds of books have been published about the Beatles. Most are pure, unadulterated crap (and fortunately, mostly out-of-print). Only a handful are worth the attention of anyone with an IQ over 70:

The Beatles--The Authorized Biography (1968) Hunter Davies
    McGraw-Hill (hardcover only)

Richard DiLello described this as the "authorized Tapioca Biography of the Beatles"--underscoring its strength and inherent weakness. With the blessing of Brian Epstein, Davies took up the task of producing a level-headed history of the Beatles from 1962 through **Sgt. Pepper**. And he did just that. Drawing no outlandish conclusions, the book only hints at the insanity later chronicled in *Lennon Remembers* and *The Man Who Gave The Beatles Away*. It does little to dispel the notion of "the four lovable mop-tops." Still, it stood heads above the trashy Beatle books appearing at the time and, in many ways, it's still the best documentation of the 1962-1967 period in Beatle history.

The Man Who Gave The Beatles Away (1975) Allan Williams and
    William Marshall Macmillan (hardcover); Ballantine Books (paperback)

Though Williams tends to exaggerate the *length* of his association as manager with the early Beatles, which only lasted from 1960-1961, there's no denying his unique perspective on their careers. He arranged their first Hamburg gig (he even drove the group out to Germany!). He helped in their early searches for a drummer. More importantly, he knew them as scruffy, aspiring young "punks" on the make—who finally made it, leaving him behind (a point he repeats constantly). His tale reads like an extended conversation—after a few pints—at a local pub: long on personal anecdotes and recrimination, but it's a great introduction to the feel of Liverpool and the beat groups of the time.

The Longest Cocktail Party (1972) Richard DiLello
    Playboy Press
    Though subtitled "an insider's view of the Beatles" it is, more accurately, an insider's view of the insanity surrounding the fab four at Apple's London headquarters. DiLello started out there as the "house hippie" and eventually, through attrition, assumed the position "Director of Public Relations." His memory is incredible. His stream-of-consciousness style weaves press releases, public relations, public reactions, casual corridor propositions and the Beatles into an intense, detailed account of the hey-day of Apple (1968-1970). He loved every minute—and it shows.

Apple To The Core (The Unmaking Of The Beatles) (1972) Peter
    McCabe and Robert Schonfeld Pocket Books
    Another look at Apple, this one juicier and much nastier. The authors mix tales of sharp personality conflicts with business wheeling and dealing. At stake: The Beatle Millions. The result: The Unmaking of the Beatles. Actually, the authors do an excellent job explaining some of the complicated business deals of the time, and they even backtrack and sort through the financial goings-on at the height of Beatlemania. The dollars-and-cents companion to Hunter Davies and Richard DiLello.

The Beatles: An Illustrated Record (1975) Roy Carr and Tony Tyler
    Harmony
    These two critical denizens of the British music weekly *New Musical Express* assembled, in effect, a giant full-color issue of *NME* devoted to the Beatles, complete with ads, publicity photos and record jackets. Since they review only each British Beatle release, chronologically through 1975, this serves as an excellent guide for the American fan who first joined the Beatlemania madness in 1964. The authors are strongly opinionated (what critic isn't) and level especially harsh blasts at Harrison. Though their coverage of "fellow travelers" (Billy J. Kramer, Cilla Black, *et al*) is spotty, this should

be required reading for American fans.

Growing Up With The Beatles (1976) Ron Schaumberg
   Pyramid
   No, Ron did not grow up on the back streets of Liverpool. Or
Hamburg. He was raised in Shawnee Mission, Kansas. But, like a
whole generation of American teenagers, he grew up following the
exploits of the Beatles. If the premise seems a bid daft, ignore the
text and zero in on the book's real strength–the photos and memorabilia. Ron and his associates contacted many of the original photo
sources and have managed to assemble a lovely collection of illustra-
tions, some previously unpublished. Actually, this book is the
Beatles seen through a fan's eyes. Distant. Inaccessible. Yet even
so, whispering secret, personal messages in their music. Perhaps un-
intentionally, this book illustrates the intense personal attachment
felt by so many people to the Beatles, and explains why, after so
many years, fans still call out longingly for a reunion.

The Beatles Complete (1976) Words and Music by John Lennon,
   Paul McCartney, George Harrison and Ringo Starr
   Warner Bros. Publications
   Though several books have been published containing the *words*
to most of the Beatles' songs, this collection is the definite *magnum
opus* of the genre. Containing both the words *and* the music, it's
the perfect companion to all those records and magazine clippings.
It omits about 19 songs, but every Beatle songbook published is
guilty of sins of omission. Now, drag out that old guitar. . .

*All Together Now, The First Complete Beatles Discography 1961-
   1975* (1976) Harry Castleman and Wally Podrazik
   Pierian Press (hardcover); Ballantine Books (paperback)
   Granted we're a biased source, but this book replaces *all* so-
called Beatle discographies printed to date. It traces group and
individual performances, and is equally authoritative on work they
did for others. The bootlegs and British & American chart sections
alone make it worthwhile. If you don't want to take our word for it,
ask the authors.

Solo efforts by the individual Beatles have yet to produce any
books devoted to George or Ringo. Paul's American tour in 1976
triggered the expected outpouring of trashy "behind the scenes"
tomes, and John's volatile artistic exploits have always made good
copy. Again, only a handful stand out:

In His Own Write (1964) John Lennon
   Simon & Schuster (hardcover only)

A Spaniard In The Works (1965) John Lennon
   Simon & Schuster (hardcover only)
Lennon Remembers: The Rolling Stone Interviews (1971) Jann
   Wenner Popular Library
   A decade later, John's only two books still wear well, while
The Rolling Stone Interviews reveals an intensely hurt John Lennon
making public the difficult transition from Beatle to ex-Beatle. First
person accounts, all worth having.

One Day At A Time (1976) Anthony Fawcett
   Grove Press
   Fawcett worked as a personal assistant to John from 1968-
1970, important years both in the growth of John Lennon as a solo
artist and in the deterioration of the Beatles as a group. He manages
to convey the uncertainty and excitement of an "emerging artist"
while also capturing the paranoia and pain of leaving old friends.
The book follows Lennon's career right up to the presentation of
his green card in July of 1976. The layout and photos are excellent,
and it's refreshing to read a history of Lennon by someone who's
not out to assassinate Yoko Ono at the same time.

The Paul McCartney Story (1975) George Tremlett
   Popular Library
The John Lennon Story (1976) George Tremlett
   Futura Publications (British Paperback)
   Tremlett observes in the opening paragraph to *The Paul Mc-
Cartney Story* that for all the material published on each of the
Beatles, very little is really known about any of them. Having seen
so many collections of rewritten press releases disguised as books,
we're inclined to agree. So saying, Tremlett reached into his personal
files of notes and put together a book on Paul (1975) and another on
John (1976). Though he doesn't quite completely escape the hopeless retelling of the same old anecdotes, he manages to transform
both books into instantly indispensible collections by devoting over
one-third of both volumes to a chronological listing of personal and
public events. Both books begin the story in the 50's and carry on to
the present. Unfortunately, the McCartney book suffers the most
here in that the "present" is pre-**Venus And Mars** and the subsequent
world-wide-super-star-status of Wings.

   That should take care of your bookshelf. Now if you'd like a
taste of current Beatle fandom, the following magazines and organi-
zations are worthwhile:

The Beatles Book Appreciation Society Magazine (Monthly)
   Subscriptions are available for $12 annually

Beat Publications, 58/60 Parker Street, London, England WC2B 5QB

In May of 1976, Johnny Dean began reprinting, from the original plates, the monthly *Beatles Book*, originally published from August 1963 through December 1969. Each issue has a wrap-around eight pages of new material. For those unfamiliar with *The Beatles Monthly* it was, in effect, a fan's monthly newsmagazine; details most newspapers would ignore are included, as well as many exclusive photos. At $1 per issue, this is a tremendous buy. (As of this writing, all the back issues are still available at the same rate.) If the series continues at its present monthly rate, it should last through 1982.

Club Sandwich (Official Newsletter of the Wings Fun Club) (Bimonthly) Membership dues are $5 annually

Wings Fun Club, PO Box 4UP, London W1A 4UP, England

Yes, that address on **Red Rose Speedway** was for real! And why not? The official "house organ" for Wings is filled with photos (many by Linda–naturally), news items, contests and album previews. All in good fun. No, Paul hasn't sent out his own Christmas record yet.

Strawberry Fields Forever (Fan Club and Newsletter)

Membership dues are $6 annually

Joe Pope, Strawberry Fields Forever, 310 Franklin St., No. 117, Boston, Massachusetts 02110

Dozens of fan clubs have been formed to celebrate the golden days of Beatlemania, to follow the Beatles' individual careers, and to await the possible Second Coming. Most publish some sort of newsletter, which relieves you of the responsibility of reading the liner notes of *every* album released–checking for Beatle appearances. Most even offer books, photos, patches and such at reasonable prices. Joe Pope's *Strawberry Fields Forever* is one of the best. Though Joe's newsletter is a bit irregular, he eventually manages to cover most news items (and then some). For the past two years, each member even received a special Christmas record. Joe staged the first Beatle Fan Convention in Boston in July of 1974.

Beatlefest (Beatle Fan Convention)

For information and location of the upcoming festivals write: Beatlefest, Box 78, North Hackensack Station, River Edge, New Jersey 07661 (201) 487-2117

Mark Lapidos has put together a series of Beatle Fan Conventions (Beatlefests) which he stages in different cities each year. In 1976 and 1977 they were held in New York, Chicago, Los Angeles and San Francisco. They're a perfect place to see old Beatle movies and TV clips, meet other Beatle fans, enter contests, buy old records and Beatle memorabilia, and even meet famous authors.

Record Stores
    Most record stores simply can't afford to store anything but the top twenty singles. Trying to find some of the more obscure 45s, even if newly released, can be a difficult, frustrating task. We recommend the following stores (in three key cities) which have a good selection of current singles, and a good selection of imports:

Chicago: Sounds Good (312) 528-8827
           3259 N. Ashland Ave.
           Chicago, Illinois 60657

Los Angeles: Tower Records (213) 477-2021
           1028 Westwood Blvd.
           Westwood, California 90024

New York: Disc-O-Phile (212) 473-1902
           26 W. 8th St.
           New York, New York 10014

           Downstairs Records (212) 221-8989
           53 W. 42nd St.
           New York, New York 10036

    You can try contacting these stores by mail, but should keep your requests limited to current (but hard for you to find) material. Though these stores do have extensive oldies sections, they *don't* have the time and personnel to check through a three page want list of out-of-print discs. The search for such records is better conducted through the hundreds of oldies/specialty/collectors shops that dot the country.
    If you still can't find the current British records you want on import, we recommend contacting Don Hughes at 2 Byron Close, Hampton, Middlesex, England. He can usually find current items, and even puts together a "British Oldies" sales list every so often.

Q: Will the Beatles ever get back together again?

A: No! Unless, of course. . .

Yesterday And Today   Capitol ST 2553 (LP)

GUMBO SOUP AND VINYL WAFERS

🍎 *I am at 3 Savile Row, most days*

Apple Records

Apple was the Beatles' dream company, offering seemingly limitless opportunities for aspiring artists, but almost from the start it was riddled with organizational problems and squeezed by clever con-men. Though many divisions quickly fell by the wayside, Apple records managed to hang on from its first releases in August of 1968 to May of 1976. Over two dozen performers released material on Apple (most in its heyday from 1968-1971), but the Beatles, of course, accounted for the label's success. Apart from the Beatles, Apple earned just two gold records and managed to push only a handful of discs to the top. With only a few exceptions, the Beatles were unable to transfer their own magic to the other artists on the label, even if they involved themselves personally in the projects. Perhaps their own presence was too powerful–Paul McCartney attending a press conference for Mary Hopkin would undoubtedly assure a good turnout, and most likely result in a news item about Paul McCartney. Perhaps they expected too much–*just* because George Harrison wrote *Try Some, Buy Some* didn't mean it was going to be a great record! Or perhaps they discovered why they needed a Brian Epstein so much. Their music might have progressed from *Love Me Do* to **Sgt. Pepper**, but their business acumen did not take a corresponding leap. They simply never really learned how to best package the monster of Apple records.

Though initially promising to be an open door for talented performers, Apple almost immediately discovered why those doors are usually so hard to keep open: too many people wanted in! Instead of openness, the Apple roster reflected only two infusions of talent: performers the individual Beatles wanted on Apple (Billy Preston, Mary Hopkin, Elephant's Memory, for example), or performers who had caught the fancy of someone who knew someone (a Mal Evans, Derek Taylor, Peter Asher) in the organization who, in effect, lobbied for them (Trash, Badfinger, James Taylor, Lon. & Derrek Van Eaton). For the most part, all of these performers were quite talented and showed signs of real greatness. Certainly the albums by James Taylor, Doris Troy, Jackie Lomax and Badfinger were superb, and most of the rest of the catalogue was at least adequate (though some of it, in all honesty, was terrible!). This section chronicles in detail the releases by all those Apple recording artists, from Badfinger to Lon & Derrek Van Eaton, who took their shot at success as part of Apple's dream machine.

The Beatles, of course, released their own records on Apple, beginning with the single *Hey Jude* and the LP **The Beatles** (*The White Album*) in 1968. These releases included the singles *Get Back, Ballad Of John & Yoko, Something, Let It Be* and *The Long And Winding Road*, and the albums **Yellow Submarine, Abbey Road, Let It Be, Hey Jude, The Beatles 1962-1966** and **The Beatles 1967-1970.** Additionally, from November of 1971 to May of 1976 all the old Beatle product (singles and albums), which originally appeared in America on Capitol, was issued on the Apple Label (though keeping the same Capitol catalogue numbers). From May of 1976, all the Beatle records, including discs originally on Apple, were issued on the Capitol label. Solo efforts by John, George and Ringo followed a similar course. Paul McCartney's singles and albums for Apple also followed the same May 1976 scheduled label shift, but since Paul had signed his own independent contract with Capitol, he was able to arrange for McCartney solo material to be released on a specially-designed Capitol label which looked like the old Capitol logo from the 1950's. The technical producing, writing and performing details of all Beatle material released before January 1976 can be found in *All Together Now.*

Badfinger. Badfinger (nee The Iveys) was Apple's only real hit group (aside from the Beatles, of course). At the persistent urging of a very enthusiastic Mal Evans (who first brought in their demo tape), the Iveys (Tom Evans: Rhythm Guitar; Pete Ham: Lead Guitar; Ron Griffith: Bass; Mike Gibbons: Drums) were signed to Apple records and publishing in July of 1968. They moved from two years of local gigs to the Beatles' Great Apple Dream Label. Their first single (*Maybe Tomorrow*) made minor ripples on the American charts, but the follow-up LP was not released to either the British or American markets. The album did find its way onto Apple's foreign release schedule (Europe and Japan), thus becoming an instant collector's item. Produced by Mal and Tony Visconti, this is one obscure disc well worth the search; it's an excellent LP and six of its tracks appeared on no other disc: *See-Saw Grampa, Think About The Good Times, Yesterday Ain't Coming Back, Sali Bloo, I've Been Waiting* and a noticeably different production of *Fisherman*. Several more Iveys tracks were released in Britain in July of 1969: a follow-up single (*Dear Angie/No Escaping Your Love*) and one track (*Storm In A Teacup*) on the special Wall's Ice Cream promotional EP.

While pondering their next move, the group changed its name (to Badfinger--they thought Iveys sounded *too nice*) and personnel (Joey Molland replaced Ron Griffith and the group shifted instruments to accommodate the change; the new line-up was: Tom Evans: Bass; Pete Ham: Lead Guitar; Joey Molland: Rhythm Guitar; Mike Gibbons: Drums). Paul McCartney then offered to help them crack the market with one song (only one--then they were back on their own). The newly rechristened Badfinger entered the studios and, with Paul writing and producing, emerged with *Come And Get It*, the opening tune to Ringo's new film, *The Magic Christian*. It hit top ten in both Britain and America, and the follow-up album (**Magic Christian Music**) sold well. That album was a half-and-half combination of the best tracks (some remixed) from the **Maybe Tomorrow** LP, and seven new tunes. The American version of the LP omitted two tracks: *Angelique* and *Give It A Try*.

Badfinger then managed a feat no other Apple artist ever accomplished: consistent, successful follow-ups. Their schedule was almost Beatle-ish: one single and one album per year for three years. The group's own Pete Ham penned *No Matter What*--and it hit top ten in Britain and America in 1971. *Without You* (written by Pete Ham and Tom Evans) from the **No Dice** LP became a worldwide success when Harry Nilsson covered it in 1972 (much to the delight of Apple publishing). George Harrison and Todd Rundgren both produced tracks for Badfinger's third LP, **Straight Up**, and the single *Day After Day* culled from this album won the group a gold disc in 1972. Badfinger (on acoustic guitars) even joined George Harrison's Concert For Bangla Desh in 1971, accompanying George on *Here Comes The Sun*.

But the success of 1972 faded into the jungle of Apple's business problems, and Badfinger jumped to Warner Brothers in 1973. The final Apple LP, **Ass**, featured the traditional selection of tracks left behind by a group that's left a label--that is, whatever fills an album. One track, *Apple Of My Eye* (ironically issued as the single), expressed some of the group's frustrations. The cover, picturing a donkey (ass to the camera) lured away by a carrot in the sky, was a none-too-subtle comment on the whole affair.

Badfinger's two Warner Brothers LPs (**Badfinger** and **Wish You Were Here**) weren't particularly successful, but the question of the group's recovery power was rendered moot when Pete Ham committed suicide. Since then, Tom Evans and brand-new member Bob Jackson split from the group and formed Dodgers, releasing several singles in 1975 and '76 on Island. Joey Molland joined Mark Clarke, Peter Wood and John Shirley in Natural Gas, which released an LP in

1976 on Private Stock. At the beginning of 1977, it was reported that Molland had left Natural Gas and was seeking to reform Badfinger.

NOV 15, 1968 (UK) Apple 5
JAN 27, 1969 (US) Apple 1803
by The Iveys Prod: Tony Visconti
A: *Maybe Tomorrow*—Tom Evans—*2:50*
*B: *And Her Daddy's A Millionaire*—Tom Evans—Pete Ham—*2:08*

JUL   4, 1969 (EUROPE) SAPCOR 8 (LP)
JUL 14, 1969 (US–Withdrawn) ST 3355 (LP)
by The Iveys
MAYBE TOMORROW Prod: Tony Visconti except † Mal Evans
side one
†*See-Saw, Grampa*—Pete Ham—*3:24*
†*Beautiful And Blue*—Tom Evans—*2:36*
  Dear Angie—Ron Griffith—*2:37*
  Think About The Good Times—Mike Gibbons—*2:13*
  Yesterday Ain't Coming Back—Pete Ham—Tom Evans—*2:55*
†*Fisherman*—Tom Evans—*2:50*
side two
  MAYBE TOMORROW—Tom Evans—*2:50*
  Sali Bloo—Pete Ham—*2:38*
  Angelique—Tom Evans—*2:25*
  I'm In Love—Pete Ham—*2:25*
†*They're Knocking Down Our Home*—Pete Ham—*3:37*
  I've Been Waiting—Pete Ham—*6:59*

JUL 18, 1969 (UK) Apple 14
by The Iveys Prod: Tony Visconti
*A: *No Escaping Your Love*—Tom Evans—*1:56*
B: *Dear Angie*—Ron Griffith—*2:37*

JUL 18, 1969 (UK SPECIAL BUSINESS PROMOTION)
  Apple CT 1 (EP)
by Various Artists
WALL'S ICE CREAM
side one
  cut one: *Storm In A Teacup*—Tom Evans—*2:26*
    by The Iveys

146

DEC 5, 1969 (UK) Apple 20
JAN 12, 1970 (US) Apple 1815
by Badfinger Prod: Paul McCartney (A side) and Tony Visconti
  (B side)
A: *Come And Get It*---Paul McCartney---*2:21*
B: *Rock Of All Ages*---Tom Evans---Pete Ham---Mike Gibbons---*3:22*

JAN 9, 1970 (UK) Apple SAPCOR 12 (LP)
FEB 16, 1970 (US) Apple ST 3364 (LP)*
by Badfinger
MAGIC CHRISTIAN MUSIC Prod: Tony Visconti except † Mal
  Evans and % Paul McCartney
side one
%*Come And Get It*---Paul McCartney---*2:21*
  Crimson Ship---Tom Evans---Pete Ham---*3:40*
  DEAR ANGIE---Ron Griffith---*2:37*
†*Fisherman (version two)*---Tom Evans---*2:22*
†*Midnight Sun*---Pete Ham---*2:45*
†*BEAUTIFUL AND BLUE*---Tom Evans---*2:37*
  Rock Of All Ages---Tom Evans---Pete Ham---Mike Gibbons---*3:22*
side two
†*Carry On 'Till Tomorrow*---Tom Evans---Pete Ham---*4:43*
  I'M IN LOVE---Pete Ham---*2:25*
†*Walk Out In The Rain*---Pete Ham---*2:23*
  ANGELIQUE---Tom Evans---*2:25*
†*THEY'RE KNOCKING DOWN OUR HOME*---Pete Ham---*3:37*
  Give It A Try---Tom Evans---Pete Ham---Mike Gibbons---Ron
    Griffith---*2:26*
  MAYBE TOMORROW---Tom Evans---*2:50*

OCT 12, 1970 (US) Apple 1822
by Badfinger Prod: Mal Evans
A: *No Matter What*---Pete Ham---*3:00*
B: *CARRY ON TILL TOMORROW*---Tom Evans---Pete Ham---*4:43*

NOV 6, 1970 (UK) Apple 31
by Badfinger Prod: Mal Evans (A side) and Geoff Emerick (B side)
A: *No Matter What*---Pete Ham---*3:00*
B: *Better Days*---Tom Evans---Joey Molland---*3:58*

*In the U.S., *Angelique* and *Give It A Try* were removed, and *Fisherman* was shifted to side two, cut four.

147

NOV 9, 1970 (US) Apple ST 3367 (LP)
NOV 27, 1970 (UK) Apple SAPCOR 16 (LP)
by Badfinger
NO DICE Prod: Geoff Emerick except † Mal Evans
side one
  I Can't Take It---Pete Ham---*2:52*
  I Don't Mind It---Tom Evans–Joey Molland---*3:12*
  Love Me Do---Joey Molland---*2:57*
  Midnight Caller---Pete Ham---*2:48*
  †No Matter What---Pete Ham---*3:00*
  Without You---Tom Evans–Pete Ham---*3:42*
side two
  Blodwyn---Pete Ham---*3:25*
  Better Days–Tom Evans–Joey Molland---*3:58*
  It Had To Be---Mike Gibbons---*2:25*
  Watford John—Tom Evans–Pete Ham–Mike Gibbons–Joey
    Molland---*3:21*
  †Believe Me---Tom Evans---*2:58*
  We're For The Dark---Pete Ham---*3:52*

NOV 10, 1971 (US) Apple 1841
by Badfinger Prod: George Harrison (A side) and Todd Rundgren
  (B side)
A: Day After Day---Pete Ham---*3:02*
B: Money—Tom Evans---*3:31*

DEC 13, 1971 (US) Apple SW 3387 (LP)
FEB 11, 1972 (UK) Apple SAPCOR 19 (LP)
by Badfinger
STRAIGHT UP Prod: Todd Rundgren except † George Harrison
side one
  Take It All—Pete Ham---*4:25*
  Baby Blue—Pete Ham---*3:38*
  Money—Tom Evans---*3:31*
  Flying--Tom Evans–Joey Molland---*2:37*
  †I'd Die Babe--Joey Molland---*2:05*
  †Name Of The Game---Pete Ham---*5:49*
side two
  †Suitcase—Joey Molland--*2:53*
  Sweet Tuesday Morning---Joey Molland---*2:31*
  †Day After Day---Pete Ham---*3:02*
  Sometimes---Joey Molland---*2:57*
  Perfection---Pete Ham---*5:10*
  It's Over---Tom Evans---*3:24*

JAN 14, 1972 (UK) Apple 40
by Badfinger Prod: George Harrison (A side) and Todd Rundgren
  (B side)
A: *Day After Day*—Pete Ham—*3:02*
B: *Sweet Tuesday Morning*—Joey Molland—*2:31*

MAR   6, 1972 (US) Apple 1844
MAR 10, 1972 (UK) Apple 42
by Badfinger Prod: Todd Rundgren
A: *BABY BLUE*—Pete Ham—*3:38*
B: *FLYING*—Tom Evans—Joey Molland—*2:37*

NOV 26, 1973 (US) Apple SW 3411 (LP)
MAR 8, 1974 (UK) Apple SAPCOR 27 (LP)
by Badfinger
ASS Prod: Chris Thomas and Badfinger except † Todd Rundgren
side one
  Apple Of My Eye—Badfinger—*3:03*
  Get Away—Badfinger—*4:00*
  Icicles—Badfinger—*2:34*
†*The Winner*—Badfinger—*3:26*
  Blind Owl—Badfinger—*3:01*
side two
  Constitution—Badfinger—*2:59*
  When I Say—Badfinger—*3:06*
  Cowboy—Badfinger—*2:40*
†*I Can Love You*—Badfinger—*3:35*
  Timeless—Badfinger—*7:43*

DEC 17, 1973 (US) Apple 1864
MAR 8, 1974 (UK) Apple 49
by Badfinger Prod: Chris Thomas and Badfinger
A: *APPLE OF MY EYE*—Badfinger—*3:03*
B: *BLIND OWL*—Badfinger—*3:01*

Black Dyke Mills Brass Band.   The Black Dyke Mills Brass Band
helped launch the new Apple label with a rousing version of McCartney's theme for the London Weekend TV comedy *Thingumybob*
(starring Stanley Holloway).   For the underbelly of that first disc,
an instrumental version of *Yellow Submarine* was recorded (after
awhile, this was used as the American A-side). Paul and the band,
conducted by Geoffrey Brand, recorded the disc on a quiet Sunday
in Bradford.   The Black Dyke Mills Band normally worked on a
record-to-record basis with another company and so, when their

Apple disc failed to click and there wasn't a request to do another, they simply continued as before. They're still going strong in England, even today.

AUG 26, 1968 (US) Apple 1800
SEP 6, 1968 (UK) Apple 4
by John Foster & Sons Ltd. Black Dyke Mills Brass Band
  Prod: Paul McCartney
*A: Thingumybob–L-McC—1:51
*B: Yellow Submarine—L-McC—2:56

Richard Brautigan. The Zapple series was conceived as a subsidiary of Apple records which would accomodate spoken word, avant garde and experimental recordings. Indeed, Zapple's first two releases were George's **Electronic Music** and John & Yoko's **Life With The Lions**. While names like Ken Kesey, Lawrence Ferlinghette, Charles Bukowski, Charles Olsen and Richard Brautigan were batted about as potential artists for the label, Brautigan was the only one who *almost* released an album. Instead, it was lost in the bureaucratic shuffle accompanying Allen Klein's ascendence to power at Apple. Capitol finally did release it in America a year later on its Harvest label (Harvest ST-424) on September 21, 1970.

On the LP, Brautigan simply read excerpts from his own works, such as *Trout Fishing In America*. On one cut (*Love Poem*) he was joined by Bob Prescott, Valerie Estes, Michael McClure, Margot Patterson Doss, Bruce Conner, Michaela Blake-Grand, Don Allen, David Schaff, Ianthe Brautigan, Imogen Cunningham, Herb Caen, Betty Kirkendall, Peter Berg, Alan Stone, Antonio, Cynthia Harwood and Price Dunn. In 1975, Brautigan authored the introduction to a paperback collection of the words to most of the Beatles' songs, *The Beatles Lyrics Illustrated*.

MAY 23, 1969 (UK–withdrawn) Zapple 03 (LP)
Released in America on September 21, 1970 as Harvest ST-424
by Richard Brautigan (All Compositions by Richard Brautigan)
LISTENING TO RICHARD BRAUTIGAN Prod: Richard Brautigan;
  Engineer: Mike Larner
side one
  The Telephone Door To Richard Brautigan—0:50
  Trout Fishing In America—7:15
  Love Poem—4:05
  A Confederate General From Big Sur—4:00
  Here Are The Sounds Of My Life In San Francisco—2:25
  The Pill Versus The Springhill Mine Disaster—6:35

side two
Revenge Of The Lawn—9:50
The Telephone Door That Leads Eventually To Some Love Poems
—7:30
In Watermelon Sugar—2:25
Here Are Some More Sounds Of My Life—1:55
Short Stories About California—6:10
Boo, Forever—0:45

Brute Force. In 1969 George Harrison assigned Apple's London office the seemingly innocuous task of releasing and promoting a single by his latest discovery, a twenty-year old singer-songwriter from New York called Brute Force (a.k.a. Steven Friedland). The single was an original Brute Force composition, produced and recorded by the singer back in New York, and titled simply *The King Of Fuh*. The song told the story of a mythical king who ruled the kingdom of Fuh. It was the tale of a Fuh king, so to speak. EMI wanted no part of such a fantasy, and refused even to press the record, much less distribute it. Undaunted, Apple itself took on the task of sales and distribution, planning to stock mail order outlets and selected retail stores. DJ copies were even sent to the BBC, who naturally didn't give it any airplay. The distribution plan never really caught fire, and the disc quickly faded away. Brute Force and Apple then parted company. The tune did turn up again in 1971 in America on Brute Force's own label, though with a different flip-side (*Tapeworm Of Love*).

MAY 16, 1969 (UK-DJ) Apple 8
Issued in America on July 20, 1971 on Brute Force Records BFR 100
by Brute Force Prod: Steven Friedland
*A: King Of Fuh—Steven Friedland
*B: Nobody Knows—Steven Friedland

Delaney & Bonnie. Ideally, Apple records was to serve as both a launching pad for talented new artists and an umbrella for musicians the individual Beatles liked. Delaney and Bonnie Bramlett were quite popular on the British music scene in 1969. In fact, they were joined on their British tour late in the year by Eric Clapton and, for the last weekend, George Harrison. The final night's concert at Croydon was even recorded for an album. The entire entourage then moved on for a quick tour of Scandinavia. Delaney & Bonnie (and their friends) seemed perfect for Apple's still-expanding stable of artists. Business complications arose, however, and the LP planned for Apple was released instead on Elektra (EKS 74039 on June 17, 1969) in America. The live LP, never intended for Apple, was even-

151

tually released by Atco, the label the two successfully recorded on for several years.

MAY 23, 1969 (UK–withdrawn) Apple SAPCOR 7 (LP)
Released in America on June 27, 1969 as Elektra EKS 74039
by Delaney & Bonnie
THE ORIGINAL DELANEY & BONNIE (ACCEPT NO SUBSTI-TUTE) Prod: Delaney Bramlett
side one
   Get Ourselves Together—Bonnie Bramlett—Carl Radle—*2:33*
   Someday—Bonnie Bramlett—Doug Gilmore—Jerry Allison—*3:30*
   Ghetto—Bonnie Bramlett—Homer Banks—Bettye Crutcher—*4:55*
   When The Battle Is Over—Mac Rebennack—Jessie Hill—*3:36*
   Dirty Old Man—Delaney Bramlett—Mac Davis—*2:32*
side two
   Love Me A Little Bit Longer—Bonnie Bramlett—*3:00*
   I Can't Take It Much Longer—Delaney Bramlett—Joey Cooper
   —3:08
   Do Right Woman, Do Right Man—Chips Moman—Dan Penn—*5:20*
   Soldiers Of The Cross—*3:10*
   Gift Of Love—Delaney Bramlett—Mac Davis—*2:55*

Elephant's Memory. Since 1969, John Lennon had been drafting basically anyone who was around into his Plastic Ono Band. Finally, in late 1971, he settled on an established band to accompany him in personal appearances and to back him on records. Elephant's Memory (a hard-ass New York rock band) worked with John and Yoko for about one intense year. The award-winning group, which received a gold record for their work on the soundtrack to *Midnight Cowboy*, consisted of Stan Bronstein: Sax; Gary Van Scyoc: Bass; Adam Ippolito: Keyboards; Rick Frank: Drums; and Wayne 'Tex' Gabriel: Guitar. In early 1972 the "Plastic Ono Elephant's Memory Band" (P.O.E.M.) hit the US TV circuit, appearing on *Dick Cavett, Mike Douglas* and several "underground" TV specials. They performed at Madison Square Garden on August 22 in two special benefit concerts (the "One-To-One" Shows) for the Willowbrook School for Children. They also backed John and Yoko on the **Sometime In New York City** LP, Yoko's **Approximately Infinite Universe** LP, and three of Yoko's singles (*Now Or Never, Death Of Samantha*, and *Jose Joi Banzaie*). Elephant's Memory recorded one LP for Apple, produced (and sometimes accompanied) by John & Yoko (naturally!). Though not an outstanding commercial success, it's a tight album revealing the talent that earned them a spot next to John Lennon–they're a tight, driving rock 'n' roll band. Elephant's Memory and John parted amicably in 1973, and since then the group has seen several labels. Member Stan Bronstein even released a solo LP.

SEP 18, 1972 (US) Apple SMAS 3389 (LP)
NOV 10, 1972 (UK) Apple SAPCOR 22 (LP)
by Elephant's Memory
ELEPHANT'S MEMORY Prod: John Lennon and Yoko Ono
side one
  Liberation Special—Rick Frank—Stan Bronstein—*5:28*
  Baddest Of The Mean—Stan Bronstein—Rick Frank—Gary Van
    Scyoc—Adam Ippolito—Wayne Gabriel—*8:46*
  Cryin' Blacksheep Blues—Rick Frank—Stan Bronstein—D. Price
    —*4:27*
  Chuck 'n' Bo—Stan Bronstein—Rick Frank—Wayne Gabriel—*4:33*
side two
  Gypsy Wolf—Stan Bronstein—Rick Frank—*3:58*
  Madness—Adam Ippolito—Rick Frank—Stan Bronstein—*3:10*
  Life—Wayne Gabriel—*3:42*
  Wind Ridge—Gary Van Scyoc—*3:20*
  Power Boogie—Stan Bronstein—Rick Frank—Chris Robison—*3:50*
  Local Plastic Ono Band—Rick Frank—*2:00*

NOV 13, 1972 (US) Apple 1854
by Elephant's Memory Prod: John Lennon and Yoko Ono
A: *LIBERATION SPECIAL*—Rick Frank—Stan Bronstein—*3:30*
B: *MADNESS*—Adam Ippolito—Rick Frank—Stan Bronstein—*3:10*

DEC 4, 1972 (US) Apple 1854
by Elephant's Memory Prod: John Lennon and Yoko Ono
A: *LIBERATION SPECIAL*—Rick Frank—Stan Bronstein—*3:30*
B: *POWER BOOGIE*—Stan Bronstein—Rick Frank—Chris Robison
    —*3:50*

DEC 8, 1972 (UK) Apple 45
by Elephant's Memory Prod: John Lennon and Yoko Ono
A: *POWER BOOGIE*—Stan Bronstein—Rick Frank—Chris Robison
    —*3:50*
B: *LIBERATION SPECIAL*—Rick Frank—Stan Bronstein—*5:28*

Bill Elliott And The Elastic Oz Band. The infamous Oz Obscenity
Trials caused quite a stir in England in 1971. It's a tale well worth
reading in Tony Palmer's paperback book, *The Trials Of Oz* (published in 1971 by Blond and Briggs in England). John testified at
the trial and even dashed off a song in support of *Oz*, donating the
proceeds from the record's sales to the defense fund. To prevent this
from being labeled "The New John Lennon Single," the Plastic Ono
Band became the Elastic Oz Band. And while John himself sang the

B-side, it fell to young Bill Elliott to deliver the message: *God Save Us (Oz)!* The single didn't sell very well, but Bill Elliott eventually went on to Dark Horse records, where he's enjoyed success as one half of Splinter (see "Dark Horse"). The Oz defendents didn't fare as well. They were found guilty on several counts. On August 4, 1971, Judge Michael Argyle sentenced Richard Neville, Jim Anderson and Felix Dennis to prison terms of fifteen, twelve and nine months, respectively.

JUL 7, 1971 (US) Apple 1835
JUL 16, 1971 (UK) Apple 36
by Bill Elliott and the Elastic Oz Band Prod: John Lennon, Yoko
   Ono, Mal Evans and Phil Spector (A side); John Lennon and Elastic
   Oz Band Prod: John Lennon, Mal Evans and Apple (B side)
*A: *God Save Us*—Lennon—Yoko Ono—*3:10*
*B: *Do The Oz*—Lennon—Yoko Ono—*3:09*

Grapefruit.   Grapefruit (so dubbed by John Lennon) was the first Apple group signed to Apple Publishing (there was no Apple Records yet!) in late 1967. The band (George Alexander: Bass; John Perry: Lead Guitar; Pete Swettenham: Rhythm Guitar; and Geoff Swettenham: Drums) released its first single (*Dear Delilah*) in January. It was given an enthusiastic push and sold reasonably well. Grapefruit made their concert debut later in the year, dressed in grapefruit-yellow suits. And all smiles. But even at this early stage of Apple's history, there was confusion (some would say chaos) in the organization. Grapefruit soured on their association with Apple in November of 1968. They never did release any material on the Apple label. Their manager, Terry Doran, eventually wound up working with another fledgling label years later, Dark Horse.

Chris Hodge. Apple probably surprised itself with the success of the UFO-invasion rocker *We're On Our Way*—so much so that repeated requests for information and biographies on singer Chris Hodge were met with an apologetic "We just don't have any." The song snuck into the top half of the American charts (no. 44), then vanished. After an unsuccessful follow-up, Hodge shifted to RCA. Then he, too, vanished. Rumors that he served as a special consultant to Nicholas Roeg have never been confirmed.

MAY 3, 1972 (US) Apple 1850
JUN 9, 1972 (UK) Apple 43
by Chris Hodge Prod: Tony Cox
*A: We're On Our Way—Chris Hodge—2:43
*B: Supersoul—Chris Hodge—3:06

JAN 22, 1973 (US) Apple 1858
by Chris Hodge Prod: Andy Black and Ray Hendriksen
*A: Goodbye Sweet Lorraine—Chris Hodge—4:38
*B: Contact Love—Chris Hodge—2:55

Mary Hopkin. Mary Hopkin seemed to fulfill the Apple promise of giving talented young performers just the break they needed to reach the top. In fact, her "overnight success" at Apple reads like a Hollywood Storybook. Mary was spotted on the all-too-appropriately named British TV show, *Opportunity Knocks.* At seventeen, she was signed to Apple and almost immediately Paul McCartney took her under his mantle. He chose and produced Mary's first single, *Those Were The Days* (a song Paul had taken a fancy to back in the Beatle touring days; in fact, he had tried to convince touring-mates the Moody Blues to record it!). The record became a world-wide smash, hot on the heels of the Beatles' own *Hey Jude*. In America, it earned Mary one of Apple's two non-Beatle gold records (Badfinger's *Day After Day* was the other). As one of the label's first four releases, *Those Were The Days* sparked an incredibly successful debut for the new company. Almost from the beginning, Apple seemed intent on developing Mary Hopkin into an international singing star. Just to be safe, the vocal track to *Those Were The Days* was sung by Mary in Italian, French, Spanish and German, though using the same instrumental backing. All these versions were released to their respective countries. The Italian recording (*Quelli Erano Giorni*) even knocked a home-grown Italian cover version right off Italy's pop charts. Mary's first two singles of 1969 continued this practice, and were aimed at particular European markets (*Lontano Dagli Occhi* for Italy and *Prince En Avignon* for France).

In November 1968, Paul ushered Mary into the studio to produce her first LP, **Postcard**. The result was an odd pastiche of contemporary tunes (Nilsson, Donovan), old standards (Irving Berlin, George and Ira Gershwin) and personal favorites (Paul had sung *The Honeymoon Song* with the Beatles back in their Cavern days). The Donovan songs (with Paul and Donovan on guitars) seemed particularly suited to Mary's voice and style, but some of the others didn't quite jell. The material seemed more suited to Peggy Lee or Lena Horne than to a Welsh folksinger. The album was moderately successful, and to help ensure higher American sales the hit single of *Those Were The Days* replaced the track *Someone To Watch Over Me*. The LP peaked at no. 28 on the American charts.

Paul then brought Mary her long-awaited follow-up to *Those Were The Days*–a new Lennon/McCartney tune, *Goodbye*. Of course, after the monster success of her first disc, everyone was prepared for a let-down, but *Goodbye* bounced into the top ten in Britain (reaching no. 2) and made the American top twenty. Not as big, but still quite respectable. Over the next two years, Mary continued her development as an international singer. She released *Que Sera Sera* (produced and arranged by Paul, his last disc for her) in France in 1969. *Knock Knock Who's There* was entered in the 1970 "Song For Europe" competition, and joined *Temma Harbour* and *Think About Your Children* in Britain's top twenty. She even cut a track in Japanese (*Let My Name Be Sorrow*). Surprisingly, though, it wasn't until 1971 that Mary finally recorded her second Apple album, **Earth Song--Ocean Song** (produced by husband Tony Visconti). The production and selections drew from her folk background rather than Tin Pan Alley. Ralph McTell, Dave Cousins and Danny Thompson provided the basic backing. It was a quiet, tasteful LP, which quietly slipped into oblivion soon after its release.

In March of 1972, Mary announced that she would not be staying with Apple any longer. Actually, Mary and Apple hadn't been getting along for awhile (both bemoaned a lack of commitment by the other), so her departure from the label was predictable. Equally predictable was Apple's release of a *Greatest Hits* package (called **Those Were The Days**) by the end of the year. Befitting her stature as a successful international artist, this LP was a welcome collection of her many hit singles in Europe, England and America (which would have been long-lost otherwise). Since leaving Apple, Mary has appeared on a number of labels in England and America, though never approaching the "overnight success" of her initial Apple releases.

AUG 26, 1968 (US) Apple 1801
AUG 30, 1968 (UK) Apple 2
by Mary Hopkin Prod: Mary Hopkin
A: Those Were The Days--Gene Raskin--*5:06*
*B: Turn! Turn! Turn! (To Everything There Is A Season)--Pete
  Seeger---*2:48*

Those Were The Days was also issued in four other languages. On each recording, the vocal track was merely replaced. Both the instrumental backing and the flip side remained intact:
Quelli Erano Giorni (Italian) Apple 2
En Aquellos Dias (Spanish) Apple 3

Le Temps des Fleurs (French) Odeon FO-131
An Jenem Tag (German) Odeon O-23910

FEB 21, 1969 (UK) Apple SAPCOR 5 (LP)
MAR 3, 1969 (US) Apple ST 3351 (LP)
by Mary Hopkin
POST CARD Prod: Paul McCartney
side one
  Lord Of The Reedy River---Donovan Leitch---*2:33*
  Happiness Runs (Pebble And The Man)---Donovan Leitch---*2:01*
  Love Is The Sweetest Thing---Ray Noble---*3:42*
  Y Blodyn Gwyn---E. J. Hughes--R. H. Jones---*3:06*
  The Honeymoon Song---Mikis Theodorakis--William Sansom---*2:05*
  The Puppy Song---Harry Nilsson---*2:42*
  Inchworm (Fram Hans Christian Andersen)---Frank Loesser---*2:31*
side two: † in America, replaced by *Those Were The Days*
  Voyage Of The Moon---Donovan Leitch---*5:52*
  Lullaby Of The Leaves---Joe Young--Bernice Petkere---*2:33*
  Young Love---Carole Joyner--Ric Cartey---*2:09*
†*Someone To Watch Over Me*---Ira Gershwin--George Gershwin---*2:01*
  Prince En Avignon---Jean Pierre Bourtayre---*3:19*
  The Game---George Martin---*2:37*
  There's No Business Like Show Business---Irving Berlin---*4:01*

MAR 7, 1969 (ITALY) Apple 7
by Mary Hopkin Prod: Paul McCartney
A: *Lontano Dagli Occhi*---Sergio Endrigo--Sergio Bardotti---*3:22*
B: *THE GAME*---George Martin---*2:37*

MAR 7, 1969 (FRANCE) Apple 9
by Mary Hopkin Prod: Paul McCartney
A: *PRINCE EN AVIGNON*---Jean Pierre Bourtayre---*3:19*
B: *THE GAME*---George Martin---*2:37*

MAR 28, 1969 (UK) Apple 10
APR 7, 1969 (US) Apple 1806
by Mary Hopkin Prod: Paul McCartney
A: *Goodbye*---L-McC---*2:23*
B: *Sparrow*---Bernard Gallagher--Graham Lyle---*3:10*

SEP 19, 1969 (FRANCE) Apple 16
JUN 15, 1970 (US) Apple 1823
by Mary Hopkin Prod: Paul McCartney
A: *Que Sera, Sera (Whatever Will Be, Will Be)*---Jay Livingston--Ray
      Evans--arr. Paul McCartney---*3:04*
B: *Fields Of St. Etienne*---Bernard Gallagher--Graham Lyle---*3:12*

JAN 16, 1970 (UK) Apple 22
JAN 29, 1970 (US) Apple 1816
by Mary Hopkin Prod: Mickie Most (A side) and Paul McCartney
  (B side)
A: *Temma Harbour*---Philamore Lincoln---*3:20*
B: *LONTANO DAGLI OCCHI*---Sergio Endrigo—Sergio Bardotti
    ---*3:22*

MAR 20, 1970 (UK) Apple 26
by Mary Hopkin Prod: Mickie Most
A: *Knock Knock Who's There*---John Carter—Geoff Stephens---*2:28*
*B: *I'm Going To Fall In Love Again*---Cyril Ornacel—Hal Shaper---*2:01*

OCT 16, 1970 (UK) Apple 30
OCT 18, 1970 (US) Apple 1825
by Mary Hopkin Prod: Mickie Most
A: *Think About Your Children*---Tony Wilson—Errol Brown—M.
    Wilson---*2:57*
B: *Heritage*---Bernard Gallagher—Graham Lyle---*2:20*

JUN 18, 1971 (UK) Apple 34
by Mary Hopkin Prod: Tony Visconti
*A: *Let My Name Be Sorrow*---Martine Habib—Bernard Estardy---*3:25*
B: *Kew Gardens*---Ralph McTell---*2:18*

OCT 1, 1971 (UK) Apple SAPCOR 21 (LP)
NOV 3, 1971 (US) Apple SMAS 3381 (LP)
by Mary Hopkin
EARTH SONG--OCEAN SONG Prod: Tony Visconti
side one
  International---Bernard Gallagher—Graham Lyle---*3:32*
  There's Got To Be More---Harvey Andrews---*3:50*
  Silver Birch And Weeping Willow---Ralph McTell---*2:43*
  How Come The Sun---Tom Paxton—David Horowitz---*5:34*
  Earth Song---Liz Thorsen---*3:48*
side two
  Martha---Harvey Andrews---*4:48*
  Streets Of London---Ralph McTell---*4:23*
  The Wind---Cat Stevens---*2:02*
  Water, Paper & Clay—Mike Sutcliffe—Reins Sutcliffe---*3:58*
  Ocean Song---Liz Thorsen---*3:58*

DEC 1, 1971 (US) Apple 1843
by Mary Hopkin Prod: Tony Visconti
A: *WATER, PAPER & CLAY*---Mike Sutcliffe—Reins Sutcliffe---*3:27*
B: *STREETS OF LONDON*---Ralph McTell---*4:23*

DEC 3, 1971 (UK) Apple 39
by Mary Hopkin Prod: Tony Visconti
A: WATER, PAPER & CLAY—Mike Sutcliffe—Reins Sutcliffe
   —*3:27*
*B: *Jefferson*—*2:35*

SEP 25, 1972 (US) SW 3395 (LP)
NOV 24, 1972 (UK) SAPCOR 23 (LP)
by Mary Hopkin
THOSE WERE THE DAYS Prod: Paul McCartney except † Mickie
  Most; % Tony Visconti
side one
   THOSE WERE THE DAYS—Gene Raskin—*5:06*
   QUE SERA, SERA (WHATEVER WILL BE, WILL BE)—Jay
      Livingston—Ray Evans—arr. Paul McCartney—*3:04*
   FIELDS OF ST. ETIENNE—Bernard Gallagher—Graham Lyle
      —*3:12*
% *KEW GARDENS*—Ralph McTell—*2:18*
† *TEMMA HARBOUR*—Philamore Lincoln—*3:20*
† *THINK ABOUT YOUR CHILDREN*—Tony Wilson—Errol Brown—
      M. Wilson—*2:57*
side two
† *KNOCK KNOCK WHO'S THERE*—John Carter—Geoff Stephens
      —*2:28*
† *HERITAGE*—Bernard Gallagher—Graham Lyle—*2:20*
   SPARROW—Bernard Gallagher—Graham Lyle—*3:10*
   LONTANO DAGLI OCCHI—Sergio Endrigo—Sergio Bardotti—*3:22*
   GOODBYE—L-McC—*2:23*

NOV 8, 1972 (US) Apple 1855
by Mary Hopkin Prod: Mickie Most (A side) and Tony Visconti
  (B side)
A: KNOCK KNOCK WHO'S THERE—John Carter—Geoff Stephens
   —*2:28*
B: INTERNATIONAL—Bernard Gallagher—Graham Lyle—*3:32*

Hot Chocolate Band. In 1969, Tony Wilson and Errol Brown, who
turned out tunes for Apple publishing (like Mary Hopkin's *Think
About Your Children*), brought in a recording of their own reggae
version of John Lennon's then-current hit *Give Peace A Chance*.
John heard it, liked it, and said: Let's release it. Press officer Marvis
Smith dubbed the "group" the Hot Chocolate Band, Apple signed
them to a one-record contract, and released the single. It bombed
and Apple didn't offer them a second disc, but the group (Errol

Brown:Lead Vocals; Tony Wilson:Bass Guitar and Vocals; Patrick Olive:Percussion; Harvey Hinsley:Lead Guitar; and Larry Ferguson:Keyboards) wanted to continue recording, and by the end of 1970 had a contract with another company. Since then Hot Chocolate has had several hits, including *Emma* and the top-ten million-seller *You Sexy Thing*.

OCT 10, 1969 (UK) Apple 18
OCT 17, 1969 (US) Apple 1812
by Hot Chocolate Band Prod: Tony Meehan
*A: *Give Peace A Chance*—L-McC—*4:31*
*B: *Living Without Tomorrow*—Tony Wilson—Errol Brown—*2:23*

Jackie Lomax. Jackie was another old Liverpool compatriot invited to join the whirlwind madness of Apple. He had been a part of the struggling, emerging music scene of the early 60's, in a group called the Undertakers. Once the Beatles opened the bridge to America, Jackie joined the ranks of the British hopefuls crossing the pond looking for that first lucky break. The Lomax Alliance didn't take off in the U.S., and shortly before his death Brian Epstein suggested that Lomax return to England.

With Apple, Jackie first found himself asked to be a writer. Then George, who wanted to take a shot at producing, offered to produce some tracks with Jackie as a solo singer. Their first effort together was the star-studded interpretation of George's composition *Sour Milk Sea*. Paul joined in on bass, Nicky Hopkins on piano, Eric Clapton on lead guitar, Ringo on drums, with George and Jackie on rhythm guitars. *Sour Milk Sea* was one of Apple's first four single releases in August of 1968. Though *Hey Jude* and *Those Were The Days* shot up the charts all around the world, Jackie was left swimming at the edges along with the Black Dyke Mills Band. Almost from the start, then, Jackie became the Apple artist who *should* have been a super-star, but wasn't *quite* there. . .yet!

Undaunted, George and Jackie continued work on enough tracks for an entire album. George made it a point to act the role of producer, rarely sitting in to play on the actual recordings. In fact, except for *You've Got Me Thinking*, which featured Eric Clapton and Ringo, the remaining tracks recorded in London were not "super-star jam sessions," but disciplined work with talented studio musicians. A few months later, George and Jackie picked up recording again in Los Angeles with session men Hal Blaine on drums, Joe Osborn on bass, and Larry Knechtel on keyboards. They finished seven more tracks (*Speak To Me, Is This What You Want?, How Can You Say Goodbye, I Fall Inside Your Eyes, Little Yellow Pills,*

Take My Word, and *I Just Don't Know*), enough material for Jackie's first LP, **Is This What You Want?**

Following the release of the LP in Britain, Jackie searched for material for a new single. The night before marrying Linda, Paul had recorded the old Coasters song *Thumbin' A Ride* with Jackie, George and Billy Preston. At that point, George expressed an interest in producing another song with Jackie, who instead wanted to record a new composition *he* had just finished, *New Day*. As a result, he took Pete Clark (drums), Tim Renick (guitar), Bill Kinsley (bass) and Chris Hatfield (piano) into the studio to produce the song himself. When Jackie had to switch to the studio to sing and play guitar, Mal Evans took over the control board. Not only was the song released as the new single in Britain and America, it was completed in time to be included on the American version of the **Is This What You Want?** LP as well (displacing *How Can You Say Goodbye?*)!

The Harrison-produced *How The Web Was Woven*, as well as the unreleased *Going Back To Liverpool*, marked the end of Jackie's recordings and releases from Apple. The individual Beatles went on to other projects, Allen Klein took over Apple, and, in the shuffle, Jackie Lomax was lost. To this day he says he's never been "official- ly" informed of his status at Apple. He soon signed with Warner Brothers, recording two albums (**Home In My Head** and **Three**). A stint as vocalist for the group Badger followed. Recently, Jackie signed with Capitol. His first LP (**Living' For Lovin'**) is actually one of his best yet.

AUG 26, 1968 (US) Apple 1802
SEP 6, 1968 (UK) Apple 3
by Jackie Lomax Prod: George Harrison
A: Sour Milk Sea—Harrison—*3:51*
B: The Eagle Laughs At You—-Jackie Lomax—-*2:22*

MAR 21, 1969 (UK) Apple SAPCOR 6 (LP)
MAY 19, 1969 (US) Apple ST 3354 (LP)
by Jackie Lomax
IS THIS WHAT YOU WANT? Prod: George Harrison
side one: in America, † replaced by *New Day*
  Speak To Me—Jackie Lomax—*3:06*
  Is This What You Want?—Jackie Lomax—*2:44*
†*How Can You Say Goodbye*—Jackie Lomax—*4:13*
  Sunset—Jackie Lomax—*3:54*
  SOUR MILK SEA—Harrison—*3:51*
  I Fall Inside Your Eyes—Jackie Lomax—*3:08*
side two
  Little Yellow Pills—Jackie Lomax—*4:01*
  Take My Word—Jackie Lomax—*3:55*
  THE EAGLE LAUGHS AT YOU—Jackie Lomax—*2:22*
  Baby You're A Lover—Jackie Lomax—*3:01*
  You've Got Me Thinking—Jackie Lomax—*2:53*
  I Just Don't Know—Jackie Lomax—*2:53*

MAY 9, 1969 (UK) Apple 11
by Jackie Lomax Prod: Jackie Lomax and Mal Evans (A side);
  George Harrison (B side)
A: New Day—Jackie Lomax—*3:18*
B: I FALL INSIDE YOUR EYES—Jackie Lomax—*3:08*

JUN 2, 1969 (US) Apple 1807
by Jackie Lomax Prod: Jackie Lomax and Mal Evans (A side);
  Paul McCartney (B side)
A: NEW DAY—Jackie Lomax—*3:18*
B: Thumbin' A Ride—Jerry Leiber—Mike Stoller—*3:58*

FEB 6, 1970 (UK) Apple 23
by Jackie Lomax Prod: George Harrison (A side); Paul McCartney
  (B side)
A: How The Web Was Woven—Clive Westlake—David Most—*3:52*
B: THUMBIN' A RIDE—Jerry Leiber—Mike Stoller—*3:58*

MAR 9, 1970 (US) Apple 1819
by Jackie Lomax Prod: George Harrison
A: HOW THE WEB WAS WOVEN—Clive Westlake—David Most
  —*3:52*
B: I FALL INSIDE YOUR EYES—Jackie Lomax—*3:08*

JUN 21, 1971 (US) Apple 1834
by Jackie Lomax Prod: George Harrison
A: SOUR MILK SEA—Harrison—3:51
B: I FALL INSIDE YOUR EYES—Jackie Lomax—3:08

Modern Jazz Quartet.   The Modern Jazz Quartet came to Apple
from Atlantic records on a special short term deal to help give the
young company additional depth and appeal. Milt Jackson (vibes),
John Lewis (piano), Percy Heath (bass) and Connie Kay (drums) had
been together for some fifteen years, and had already tasted success,
unlike the struggling new artists in the rest of the catalogue. In all
honesty, Apple could add little to the MJQ's well-established reputation, and perhaps for this reason didn't lavish much attention at all
on promotion. After two LPs, the group parted ways with Apple (in
1969) and continued a successful performing and recording career
with Atlantic.

DEC   6, 1968 (UK) Apple SAPCOR 4 (LP)
FEB 17, 1969 (US) Apple ST 3353 (LP)
by The Modern Jazz Quartet
UNDER THE JASMINE TREE Prod: John Lewis
side one
  Blue Necklace—John Lewis—*5:00*
  Three Little Feelings (Parts I, II, III)—John Lewis—*14:07*
side two
  Exposure—John Lewis—*9:15*
  The Jasmine Tree—John Lewis—*5:15*

OCT 24, 1969 (UK) SAPCOR 10 (LP)
NOV 10, 1969 (US) Apple STAO 3360 (LP)
by The Modern Jazz Quartet
SPACE Prod: John Lewis
side one
  Visitor From Venus—John Lewis—*5:40*
  Visitor From Mars—John Lewis—*7:18*
  Here's That Rainy Day—James Van Heusen—Johnny Burke—*4:20*
side two
  Dilemma—Miljenko Prohaska—*5:48*
  Adagio From Concierto De Aranjuez—Jaoquin Rodrigo—*10:18*

Yoko Ono. Yoko Ono was an already established (though certainly
not famous) avant garde artist before she ever met John Lennon.
She had staged art exhibitions, "events," and public "happenings" in

both the United States and Japan. It was at the preview of her London exhibition of "Unfinished Paintings And Objects" in 1966 that she met John. At first, Lennon, fascinated with her nihilistic art (not to mention her aggressive personality), played the part of sponsor and benefactor, but by mid-1968, "John and Yoko" were fast becoming public property. Their five intense years together (1968-1973) staging events for peace, then for radical political causes, helped fill gossip columns, editorial pages, and sometimes even the front page. Among Yoko's many activities with John were records released, of course, on Apple. Some were even recorded with the Beatles–*Revolution No. 9, Birthday* (Yoko in the backing chorus), the unreleased *What's The News Maryjane* (John, George and Yoko), and the Beatles' 1968 and 1969 Christmas messages. The records which gathered the most attention, though, were her direct collaborations with John, especially those which could be snidely dismissed with a few barbed phrases (**Two Virgins**, *Baby's Heartbeat*, **Wedding Album**). (Almost from the beginning, Yoko–perceived as an unwelcome foreign intruder to the Beatles' world–was recipient of some of the most vicious press in pop history.) Actually, all those "John & Yoko" discs can best be looked on as two people playing around in the studio. It just so happened that *one* of the pair owned his own record company, so that *anything* he waxed could be released to the world. (Whether they *should* have been is another matter.) Taken as merely souvenirs of events or just playing around, the records were tolerable if quite self-indulgent. When taken too seriously as Important Art both by the performers and the public, they were an oppressive bore. Nonethless, once exposed to the medium of records, Yoko struggled to express herself on disc as a solo artist. At first, this took place on the B-sides of John's solo records (*Give Peace A Chance, Cold Turkey,* **Live Peace In Toronto** and *Instant Karma!*). Her writing and recording ambitions immediately expanded, however, and between 1970 and 1973, whenever a John Lennon solo effort would be released, a companion Yoko Ono record would surely follow. And unlike the other Apple artists, Yoko had "Beatle-status" in the company. Even if her records didn't sell, as long as she was Mrs. Lennon, Apple would keep putting them out.

The companion disc to **John Lennon/Plastic Ono Band** was (no surprise) **Yoko Ono/Plastic Ono Band**. Drawing from some of the same "primal" background as John's classic disc, and using session men Klaus Voorman, Ringo Starr and John, the record showcased Yoko's voice as an abstract rock instrument. (It was difficult to tell when a guitar riff ended and her voice took over.) The record was alternately puzzled over ("There are no words. . ."), mocked, or just dismissed as some more John & Yoko garbage. Strangely enough, this first LP has worn better with time than any other Yoko Ono effort, probably because it drew on her familiar background in abstract sounds and jazz-type riffs with which she had been experimenting for a couple of years. One cut on the LP (*AOS*) is actually from February 1968; on it Yoko is even joined by Ornette Coleman (trumpet) and Charlie Haden (bass). Her companion release to John's **Imagine** was the two record set **Fly**. It was a sort of *Yoko's Greatest Hits* (5 of the 13 cuts were on singles), chiefly remembered for its 22 minute title track (to match the film of the same name) of a fly buzzing and crawling up a woman's body. Other tracks featured a flushing toilet and a ringing telephone. The LP also included the previously banned-in-America track *Open Your Box* intact, but simply retitled *Hirake*. There were even a few "normal" songs included. *Mrs. Lennon*, for instance, was a catchy, almost haunting track on the difficulties of being an artist and John Lennon's wife. Yoko ended 1971 with a pleasant, gentle ode to the season (*Listen, The Snow Is Falling*) on the flip of *Happy Christmas*. A legal dispute over the publishing of the A-side held up release of the Christmas single in Britain, so *Listen, The Snow Is Falling* greeted 1972 in the U.K. as the B-side of a cut-down of *Mind Train* (from **Fly**).

During the whirlwind political days of 1972, Yoko and John seemed to pop up everywhere — in print, on the radio, and on America's talk show circuit. **Sometime In New York City** captured them at the height of their affection for political catch-phrases and radical causes. Yoko must certainly take her share of blame for this disasterous package (*Angela* was a co-composition), which should have been filed away as another "John & Yoko" souvenir disc. Unfortunately, no other ex-Beatle released *any* sort of album in 1972, so this was treated not like **Life With The Lions** but like a new (Beatle) John Lennon LP. It was torn to pieces.

Yoko's next solo effort (**Approximately Infinite Universe**) was, in many ways, a radical departure. She put aside the abstract voice concept and tried to produce a normal rock album, though still from a feminist point of view. Some cuts were pretty good (*Winter Song* featuring John and Mick Jagger on guitars), but most were merely average and too often caught up in the "message" of feminism. Out of her avant-garde element, she had to compete on the same level as any other aspiring rock artist. The disc didn't fair well. Neither did her later attempts to perform live as a solo rock act (without the John-&-Yoko-event magic). She earned largely negative reviews.

Her last album, released shortly after her separation from John in 1973, was **Feeling The Space**. It was an OK album, with a better feel for lyrics, and more control in her music. Yoko produced it herself and John appeared on only three cuts (*She Hits Back, Woman Power* and *Men Men Men*). Though Yoko and John ended their separation in 1975, she hasn't yet resumed her recording career.

Note: Only Yoko Ono's *solo* efforts are listed in detail here. Her collaborations with John are fully chronicled in *All Together Now*. These John and Yoko collaborations include: **Unfinished Music No. 1--Two Virgins, Unfinished Music No. 2--Life With The Lions, Wedding Album** and **Sometime In New York City** plus producing the discs **The Pope Smokes Dope** (David Peel), **Elephant's Memory** (Elephant's Memory) and *God Save Us* (Elastic Oz Band). She worked with John on his Plastic Ono Band solo efforts, co-producing the singles *Give Peace A Chance* and *Cold Turkey*, and the album **Live Peace In Toronto**. She shared production credits with John and Phil Spector for John's **John Lennon/Plastic Ono Band** and **Imagine** LPs, and the single *Power To The People*. Additionally, she co-authored *Oh My Love* on **Imagine**.

Again, Yoko's first solo recordings were the flip sides of John's discs (both as John Lennon and under the Plastic Ono Band umbrella).

JUL 4, 1969 (UK) Apple 13
JUL 7, 1969 (US) Apple 1809
by Plastic Ono Band Prod: John Lennon and Yoko Ono
*B: Remember Love--Yoko Ono--4:01
*A: Give Peace A Chance--L-McC--4:49

OCT 20, 1969 (US) Apple 1813
OCT 24, 1969 (UK) Apple 1001
by Plastic Ono Band Prod: John Lennon and Yoko Ono
B: Don't Worry Kyoko (Mummy's Only Looking For A Hand In
    The Snow)--Yoko Ono--4:52
A: Cold Turkey--Lennon--4:59

DEC 12, 1969 (UK) Apple CORE 2001 (LP)
DEC 12, 1969 (US) Apple SW 3362 (LP)
by The Plastic Ono Band
THE PLASTIC ONO BAND--LIVE PEACE IN TORONTO
 Prod: John Lennon and Yoko Ono
side two
  *Don't Worry Kyoko (Mummy's Only Looking For Her Hand In
    The Snow)--Yoko Ono--4:44
  John, John (Let's Hope For Peace)--Yoko Ono--12:54*

FEB 6, 1970 (UK) Apple 1003
FEB 20, 1970 (US) Apple 1818
by Yoko Ono Lennon with The Plastic Ono Band Prod: John Lennon
   (B side); John Ono Lennon with The Plastic Ono Band Prod: Phil
   Spector (A side)
*B: Who Has Seen The Wind?—Yoko Ono—2:02
A: Instant Karma! (We All Shine On)—Lennon—3:18

DEC 11, 1970 (UK) Apple SAPCOR 17 (LP)
DEC 11, 1970 (US) Apple SW 3373 (LP)
by Yoko Ono Plastic Ono Band
YOKO ONO/PLASTIC ONO BAND Prod: John Lennon and Yoko
   Ono
side one
   Why—Yoko Ono—5:30
   Why Not—Yoko Ono—10:39
   Greenfield Morning I Pushed An Empty Baby Carriage All Over The
      City—Yoko Ono—5:40
side two
   AOS—Yoko Ono—7:06
   Touch Me—Yoko Ono—3:40
   Paper Shoes—Yoko Ono—8:10

DEC 28, 1970 (US) Apple 1827
by Yoko Ono Plastic Ono Band Prod: John Lennon and Yoko Ono
   (B side); John Lennon Plastic Ono Band Prod: John Lennon, Yoko
   Ono and Phil Spector (A side)
B: WHY—Yoko Ono—5:30
A: MOTHER—Lennon—3:55

MAR 12, 1971 (UK) Apple R 5892
by Yoko Ono Plastic Ono Band Prod: John Lennon and Yoko Ono
   (B side); John Lennon Plastic Ono Band Prod: John Lennon, Yoko
   Ono and Phil Spector (A side)
B: Open You Box (later called: Hirake)—Yoko Ono—3:23
A: Power To The People—Lennon—3:15

MAR 22, 1971 (US) Apple 1830
by Yoko Ono Plastic Ono Band Prod: John Lennon and Yoko Ono
   (B side); John Lennon Plastic Ono Band Prod: John Lennon, Yoko
   Ono and Phil Spector (A side)
B: TOUCH ME—Yoko Ono—3:40
A: Power To The People—Lennon—3:15

SEP 20, 1971 (US) Apple SVBB 3380 (2 LPs)
DEC 3, 1971 (UK) Apple SAPTU 101/2 (2 LPs)
by Yoko Ono Plastic Ono Band with Joe Jones Tone Deaf Music Co.
FLY Prod: John Lennon and Yoko Ono
side one
  Midsummer New York---Yoko Ono---*3:50*
  Mind Train---Yoko Ono---*16:52*
side two
  Mind Holes---Yoko Ono---*2:45*
  DON'T WORRY KYOKO---Yoko Ono---*4:52*
  Mrs. Lennon---Yoko Ono---*4:10*
  HIRAKE (previously called: *Open Your Box*)---Yoko Ono---*3:23*
  Toilet Piece/Unknown---Yoko Ono---*0:30*
  O' Wind (Body Is The Scar Of Your Mind)---Yoko Ono---*5:22*
side three
  Airmale (Tone Deaf Jam)---Yoko Ono---*10:40*
  Don't Count The Waves---Yoko Ono---*5:26*
  You---Yoko Ono---*9:00*
side four
  Fly---Yoko Ono---*22:53*
  Telephone Piece---Yoko Ono---*1:01*

SEP 29, 1971 (US) Apple 1839
OCT 29, 1971 (UK) Apple 38
by Yoko Ono Plastic Ono Band Prod: John Lennon and Yoko Ono
A: *Mrs. Lennon*---Yoko Ono---*4:10*
B: *Midsummer New York*---Yoko Ono---*3:50*

DEC 1, 1971 (US) Apple 1842
NOV 24, 1972 (UK) Apple R 5970
by Yoko Ono Plastic Ono Band (B side), and John Lennon and Yoko
  Ono Plastic Ono Band (A side) Prod: John Lennon, Yoko Ono and
  Phil Spector
*B: *Listen, The Snow Is Falling*---Yoko Ono---*3:10*
A: *Happy Xmas (War Is Over)*--Lennon--Yoko Ono---*3:25*

JAN 21, 1972 (UK) Apple 41
by Yoko Ono Plastic Ono Band Prod: John Lennon and Yoko Ono
  (A side); John Lennon, Yoko Ono and Phil Spector (B side)
A: *MIND TRAIN*---Yoko Ono---*4:43*
*B: *LISTEN, THE SNOW IS FALLING*---Yoko Ono---*3:10*

NOV 13, 1972 (US) Apple 1853
by Yoko Ono Plastic Ono Band (A side) and Yoko Ono Plastic Ono
  Band with Elephant's Memory (B side) Prod: John Lennon and
  Yoko Ono
A: *Now Or Never*---Yoko Ono---*4:57*
B: *Move On Fast*---Yoko Ono---*3:40*

JAN   8, 1973 (US) Apple SVBB 3399 (2 LPs)
FEB 16, 1973 (UK) Apple SAPDO 1001 (2 LPs)
by Yoko Ono Plastic Ono Band with Elephant's Memory, The
  Endless Strings and Choir Boys
APPROXIMATELY INFINITE UNIVERSE Prod: Yoko Ono and
  John Lennon
side one
  Yang Yang---Yoko Ono---*3:52*
  Death Of Samantha---Yoko Ono---*6:23*
  I Want My Love To Rest Tonight---Yoko Ono---*5:11*
  What Did I Do!---Yoko Ono---*4:11*
  Have You Seen A Horizon Lately---Yoko Ono---*1:55*
side two
  Approximately Infinite Universe---Yoko Ono---*3:19*
  Peter The Dealer---Yoko Ono---*4:43*
  Song For John---Yoko Ono---*2:02*
  Catman (The Rosies Are Coming)---Yoko Ono---*5:29*
  What A Bastard The World Is---Yoko Ono---*4:33*
  Waiting For The Sunrise---Yoko Ono---*2:32*
side three
  I Felt Like Smashing My Face In A Clear Glass Window---Yoko Ono
    ---*5:07*
  Winter Song---Yoko Ono---*3:37*
  Kite Song---Yoko Ono---*3:19*
  What A Mess---Yoko Ono---*2:41*
  Shirankatta (I Didn't Know)---Yoko Ono---*3:13*
  Air Talk---Yoko Ono---*3:21*
side four
  I Have A Woman Inside My Soul---Yoko Ono---*5:31*
  Move On Fast---Yoko Ono---*3:40*
  Now Or Never---Yoko Ono---*4:57*
  Is Winter Her To Stay?---Yoko Ono---*4:27*
  Looking Over From My Hotel Window---Yoko Ono---*3:30*

FEB 26, 1973 (US) Apple 1859
MAY 4, 1973 (UK) Apple 47
by Yoko Ono Plastic Ono Band with Elephant's Memory, The
Endless Strings and Choir Boys Prod: Yoko Ono and John Lennon
A: *DEATH OF SAMANTHA*—Yoko Ono—*3:40*
B: *YANG YANG*—Yoko Ono—*3:52*

MID 1973 (JAPAN) Apple 10344
by Yoko Ono Plastic Ono Band with Elephant's Memory Prod: Yoko
Ono
*A: *Jose Joi Banzaie*—Yoko Ono—*2:51*
*B: *Jose Joi Banzaie (Part 2)*—Yoko Ono—*5:11*

SEP 24, 1973 (US) Apple 1867
by Yoko Ono Prod: Yoko Ono
A: *Woman Power*—Yoko Ono—*4:50*
B: *Men, Men, Men*—Yoko Ono—*4:01*

NOV 2, 1973 (US) Apple SW 3412 (LP)
NOV 23, 1973 (UK) Apple SAPCOR 26 (LP)
by Yoko Ono Plastic Ono Band and Something Different
FEELING THE SPACE Prod: Yoko Ono
side one
 Growing Pain—Yoko Ono—*3:50*
 Yellow Girl (Stand By For Life)—Yoko Ono—*3:13*
 Coffin Car—Yoko Ono—*3:29*
 Woman Of Salem—Yoko Ono—*3:09*
 Run, Run, Run—Yoko Ono—*5:07*
 If Only—Yoko Ono—*3:40*
side two
 A Thousand Times Yes—Yoko Ono—*3:00*
 Straight Talk—Yoko Ono—*2:50*
 Angry Young Woman—Yoko Ono—*3:51*
 She Hits Back—Yoko Ono—*3:48*
 Woman Power—Yoko Ono—*4:50*
 Men, Men, Men—Yoko Ono—*4:01*

NOV 9, 1973 (UK) Apple 48
by Yoko Ono Prod: Yoko Ono
A: *Run, Run, Run*—Yoko Ono—*5:07*
B: *Men, Men, Men*—Yoko Ono—*4:01*

David Peel. When John & Yoko came to New York in 1971, they
found David Peel. A cult figure since 1967, with his two aptly

named LPs (**Have A Marijuana** and **The American Revolution**), Peel personified the term "street singer." The streets were his *raison d'etre*, specifically the streets of Greenwich Village. Inasmuch as John & Yoko were at the height of their political consciousness phase, Peel was the perfect companion, introducing them to a whole new circle of friends. In December of 1971 they combined musical forces for a late night appearance at an Ann Arbor rally for imprisoned radical John Sinclair. Observers noted the amazing physical resemblance between Peel and Lennon (well, it was dark out). Also commented upon was the inspired bongo work of Jerry Rubin (later seen advertising 60's memorabilia on *NBC's Saturday Night*). In 1972, John and Yoko produced David's memorable album on Apple (not released in Britain). Peel wrote all the songs on the LP, including *I'm A Runaway, Everybody's Smoking Marijuana, The Hippie From New York City* and *I'm Gonna Start Another Riot*. The back of the album listed the demands of Peel's latest project, the Rock Liberation Front, whose basic philsosphy was. . .well, you have to read it yourself to get the full flavor. The heavy use of "street-wise vocabulary" prevented Peel from getting much airplay. To rectify this, Apple issued a specially edited DJ single of *F Is Not A Dirty Word* (you figure it out). As the 70's meandered their way to the midway point and political tempers cooled, Peel and Lennon saw less and less of each other. David now busies himself by recording for Orange Records (Orange Records. . .David Peel. . .Get it?). He's released two albums for them (**Bring Back The Beatles** and **An Evening With David Peel**). He regularly performs at New York bars, and his latest single (*Bring Back The Beatles*) makes him a familiar sight at all Eastern Beatle Conventions.

Peel is perhaps best summarized by two quotes about him: "His (Peel's) *Up Against The Wall* is true urban folk." – Lillian Roxon's *Rock Encyclopedia*; and "David Peel, that well known stupid person." – *Rolling Stone*.

APR 17, 1972 (US) Apple SW 3391 (LP)
by David Peel & The Lower East Side
THE POPE SMOKES DOPE Prod: John Lennon and Yoko Ono
side one
  I'm A Runaway—David Peel—*3:39*
  Everybody's Smoking Marijuana—David Peel—*4:06*
  F Is Not A Dirty Word—David Peel—*3:12*
  The Hippie From New York City—David Peel—*3:01*
  McDonald's Farm—David Peel—*3:13*
  The Ballad Of New York City–John Lennon/Yoko Ono—David
    Peel—*3:19*
side two
  The Ballad Of Bob Dylan—David Peel—*4:12*
  The Chicago Conspiracy—David Peel—*3:47*
  The Hip Generation—David Peel—*1:50*
  I'm Gonna Start Another Riot—David Peel—*2:37*
  The Birth Control Blues—David Peel—*4:48*
  The Pope Smokes Dope—David Peel—*2:15*

APR 20, 1972 (US–DJ PROMO) Apple 6498/6499
by David Peel and The Lower East Side Prod: John Lennon and
  Yoko Ono
A: F Is Not A Dirty Word (edited)—David Peel—*3:12*
B: The Ballad Of New York City–John Lennon/Yoko Ono—David
    Peel—*3:19*

JUN 16, 1972 (US–DJ PROMO) Apple 6545/6546
by David Peel and The Lower East Side Prod: John Lennon and
  Yoko Ono
A: HIPPIE FROM NEW YORK CITY—David Peel—*3:01*
B: THE BALLAD OF NEW YORK CITY–JOHN LENNON/YOKO ONO
    —David Peel—*3:19*

Billy Preston. Billy Preston brought his Gospel and Rock keyboards
to Apple in 1969, when he joined in on the Beatles' *Get Back/Let
It Be* sessions. Their very first contact, though, came 'way back in
the Hamburg era when Billy was working with Little Richard and
Sam Cooke, two stars who showed him it wasn't all that hard to take
his strong gospel background and step right into the world of rock
'n' roll. Billy was hooked and never stopped rockin'. He won the
spot as resident keyboard player for the *Shindig* TV show, and there
caught the interest of Ray Charles. The two recorded an album
together (**The Most Exciting Organ Ever**) for Vee Jay, and then
toured together in 1967 and 1968. It was while touring in England

that Billy was spotted again by George Harrison, who asked him to come on over to Apple. The Beatles and Billy instantly jelled. Together they recorded the single *Get Back*, and the Beatles even shared the by-line with Billy (it was released as "The Beatles with Billy Preston"). The Beatles then bought Billy's contract from Vee Jay and signed him to Apple. During his three-year stint with the label, Billy cut two albums, both co-produced by George: **That's The Way God Planned It** and **Encouraging Words**. More importantly, he began a long career of sitting-in on sessions with the individual Beatles, which has continued to this day. Billy sat in on piano for *God* on John's first solo LP, played some keyboards for **All Things Must Pass**, and was one of the featured performers at the Concert for Bangla Desh. Even after moving over to A&M records in 1971, he continued working closely with George, John and Ringo. Though he never had a hit single at Apple (*That's The Way God Planned It* came closest), he has since earned several Gold Records with tunes like *Outta Space* and *Will It Go 'Round In Circles?*

APR 11, 1969 (UK) Apple R 5777
MAY 5, 1969 (US) Apple 2490
by The Beatles with Billy Preston Prod: George Martin
A: Get Back---3:11
B: Don't Let Me Down---3:34

JUN 27, 1969 (UK) Apple 12
JUL 7, 1969 (US) Apple 1808
US Reissue: June 26, 1972
by Billy Preston Prod: George Harrison
A: That's The Way God Planned It---Billy Preston---3:22
B: What About You?---Billy Preston---2:07

AUG 22, 1969 (UK) Apple SAPCOR 9 (LP)
SEP 10, 1969 (US) Apple ST 3359 (LP)
by Billy Preston
THAT'S THE WAY GOD PLANNED IT Prod: George Harrison
  except † Wayne Shuler
side one
  Do What You Want---Billy Preston---*3:40*
  †*I Want To Thank You*---Billy Preston---*3:04*
  Everything's All Right---Billy Preston—Doris Troy---*2:41*
  She Belongs To Me---Bob Dylan---*4:06*
  It Doesn't Matter---Billy Preston---*2:37*
  Morning Star---W. C. Handy—Mack David---*3:16*
side two
  †*Hey Brother*---Billy Preston—Jesse J. Kirkland---*2:30*
  What About You?---Billy Préston---*2:07*
  Let Us All Get Together Right Now---Billy Preston—Doris Troy
      ---*3:05*
  This Is It---Billy Preston—Doris Troy---*2:38*
  †*Keep To Yourself*---Billy Preston---*2:35*
  That's The Way God Planned It---Billy Preston---*5:34*

OCT 17, 1969 (UK) Apple 19
OCT 24, 1969 (US) Apple 1814
by Billy Preston Prod: George Harrison (A side) and Wayne Shuler
  (B side)
A: EVERYTHING'S ALL RIGHT—Billy Preston—Doris Troy---*2:41*
B: I WANT TO THANK YOU---Billy Preston---*3:04*

JAN 30, 1970 (UK) Apple 21
FEB 16, 1970 (US) Apple 1817
by Billy Preston Prod: George Harrison (A side) and Ray Charles
  (B side)
*A: All That I've Got (I'm Gonna Give It To You)---Billy Preston—
      Doris Troy---*3:34*
*B: As I Get Older---Billy Preston—Sylvester Stewart---*3:40*

SEP 4, 1970 (UK) Apple 29
by Billy Preston Prod: George Harrison and Billy Preston
A: My Sweet Lord---Harrison---*3:21*
*B: Long As I Got My Baby

174

SEP 11, 1970 (UK) Apple SAPCOR 14 (LP)
NOV 9, 1970 (US) Apple ST 3370 (LP)
by Billy Preston
ENCOURAGING WORDS Prod: George Harrison and Billy Preston
side one
  Right Now—Billy Preston—*3:13*
  Little Girl—Billy Preston—*3:28*
  Use What You Got—Billy Preston—*4:21*
  My Sweet Lord—Harrison—*3:21*
  Let The Music Play—Billy Preston—Joe Greene—Jesse Kirkland
    —*2:42*
  The Same Thing Again—Billy Preston—Herndon—*4:32*
side two
  I've Got A Feeling—L-McC—*2:49*
  Sing One For The Lord—Harrison—Billy Preston—*3:47*
  When You Are Mine—Billy Preston—*2:44*
  I Don't Want You To Pretend—Billy Preston—*2:35*
  Encouraging Words—Billy Preston—*3:32*
  All Things (Must) Pass—Harrison—*3:38*
  You've Been Acting Strange—Billy Preston—*3:20*

DEC 3, 1970 (US) Apple 1826
by Billy Preston Prod: George Harrison and Billy Preston
A: MY SWEET LORD—Harrison—*3:21*
B: LITTLE GIRL—Billy Preston—*3:28*

DEC 20, 1971 (US) Apple STCX 3385 (3 LPs)
JAN 10, 1972 (UK) Apple STCX 3385 (3 LPs)
by George Harrison and Friends
THE CONCERT FOR BANGLA DESH Prod: George Harrison and
  Phil Spector
side two
  cut four: *That's The Way God Planned It*—Billy Preston—*4:05*
    by Billy Preston

Radha Krsna Temple. Hoping to convey the words and feelings of
Krsna Consciousness, an enthusiastic George Harrison took members
of the Radha Krsna Temple of London into the Apple studios in
1969. They recorded the *Hare Krsna Mantra*, released as a single
that summer, then an entire album of material eventually released in
1971. In a year when every song from the rock musical *Hair* seemed
to be covered by a dozen different artists, the energy and sincerity
of Apple's *Hare Krsna Mantra* single actually propelled it over some
of the din. Though failing to chart in America, it just missed top ten

in Britain.   The album package was a quick mini-course in Krsna Consciousness, complete with the words to all the chants on the record, a biography of the Spiritual Master, a History of Krsna Consciousness, the Message of Krsna, and the addresses of Krsna Temples throughout the world.   And how many top twenty hits has Rev. Moon had?

AUG 22, 1969 (US) Apple 1810
AUG 29, 1969 (UK) Apple 15
by Radha Krishna Temple (London) Prod: George Harrison
A: *Hare Krishna Mantra*—Traditional—arr. Makunda Das Adhikary —*3:35*
*B: *Prayer To The Spiritual Masters*—Traditional—arr. Makunda Das Adhikary—*4:00*

MAR   6, 1970 (UK) Apple 25
MAR 24, 1970 (US) Apple 1821
by Radha Krishna Temple (London) Prod: George Harrison
A: *Govinda*—Traditional—arr. Makunda Das Adhikary—*3:18*
B: *Govinda Jai Jai*—Traditional—arr. Makunda Das Adhikary—*5:58*

MAY 21, 1971 (US) Apple SKAO 3376 (LP)
MAY 28, 1971 (UK) Apple SAPCOR 18 (LP)
by Radha Krsna Temple (London)
THE RADHA KRSNA TEMPLE Prod: George Harrison
side one
   GOVINDA—Traditional—arr. Makunda Das Adhikary—*4:39*
   Sri Gurvastakam—Traditional—arr. Makunda Das Adhikary—*3:07*
   Bhaja Bhakata/Arati—Traditional—arr. Makunda Das Adhikary —*8:28*
   HARE KRSNA MANTRA—Traditional—arr. Makunda Das Adhikary—*3:35*
side two
   Sri Isopanisad—Traditional—arr. Makunda Das Adhikary—*4:00*
   Bhaja Hunre Mana—Traditional—arr. Makunda Das Adhikary—*8:43*
   GOVINDA JAYA JAYA—Traditional—arr. Makunda Das Adhikary —*5:58*

Ravi Shankar. Ravi Shankar brought the sitar, and Indian music, to two generations of Americans.   In the 1950's, he cultivated the interest of Western classical music buffs with his solo sitar concerts, and then with his joint appearances with other respected performers such as Yehudi Menuhin.   (The two recorded and released two volumes of **West Meets East**, and an excerpt from volume two was included on the **Raga** album.) In the 1960's, George Harrison's use of a sitar on several Beatle tracks introduced the rock generation to his teacher, Ravi Shankar, and the realm of Indian music. Shankar, of course, had recorded and released albums on several labels over the years, so when George brought Ravi over to Apple, it presented him the opportunity to pursue a number of special projects. The most famous, of course, was the Concert for Bangla Desh. Ravi asked George if there might be *something* that could be done to help the suffering people of the ravaged Bangla Desh, more and more of whom were pouring into India every day, sick and homeless. The idea of a benefit concert, record, and film emerged. and that super-star show still stands today as one of the genuine high points in rock's history. Ravi's other releases on Apple included the sound-track to a special filmed documentary on India called **Raga**, and a two record set of a concert in New York with Ali Akbar Khan (October 8, 1972). When George set up Dark Horse records, he invited Ravi to join that label (see "Dark Horse").

AUG   9, 1971 (US) Apple 1838
AUG 27, 1971 (UK) Apple 37
by Ravi Shankar & Chorus (side one), and Ravi Shankar and Ali
  Akbar Khan with Alla Rakah (side two) Prod: George Harrison
side one
Joi Bangla---Ravi Shankar---*3:18*
Oh Bhaugowan---Ravi Shankar---*3:35*
side two
Raga Mishra—Jhinjhoti---P. D.---*6:52*

DEC   7, 1971 (US) Apple SWAO 3384 (LP)
by Ravi Shankar
RAGA (Original Soundtrack Album) Prod: George Harrison
side one
  Dawn To Dusk---Ravi Shankar---*3:38*
  Vedic Hymns---P. D.---*1:30*
  Baba Teaching---P. D.---*1:08*
  Birth To Death---Ravi Shankar---*3:10*
  Vinus House---Ravi Shankar---*3:10*
  Gurur Bramha---Ravi Shankar---*1:10*
  United Nations---Ravi Shankar—Yehudi Menuhin---*4:33*

side two
  medley: 4:31
    Raga Parameshwari—Ravi Shankar—*2:51*
    Rangeswhart—Ravi Shankar—*1:40*
    Banaras Ghat—Ravi Shankar—*2:45*
    Bombay Studio—Ravi Shankar—*2:45*
    Kinnara School—Ravi Shankar—*1:51*
    Frenzy And Distortion—Ravi Shankar—*1:06*
    Raga Desh—Ravi Shankar—*8:50*

DEC 20, 1971 (US) Apple STCX 3385 (3 LPs)
JAN 10, 1972 (UK) Apple STCX 3385 (3 LPs)
by George Harrison and Friends
THE CONCERT FOR BANGLA DESH Prod: George Harrison and
  Phil Spector
side one: Ravi Shankar, Ali Akbar Khan, Alla Rakah and Kamala
Chakrauarty
George Harrison/Ravi Shankar Introduction—*6:16*
Bangla Dhun—P. D.—*16:19*
  Sitar And Sarod Duet
  Dadratal
  Teental

JAN 22, 1973 (US) Apple SVBB 3396 (2 LPs)
APR 13, 1973 (UK) Apple SAPDO 1002 (2 LPs)
by Ravi Shankar and Ali Akbar Khan
IN CONCERT 1972 Prod: George Harrison, Zakir Hussein and
  Phil McDonald
side one
Raga—Hem Bihag—Ravi Shankar—Ali Akbar Khan—*25:17*
side two
Raga—Manj Khamaj (Part One)—Ravi Shankar—Ali Akbar Khan
  —*26:16*
side three
Raga—Manj Khamaj (Part Two)—Ravi Shankar—Ali Akbar Khan
  —*25:06*
side four
Raga—Sindhi Bhairabi—Ravi Shankar—Ali Akbar Khan—*25:20*

Soundtracks. Apple released a number of Beatle-related soundtrack
LPs, including **Yellow Submarine**, George Harrison's **Wonderwall
Music** and **Concert For Bangla Desh**, and Ravi Shankar's **Raga**. When
Allen Klein took over management of Apple, he added two Abkco
film soundtracks to the Apple catalogue: **Come Together** and

El Topo, both released in the last months of 1971.

Of the two, the film *El Topo* (released in November of 1971) was at least mildly intriguing, musically. A sort of "South-of-the-Border-*Satyricon*, " the score (written by Alexandro Jodorowsky, who also wrote, directed and starred in the film) was a bit avant-garde and somehow appropriate to such scenes as *The Soul Born In The Blood, The Flowers Born In The Mind* and *300 Rabbits*. Running over two hours, the film was either too arty, too esoteric, or too boring to catch one.

Come Together, on the other hand, was one of those "this-week-only!" first-run neighborhood flicks, probably on a twin bill with *Chainsaw Murder* (or some such nonsense). It starred Ringo's *Blindman* buddy, the man with two first names, Tony Anthony. He played a young American actor in Rome named Tony (surprise!), who gets quite involved there with two women, Lisa (Luciana Paluzzi) and Ann (Rosemary Dexter). Anthony wrote the screenplay with Saul Swimmer (the two also shared producing chores), but the juicy lead role was all his. The *New York Times'* Vincent Canby singled Anthony out, describing him as "the least magnetic movie personality to come along since Frankie Vaughn." The soundtrack album itself was a mixture of travelogue muzak, insipid dialogue ("Hey, I'm a virgin!"), a fruity version of the hit *Love Is Blue* plus two established hits, the Dells' *I Can Sing A Rainbow* and Joe South's *Games People Play*. The Beatles' song *Come Together* had *nothing* to do with this film.

Neither album was released in Britain.

SEP 17, 1971 (US) Apple SW 3377 (LP)
by Stelvio Cipriani except † Joe South and % The Dells
COME TOGETHER (Original Soundtrack Album) Prod: Allan
  Steckler
side one
†*Games People Play*—Joe South—*3:29*
  Come Together (Arrival In Rome)—Stelvio Cipriani—*1:39*
  Love Is Blue—Andre Popp—Pierre Cour—Bryan Blackburn—*2:46*
  Fascinum—Stelvio Cipriani—*2:07*
  Monument To Love—Stelvio Cipriani—*3:20*
  Love Is Blue—Andre Popp—Pierre Cour—Bryan Blackburn—*2:34*

side two
%medley: 3:25
   Love Is Blue---Andre Popp--Pierre Cour--Bryan Blackburn
   I Can Sing A Rainbow---A. Hamilton
Come Together---Stelvio Cipriani--*2:11*
Love Is Blue---Andre Popp--Pierre Cour--Bryan Blackburn---*2:23*
Bad Vibrations---Stelvio Cipriani---*2:26*
medley: 2:54
   Come Together---Stelvio Cipriani
   Get Together---Chet Powers

DEC 27, 1971 (US) Apple SWAO 3388 (LP)
by Alexandro Jodorowsky (All compositions by Alexandro
Jodorowsky)
EL TOPO Prod: Allan Steckler
side one
Entiero Del Primer Juguete (Burial Of The First Toy)---*2:22*
Bajo Tierra (Under The Earth)---*1:38*
La Cathedral De Los Puerlos (The Pig's Monastery)---*1:30*
Los Mendigos Sagrados (The Holy Beggars)---*2:28*
La Muerte Es Un Nacimiento (Death Is Birth)---*2:15*
Curios Mexicano (Mexican Curios)---*2:33*
El Agua Viva (Living Water)---*1:12*
Vals Fantasma---*3:15*
side two
El Alma Nace En La Sangre (The Soul Born In The Blood)--*2:42*
Topo Triste---*2:41*
Los Dioses De Azucar (The Sugar Gods)---*1:36*
Las Flores Nacen En El Barro (Flowers Born In The Mud)---*1:49*
*El Infierno De Las Angeleses Prostitutos (The Hall Of The
   Prostituted Angels)*---*1:52*
*Marcha De Los O Jos En El Trianqulos (March Of The Eyes In The
   Triangles)*---*1:34*
La Mieldel Dolor (The Pain Of The Honey)---*1:06*
300 Conejos (300 Rabbits)---*0:55*
Conocimiento A Traves De La Musica (Knowledge Through Music)
   ---*0:39*
*La Primera Flor Despues Del Diluvio (The First Flower After The
   Flood)*---*3:27*

Phil Spector and Ronnie Spector. Phil Spector was the eccentric boy
genius of the late 1950's and early 1960's, who made the producer,
as well as the artist, a star. He wrote, produced and performed (as
one of the Teddy Bears) his first big hit, *To Know Him Is To Love*

Him, which topped the charts in late 1958. Spector started his own label (Phillies), gathered his own stable of artists (Darlene Love, the Crystals, the Ronettes–featuring Ronnie!), and set about producing hit records. Of course, each release didn't become a hit, but there was no denying the distinctive sound in each Phil Spector production. Spector set about turning singles into what he called "symphonies for kids"–voices, instruments, echo dubbed over and over in layers until a virtual "wall of sound" was created. It was this distinctive work the Beatles greatly admired. *To Know Her Is To Love Her* was a part of their early stage show, and George Harrison called Spector's production (for Tina Turner) of *River Deep–Mountain High* "a perfect record." They even met Phil on one of their tours of America. At first, the atmosphere was awkward and uncomfortable, but once they all started singing Phil's old hits, gathered around the piano, not only was the ice broken, they all became great friends. In fact, Lennon once said that if the Beatles considered working with any producer other than George Martin, it would be Phil.

Strangely enough, though, Spector's only project with the Beatles as a group involved the post-mortem work on the *Let It Be* tapes in 1970, after the group had, in effect, split. Reactions to the album as it was finally released in May of 1970 ranged from outrage (especially over his doctoring of *The Long And Winding Road*) to grudging admiration (for his handling of *Across The Universe*). Nonetheless, over the next few years, Phil worked with John and George on several of their most critically acclaimed solo albums, such as **John Lennon/Plastic Ono Band**, **Imagine**, **All Things Must Pass** and **The Concert For Bangla Desh**. Two of his most exciting projects were singles with John: *Instant Karma!* (written, recorded and remixed in one day–January 26, 1970) and *Happy Christmas* (for the 1971 Christmas season). Both showcased the Phil Spector "wall of sound" technique, and tight rock 'n' roll from Lennon. *Instant Karma!* hit top five in both Britain and America, and *Happy Christmas* became a standard for rock stations every Christmas holiday. George and Phil got together in early 1971 to try and produce a hit single (*Try Some Buy Some*) for Phil's wife, Ronnie, but this record was much less successful, reaching only number 77 in America. In 1972 Apple even reissued (in glorious mono) Phil's old Christmas album (originally released in 1963 on Phillies) in a bright new Christmas cover featuring Phil dressed as Santa Claus. The album contained all the old Spector favorites--the Ronettes, Darlene Love, the Crystals, Bobb B. Soxx and the Blue Jeans--and even Phil himself, delivering a personal Christmas message.

By 1973, John and George were producing all their own material, and there were no other artists at Apple for Phil to handle. Phil's last Beatle-production was with John in late 1973 on Lennon's **Rock** 'n' **Roll** oldies album.   Even then, only four cuts from the Spector sessions were included in the final product.

Ronnie Spector, on the other hand, has resumed her performing career with vigor. She's toured and recorded with Bruce Springsteen-buddies South Side Johnny and the Asbury Jukes, and the 'E' Street Band.

During his time at Apple, Phil Spector produced the following material with John Lennon and George Harrison:

With John Lennon: the albums **John Lennon/Plastic Ono Band, Imagine, Sometime In New York City,** and four tracks (*Bony Moronie, Just Because, Sweet Little Sixteen* and *You Can't Catch Me*) on **Rock 'n' Roll**; and the singles *Instant Karma!, Power To The People, God Save Us* (Elastic Oz Band), and *Happy Christmas/Listen, The Snow Is Falling.*

With George Harrison: the albums **All Things Must Pass** and **The Concert For Bangla Desh**; the singles *Bangla Desh/Deep Blue* and *Try Some Buy Some/Tandoori Chicken* (Ronnie Spector); and George used the basic instrumental track from *Try Some Buy Some* for his own version appearing on **Living In The Material World.**

Plus, of course, the **Let It Be** album.

APR 16, 1971 (UK) Apple 33
APR 19, 1971 (US) Apple 1832
by Ronnie Spector Prod: George Harrison and Phil Spector
*A: *Try Some, Buy Some*---Harrison---*4:08*
*B: *Tandoori Chicken*---Harrison--Phil Spector---*2:14*

DEC 8, 1972 (UK) Apple APCOR 24 (LP)
DEC 11, 1972 (US) Apple SW 3400 (LP)
by Various Artists
   (By Darlene Love; † The Ronettes; % The Crystals; $ Bob B. Soxx
      and the Blue Jeans; + Phil Spector)
PHIL SPECTOR'S CHRISTMAS ALBUM Prod: Phil Spector
side one
   White Christmas---Irving Berlin---*2:45*
   †*Frosty The Snowman*---Steve Nelson--Jack Rollins---*2:29*
   $*The Bells Of St. Mary's*---A. Emmett Adams--Douglas Furber---*2:30*
   %*Santa Claus Is Coming To Town*---John Coots--Haven Gillespie
      ---*2:29*
   †*Sleigh Ride*---Leroy Anderson--Mitchell Parish---*3:45*
   It's A Marshmallow World---Peter De Rose--Carl Sigman---*2:30*

side two
†*I Saw Mommy Kissing Santa Claus*---Tommie Connor---*2:19*
%*Rudolph The Red-Nosed Reindeer*---Johnny Marks---*2:20*
  Winter Wonderland---Felix Bernard–Dick Smith---*2:32*
%*Parade Of The Wooden Soldiers*---Leon Jessel---*3:00*
  Christmas (Baby Please Come Home)---Phil Spector–Jeff Barry–
    Ellie Greenwich---*2:30*
$*Here Comes Santa Claus*---Oakley Haldeman–Gene Autry---*2:24*
+*Silent Night*---Traditional---*2:35*

Sundown Playboys. During the week, Lesa and Larry worked for an oil refinery, Darryl was a vending route candy-man, Wallace operated a grocery store, and Pat and Danny attended school. Come Saturday night, they'd put away the work clothes, gather up the guitars, accordion, fiddle and pedal steel, let loose and play! Their one and only single for Apple (released during the "Back To Mono" movement) is as perfect an example of the Louisiana French Cajun style of music as you are likely to find. Though Apple offered only a taste, there are many other albums like it if you search hard enough.

SEP 26, 1972 (US) Apple 1852
NOV 24, 1972 (UK) Apple 44
by Sundown Playboys Prod: Swallow Records
*A: Saturday Night Special---Darryl Higginbotham---*2:10*
*B: Valse De Soleil Coucher (Sundown Waltz)---Darryl Higginbotham
  ---*3:35*

John Tavener. Apple's classical catalogue consisted of two excellent LPs by the British composer-conductor-performer, John Tavener. Tavener was born in 1944, studied at the Highgate School and the Royal Academy of Music, and first came into prominence with his 1966 composition, *The Whale*. The first performance of *The Whale* was on January 24, 1968. This also marked the first appearance of the London Sinfonietta, a group dedicated to performing music written in the twentieth century, particularly by British composers. Tavener was then spotted by Ringo and signed to Apple Records. He recorded *The Whale* for Apple on July 22, 23, 24, 1970 at the Church of St. John the Evangelist, Islington, London. Dave Atherton conducted the London Sinfonietta and London Sinfonietta Chorus. Anna Reynolds was the Mezzo Soprano, Raimund Herincx was the Baritone, Alvar Lidell was the Speaker, and John Tavener himself played the Organ and Hammond Organ.

Tavener's follow-up album for Apple in 1971 (released only in Britain), contained three compositions: *Celtic Requiem, Nomine*

183

Jesu and *Coplas*.   Again, all were recorded at the Church of St. John
the Evangelist, Islington, London.   *Celtic Requiem*, commissioned
by the London Sinfonietta and the Calouste Gulbenkian Foundation,
was first performed on July 16, 1969 at the Royal Festival Hall,
London.   The Apple recording was made on September 28, 29, 30,
1970.   David Atherton conducted the London Sinfonietta and Sinfonietta Chorus, joined by children from Little Missenden Village
School.   June Barton was the Soprano, John Tavener played the
organ.   *Nomine Jesu* (composed for a BBC television program about
Tavener) was first performed on August 14, 1970, in Dartington.
The Apple recording was made on February 19, 1971.   John Tavener
himself conducted members of the London Sinfonietta and the
London Sinfonietta Chorus.   Margaret Lensky was the Mezzo Soprano.   *Coplas* was commissioned by the Cheltenham Festival and was
first performed there on July 9, 1970.   The Apple recording was
made on February 18 & 19, 1971.   David Atherton again conducted
the London Sinfonietta and London Sinfonietta Chorus.

SEP 25, 1970 (UK) Apple SAPCOR 15 (LP)
NOV 9, 1970 (US) Apple SMAS 3369 (LP)
by John Tavener
THE WHALE
side one
  The Whale (Part One)---John Tavener---*18:30*
side two
  The Whale (Part Two)---John Tavener---*13:15*

JUL 2, 1971 (UK) Apple SAPCOR 20 (LP)
by John Tavener
CELTIC REQUIEM
side one
  Celtic Requiem---John Tavener---*23:54*
side two
  Nomine Jesu---John Tavener---*11:28*
  Coplas---John Tavener---*9:27*

James Taylor.   James Taylor, one of the super-star singer-songwriters
of the early 70's, was an unknown, stoned-out hippie when he met
Peter Asher (of Peter and Gordon) in 1968. Taylor had been in the
group Flying Machine which included long-time friend and guitarist,
Danny Kortchmar (known as "Kootch" and now a member of Dark
Horse's band Attitudes). In 1967, they recorded a number of tracks,
not released until Taylor reached fame some three years later. Asher
(an A&R Man and staff producer to Apple records in 1968) saw

184

promise in Taylor's work and got him signed as one of the first artists on Apple records. He then began producing Taylor's first album. Asher's friend, Paul McCartney, helped out on bass on one song (*Carolina In My Mind*). Another song (*Something In The Way She Moves*) obviously affected George Harrison in that George's song *Something* from 1969 uses the same first line. The album's twelve songs are all connected by folk and classical flavored musical links (a very unconventional idea at that time). Both the album and its single (*Carolina In My Mind*) went absolutely nowhere when released in December of 1968. Taylor, apparently going through some complicated personal problems, was further disturbed by what he saw (quite rightly) as Apple's failure to promote him, and left Apple and England in 1969.

Back home in America he signed with Warner Brothers and, retaining Peter Asher as producer, recorded the LP **Sweet Baby James** (released in March 1970) whose single, *Fire And Rain*, made Taylor a national star by the fall. He's released eight albums since then and, while not the superstar he was (the curse of being on the cover of *Time* magazine still holds), his albums still sell well and he often has hit singles. He now records for Columbia Records.

Taylor is currently happily married to another rock star, Carly Simon, and still seems to keep in contact with Paul McCartney (Paul and Linda have sung on both Taylor's and Simon's albums).

DEC 6, 1968 (UK) Apple SAPCOR 3 (LP)
FEB 17, 1969 (US) Apple SKAO 3352 (LP)
by James Taylor
JAMES TAYLOR Prod: Peter Asher
side one
  Don't Talk Now---James Taylor---*2:36*
    Link: Greensleeves---arr. and played by James Taylor---*0:40*
  Something's Wrong---James Taylor---*2:30*
    Link---arr. by Richard Hewson and played by Aeolian String
      Quartet---*0:33*
  Knocking 'Round The Zoo---James Taylor---*2:54*
  Sunshine Sunshine---James Taylor---*2:50*
    Link---arr. by Richard Hewson and played by Skaila Kanga---*0:41*
  Taking It In---James Taylor---*2:25*
    Link---arr. and played by Don Schinn---*0:37*
  Something In The Way She Moves---James Taylor---*2:26*

side two
  Carolina In My Mind—James Taylor—*3:36*
  Brighten Your Night With My Day—James Taylor—*2:28*
    Link—arr. and conducted by Richard Hewson—*0:37*
  Night Owl—James Taylor—*2:59*
    Percussion Link—arr. and played by Bishop O'Brien, James
      Taylor and Peter Asher—*0:35*
  Rainy Day Man—James Taylor—*3:00*
  Circle 'Round The Sun—Traditional—*3:26*
    Link—arr. and conducted by Richard Hewson—*0:48*
  The Blues Is Just A Bad Dream—James Taylor—*2:54*

MAR 17, 1969 (US) Apple 1805
by James Taylor Prod: Peter Asher
A: *CAROLINA IN MY MIND*—James Taylor—*3:36*
B: *TAKING IT IN*—James Taylor—*2:25*

OCT 26, 1970 (US) Apple 1805
NOV   6, 1970 (UK) Apple 32
by James Taylor Prod: Peter Asher
A: *CAROLINA IN MY MIND*—James Taylor—*3:36*
B: *SOMETHING'S WRONG*—James Taylor—*2:30*

Trash. In 1968, producer Tony Meehan, former drummer from the Shadows, went up to Glasgow to see a group said to be one of the best rock bands in Scotland, the Pathfinders (Ian Clews: Lead Singer; Fraser Watson:Lead Guitar; Colin Hunter-Morrison:Bass; Ronald Leahy:Organ; Timi Donald:Percussion). He had heard the group play on a demo tape of new songs which George Gallagher, co-author of several tunes for Mary Hopkin, had brought to his office. Meehan liked what he heard, brought the group to London, and produced a recording of their version of *Road To Nowhere*, a Goffin/King tune. He brought it to Apple, George and Paul liked it, signed the group to a single record contract with Apple, and scheduled the song for release. First, though, the group wanted a new name. So, house-hippie (later turned author) Richard DiLello dubbed them: White Trash. The BBC found the name offensive and refused to play the single.   Fearing the same reaction in the U.S., Apple quickly redubbed the group simply: Trash. All the same, *Road to Nowhere* went nowhere. Trash kicked around Apple for a few months, recording some tracks and eventually had an album's worth. Then, at Richard DiLello's urging and in a concerted effort to break the group, Trash was allowed to preview **Abbey Road** and choose a song to cover. They selected *Golden Slumbers/Carry That Weight*. Their single, however, released shortly after **Abbey Road**, was simply lost in the shadows of the Beatles' most successful LP. Apple didn't pick up its option on Trash, and the group faded away.

JAN 24, 1969 (UK) Apple 6
MAR 3, 1969 (US) Apple 1804
by Trash Prod: Tony Meehan
*A: Road To Nowhere---Gerry Goffin--Carole King--5:07
*B: Illusions--Hugh Nicholson--3:11

OCT 3, 1969 (UK) Apple 17
OCT 15, 1969 (US) Apple 1811
by Trash Prod: Tony Meehan
*A: Golden Slumbers/Carry That Weight---L-McC--3:59
*B: Trash Can---D. Tennent--Trash--4:50

Doris Troy. Doris Troy had had a number of R&B hits in the early 1960's, but had been largely inactive on the recording scene for awhile. In 1969 she joined Billy Preston for the recording of his first Apple album, and even co-authored several tracks with him. By 1970, she was signed up with Apple herself. She produced an *excellent* LP which featured the talents of George Harrison, Ringo Starr, Jackie Lomax, Klaus Voorman and Steve Stills. The vocals were powerful, the musicianship incredibly tight. Apple never seemed to realize, though, that while understatement worked for the Beatles, in all other cases, unless people were *told* about such super-star collaborations right on the album package, they'd never give the LP a second glance. The Apple LPs by James Taylor and Jackie Lomax suffered such fates--neither cover even listed the contents, much less the personnel. (Long after its initial release, a sticker was *finally* put on the Lomax LP indicating who some of its performers were!) Doris' plain black cover with her picture at a piano suffered this fate. Even a couple of singles from the LP failed to stir suffi-cient interest in the project. She neither recorded nor released any more tracks for Apple. Like Jackie Lomax, Doris Troy should have turned into a star, but didn't. She's still an active performer, and a powerful vocalist who unexpectedly turns up every so often on some excellent discs.

FEB 13, 1970 (UK) Apple 24
MAR 16, 1970 (US) Apple 1820
by Doris Troy Prod: George Harrison (A side); Doris Troy (B side)
A: Ain't That Cute---Harrison--Doris Troy--3:48
*B: Vaya Con Dios---Larry Russell--Jack R. Starkey--Inez James--
    Carl Hoff--3:27

AUG 28, 1970 (UK) Apple 28
SEP 21, 1970 (US) Apple 1824
by Doris Troy Prod: Doris Troy
A: *Jacob's Ladder*---Traditional—arr. Harrison—Doris Troy---*3:18*
*B: *Get Back*---L-McC---*3:04*

SEP 11, 1970 (UK) Apple SAPCOR 13 (LP)
NOV 9, 1970 (US) Apple ST 3371 (LP)
by Doris Troy
DORIS TROY Prod: Doris Troy except † George Harrison
side one
†*AIN'T THAT CUTE*---Harrison—Doris Troy---*3:48*
  Special Care---Steve Stills---*2:54*
  Give Me Back My Dynamite---Harrison—Doris Troy---*4:53*
  You Tore Me Up Inside---Doris Troy—Ray Schinnery---*2:27*
  Games People Play---Joe South---*3:06*
  Gonna Get My Baby Back---Harrison—Starkey—Doris Troy—Steve
    Stills---*2:17*
  I've Got To Be Strong---Jackie Lomax—Doris Troy---*2:33*
side two
  Hurry---Doris Troy—Greg Carroll---*3:10*
  So Far---Klaus Voorman—Doris Troy---*4:22*
  Exactly Like You—Jimmy McHugh—Doroth Fields---*3:08*
  You Give Me Joy Joy---Harrison--Starkey—Doris Troy—Steve Stills
    ---*3:38*
  Don't Call Me No More---Doris Troy—Ray Schinnery---*2:04*
  Jacob's Ladder---Traditional—arr. Harrison—Doris Troy---*3:18*

Lon & Derrek Van Eaton. The Van Eaton brothers came to Apple
during its swan song days as an active label, yet their story reads
like a page from Apple's 1968 script for struggling artists. (One of
the first Apple ads urged talented musicians to tape record some of
their music, send it to Apple, and—magically—they'd one day be rich
and famous and driving a Bentley.) Lon and Derrek had been part
of the group Jacob's Creek. When it disbanded in March of 1971,
they spent a month in a makeshift studio at home (in Trenton, New
Jersey!), singing, playing, and recording their own original songs on
two tape recorders. Robin Garb, their manager, sent a tape containing seven songs from these sessions to several producers and record
companies, including Apple. Apple A&R Man Tony King took the
tape to Harrison, who liked it. Ringo and John did, too. A few days
after signing with Apple, Lon and Derrek flew out to London to
record their first LP. George produced the first song (and the
eventual American single), *Sweet Music*, joined by Ringo and Jim

188

Gordon on drums. Then Klaus Voorman took over, producing the rest over the next few months. After some delay, the **Brother** album was finally released in late 1972. *Warm Woman*, one of the original tracks recorded by Lon and Derrek on their home tape recorders, was taken from the LP and issued in England as a single in 1973. By then, Apple was rapidly becoming just a label for Beatle catalogue material and Beatle solo efforts. Lon and Derrek soon moved over to A&M records and released their next LP there. Since then, they've appeared as backing performers, together and separately, on a number of Beatle solo efforts, including George's **Dark Horse** and Ringo's **"Ringo"**, **Goodnight Vienna**, **Rotogravure**, and **Ringo The 4th**.

MAR   6, 1972 (US) Apple 1845
by Lon and Derrek Van Eaton Prod: George Harrison (A side);
   Klaus Voorman (B side)
A: Sweet Music—Lon & Derrek Van Eaton—*3:41*
*B: Song of Songs—Lon & Derrek Van Eaton—*1:25*

SEP 22, 1972 (US) Apple SMAS 3390 (LP)
FEB   9, 1973 (UK) Apple SAPCOR 25 (LP)
by Lon and Derrek Van Eaton
BROTHER Prod: Klaus Voorman except † George Harrison
side one
   Warm Woman—Lon & Derrek Van Eaton—*3:01*
   Sun Song—Lon & Derrek Van Eaton—*3:57*
   More Than Words—Lon & Derrek Van Eaton—*2:16*
   Hear My Cry—Lon & Derrek Van Eaton—*3:00*
   Without The Lord—Lon & Derrek Van Eaton—*1:37*
   †SWEET MUSIC—Lon & Derrek Van Eaton—*3:41*
side two
   Help Us All—Lon & Derrek Van Eaton—*2:53*
   Maybe There's Another—Lon & Derrek Van Eaton—*2:42*
   Ring—Lon & Derrek Van Eaton—*2:24*
   Sunshine—Lon & Derrek Van Eaton—*3:48*
   Another Thought—Lon & Derrek Van Eaton—*3:41*

MAR   9, 1973 (UK) Apple 46
by Lon and Derrek Van Eaton Prod: Klaus Voorman
A: WARM WOMAN—Lon & Derrek Van Eaton—*3:01*
B: MORE THAN WORDS—Lon & Derrek Van Eaton—*2:16*

Wall's Ice Cream EP. As part of a special promotion in connection with the Wall's Ice Cream company in England, Apple issued an EP of selections by four Apple artists (Mary Hopkin, the Iveys, Jackie

Lomax, and James Taylor). Three were from recent Apple albums, but the Iveys' selection never turned up on any other record, not even their **Maybe Tomorrow** LP. The EP is extremely rare, even in England. Any extra copies should please be sent to us, in care of the publisher. We'll deliver a gallon of ice cream (Wall's, if you insist) in return. (That's a promise!)

JUL 18, 1969 (UK SPECIAL BUSINESS PROMOTION) Apple CT 1 (EP)
by Various Artists
WALL'S ICE CREAM
side one
  Storm In A Teacup---Tom Evans---*2:26*
    by The Iveys
  SOMETHING'S WRONG--James Taylor--*2:30*
    by James Taylor Prod: Peter Asher
side two
  LITTLE YELLOW PILLS---Jackie Lomax---*4:01*
    by Jackie Lomax Prod: George Harrison
  HAPPINESS RUNS (PEBBLE AND THE MAN)---Donovan Leitch
    ---*2:01*
    by Mary Hopkin Prod: Paul McCartney

Apple By The Numbers

US Singles

All selections by the Beatles unless otherwise noted.

From May 1976, all the Beatles' Apple records and all solo efforts were reissued on Capitol, if they were kept in print.

*Originally issued on Capitol; between November 1971 and May of 1976, issued on the Apple label. After May of 1976, returned to the Capitol label.

1800	(Black Dyke Mills Band) *Yellow Submarine/Thingumybob*
1801	(Hopkin) *Those Were The Days/Turn Turn Turn*
1802	(Lomax) *Sour Milk Sea/Eagle Laughs At You*
1803	(Iveys) *Maybe Tomorrow/Daddy's A Millionaire*
1804	(Trash) *Road To Nowhere/Illusions*
1805	(Taylor) *Carolina In My Mind/Taking It In*
1805	(Taylor) *Carolina In My Mind/Something's Wrong*
1806	(Hopkin) *Goodbye/Sparrow*
1807	(Lomax) *New Day/Thumbin' A Ride*
1808	(Preston) *That's The Way God Planned It/What About You*
1809	(John) *Give Peace A Chance/Remember Love*
1810	(Radha Krsna Temple) *Hare Krishna Mantra/Prayer To Spiritual Masters*
1811	(Trash) *Golden Slumbers/Carry That Weight/Trash Can*
1812	(Hot Chocolate) *Give Peace A Chance/Living Without Tomorrow*
1813	(John) *Cold Turkey/Don't Worry Kyoko*
1814	(Preston) *Everything's All Right/I Want To Thank You*
1815	(Badfinger) *Come & Get It/Rock Of All Ages*
1816	(Hopkin) *Temma Harbour/Lontano Dagli Occhi*
1817	(Preston) *All That I've Got/As I Get Older*
1818	(John) *Instant Karma!/Who Has Seen The Wind*
1819	(Lomax) *How The Web Was Woven/I Fall Inside Your Eyes*
1820	(Troy) *Ain't That Cute/Vaya Con Dios*
1821	(Radha Krsna Temple) *Govinda/Govinda Jai Jai*
1822	(Badfinger) *No Matter What/Carry On 'Till Tomorrow*
1823	(Hopkin) *Que Sera Sera/Fields Of St. Etienne*
1824	(Troy) *Jacob's Ladder/Get Back*
1825	(Hopkin) *Think About Your Children/Heritage*
1826	(Preston) *My Sweet Lord/Little Girl*
1827	(John) *Mother/Why*
1828	(George) *What Is Life/Apple Scruffs*
1829	(Paul) *Another Day/Oh Woman Oh Why*
1830	(John) *Power To The People/Touch Me*
1831	(Ringo) *It Don't Come Easy/Early 1970*
1832	(R. Spector) *Try Some Buy Some/Tandoori Chicken*
1833	(NOT USED)
1834	(Lomax) *Sour Milk Sea/I Fall Inside Your Eyes*
1835	(B. Elliott) *God Save Us/Do The Oz*
1836	(George) *Bangla Desh/Deep Blue*
1837	(Paul) *Uncle Albert/Admiral Halsey/Too Many People*
1838	(Shankar) *Joi Bangla/Oh Bhaugowan/Raga Mishra-Jhinjhoti*
1839	(Y. Ono) *Mrs. Lennon/Midsummer New York*
1840	(John) *Imagine/It's So Hard*
1841	(Badfinger) *Day After Day/Money*
1842	(John) *Happy Xmas/Listen The Snow Is Falling*
1843	(Hopkin) *Water Paper Clay/Streets Of London*
1844	(Badfinger) *Baby Blue/Flying*
1845	(Van Eaton) *Sweet Music/Song Of Songs*

1846	(NOT USED)
1847	(Paul) *Give Ireland Back To The Irish/Instrumental*
1848	(John) *Woman Is The Nigger/Sisters O Sisters*
1849	(Ringo) *Back Off Boogaloo/Blindman*
1850	(Hodge) *We're On Our Way/Supersoul*
1851	(Paul) *Mary Had A Little Lamb/Little Woman Love*
1852	(Sundown Playboys) *Saturday Night Special/Valse De Soleil Coucher*
1853	(Y. Ono) *Now Or Never/Move On Fast*
1854	(Elephant's Memory) *Liberation Special/Madness*
1854	(Elephant's Memory) *Liberation Special/Power Boogie*
1855	(Hopkin) *Knock Knock/International*
1856	(NOT USED)
1857	(Paul) *Hi Hi Hi/C Moon*
1858	(Hodge) *Goodbye Sweet Lorraine/Contact Love*
1859	(Y. Ono) *Death Of Samantha/Yang Yang*
1860	(NOT USED)
1861	(Paul) *My Love/The Mess*
1862	(George) *Give Me Love/Miss O'Dell*
1863	(Paul) *Live & Let Die/I Lie Around*
1864	(Badfinger) *Apple Of My Eye/Blind Owl*
1865	(Ringo) *Photograph/Down & Out*
1866	(NOT USED)
1867	(Y. Ono) *Woman Power/Men Men Men*
1868	(John) *Mind Games/Meat City*
1869	(Paul) *Helen Wheels/Country Dreamer*
1870	(Ringo) *You're Sixteen/Devil Woman*
1871	(Paul) *Jet/Mamunia*
1871	(Paul) *Jet/Let Me Roll It*
1872	(Ringo) *Oh My My/Step Lightly*
1873	(Paul) *Band On The Run/1985*
1874	(John) *Whatever Gets You Thru The Night/Beff Jerky*
1875	(Paul) *Junior's Farm/Sally G*
1876	(Ringo) *Only You/Call Me*
1877	(George) *Dark Horse/I Don't Care Anymore*
1878	(John) *No. 9 Dream/What You Got*
1879	(George) *Ding Dong/Hari's On Tour*
1880	(Ringo) *No No Song/Snookeroo*
1881	(John) *Stand By Me/Move Over Ms. L*
1882	(Ringo) *Goodnight Vienna/Oo-Wee*
1883	(John — DJ only) *Slippin' And Slidin'/Ain't That A Shame*
1884	(George) *You/World Of Stone*
1885	(George) *This Guitar/Maya Love*
*2056	*Hello Goodbye/I Am The Walrus*
*2138	*Lady Madonna/Inner Light*
2276	*Hey Jude/Revolution*
2490	*Get Back/Don't Let Me Down*
2531	*Ballad Of John & Yoko/Old Brown Shoe*
2654	*Something/Come Together*
2764	*Let It Be/You Know My Name*
2832	*Long And Winding Road/For You Blue*
2969	(Ringo) *Beaucoups Of Blues/Coochy Coochy*
2995	(George) *My Sweet Lord/Isn't It A Pity*
*5112	*I Want To Hold Your Hand/I Saw Her Standing There*
*5150	*Can't Buy Me Love/You Can't Do That*
*5222	*A Hard Day's Night/I Should Have Known Better*
*5234	*I'll Cry Instead/I'm Happy Just To Dance With You*
*5235	*And I Love Her/If I Fell*
*5255	*Slow Down/Matchbox*
*5327	*I Feel Fine/She's A Woman*
*5371	*Eight Days A Week/I Don't Want To Spoil The Party*
*5407	*Ticket To Ride/Yes It is*

192

*5476	*Help/I'm Down*	
*5498	*Yesterday/Act Naturally*	
*5555	*We Can Work It Out/Day Tripper*	
*5587	*Nowhere Man/What Goes On*	
*5651	*Paperback Writer/Rain*	
*5715	*Yellow Submarine/Eleanor Rigby*	
*5810	*Penny Lane/Strawberry Fields Forever*	
*5964	*All You Need Is Love/Baby You're A Rich Man*	

US Albums

All selections by the Beatles unless otherwise noted.

From May 1976, all the Beatles' Apple records and all solo efforts were reissued on Capitol, if they were kept in print.

*Originally issued on Capitol; between November 1971 and May of 1976, issued on the Apple label. After May of 1976, re-- turned to the Capitol label.

(LP Letter Prefix)

SBC	100	(Fan Club) **The Beatles Christmas Album**
SWBO	101	**The Beatles**
SW	153	**Yellow Submarine**
SO	383	**Abbey Road**
SW	385	**Hey Jude**
STCH	639	(George) **All Things Must Pass**
ST	2047	*Meet The Beatles
ST	2080	*Beatles 2nd Album
ST	2108	*Something New
STBO	2222	*The Beatles Story
ST	2228	*Beatles '65
ST	2309	*Early Beatles
ST	2358	*Beatles VI
SMAS	2386	*Help
ST	2442	*Rubber Soul
ST	2553	*Yesterday And Today
ST	2576	*Revolver
SMAS	2653	*Sgt. Pepper
SMAL	2835	*Magical Mystery Tour
ST	3350	(George) **Wonderwall Music**
ST	3351	(Hopkin) **Post Card**
SKAO	3352	(Taylor) **James Taylor**
ST	3353	(Modern Jazz Quartet) **Under The Jasmine Tree**
ST	3354	(Lomax) **Is This What You Want**
ST	3355	(Iveys–withdrawn) **Maybe Tomorrow**
	3356	(NOT USED)
ST	3357	(John) **Life With The Lions**
ST	3358	(George) **Electronic Sound**
ST	3359	(Preston) **That's The Way God Planned It**
STAO	3360	(Modern Jazz Quartet) **Space**
SMAX	3361	(John) **Wedding Album**
SW	3362	(John) **Live Peace In Toronto**
SMAS	3363	(Paul) **McCartney**
ST	3364	(Badfinger) **Magic Christian Music**
SW	3365	(Ringo) **Sentimental Journey**
	3366	(NOT USED)
SKAO	3367	(Badfinger) **No Dice**
SMAS	3368	(Ringo) **Beaucoups Of Blues**
SMAS	3369	(Tavener) **The Whale**
ST	3370	(Preston) **Encouraging Words**

ST	3371	(Troy) **Doris Troy**
SW	3372	(John) **Plastic Ono Band**
SW	3373	(Y. Ono) **Plastic Ono Band**
	3374	(NOT USED)
SMAS	3375	(Paul) **Ram**
SKAO	3376	(Radha Krsna Temple) **Radha Krsna Temple**
SW	3377	(Soundtrack) **Come Together**
	3378	(NOT USED)
SW	3379	(John) **Imagine**
SVBB	3380	(Y. Ono) **Fly**
SMAS	3381	(Hopkin) **Earth Song–Ocean Song**
3382/	3383	(USED to identify 2--tape package of 3380)
SWAO	3384	(Soundtrack) **Raga**
STCX	3385	(George) **Concert For Bangla Desh**
SW	3386	(Paul) **Wild Life**
SW	3387	(Badfinger) **Straight Up**
SWAO	3388	(Soundtrack) **El Topo**
SMAS	3389	(Elephant's Memory) **Elephant's Memory**
SMAS	3390	(Van Eaton) **Brother**
SW	3391	(Peel) **Pope Smokes Dope**
SVBB	3392	(John) **Sometime In New York City**
3393/	3394	(USED to identify 2--tape package of 3392)
SW	3395	(Hopkin) **Those Were The Days**
SVBB	3396	(Shankar) **In Concert 1972**
3397/	3398	(USED to identify 2--tape package of 3396)
SVBB	3399	(Y. Ono) **Approximately Infinite Universe**
SW	3400	(P. Spector) **Christmas Album**
3401/	3402	(USED to identify 2--tape package of 3399)
SKBO	3403	**The Beatles, 1962--1966**
SKBO	3404	**The Beatles, 1967--1970**
3405/	3406	(USED to identify 2--tape package of 3403)
3407/	3408	(USED to identify 2--tape package of 3404)
SMAL	3409	(Paul) **Red Rose Speedway**
SMAS	3410	(George) **Living In The Material World**
SW	3411	(Badfinger) **Ass**
SW	3412	(Y. Ono) **Feeling The Space**
SWAL	3413	(Ringo) **"Ringo"**
SW	3414	(John) **Mind Games**
SO	3415	(Paul) **Band On The Run**
SW	3416	(John) **Walls And Bridges**
SW	3417	(Ringo) **Goodnight Vienna**
SW	3418	(George) **Dark Horse**
SW	3419	(John) **Rock 'n' Roll**
SW	3420	(George) **Extra Texture**
SW	3421	(John) **Shaved Fish**
SW	3422	(Ringo) **Blast From Your Past**
T	5001	(John) **Two Virgins**
AR	34001	**Let It Be**

UK Singles

All selections by the Beatles unless otherwise noted.

2 (Hopkin) *Those Were The Days/Turn Turn Turn*
3 (Lomax) *Sour Milk Sea/Eagle Laughs At You*
4 (Black Dyke Mills Band) *Thingumybob/Yellow Submarine*
5 (Iveys) *Maybe Tomorrow/And Her Daddy's A Millionaire*
6 (Trash) *Road To Nowhere/Illusions*
7 (Hopkin--Italy) *Lontano Dagli Occhi/The Game*
8 (Brute Force--DJ only) *King Of Fuh/Nobody Knows*

9	(Hopkin--France) *Prince En Avignon/The Game*
10	(Hopkin) *Goodbye/Sparrow*
11	(Lomax) *New Day/I Fall Inside Your Eyes*
12	(Preston) *That's The Way God Planned It/What About You*
13	(John) *Give Peace A Chance/Remember Love*
14	(Iveys) *No Escaping Your Love/Dear Angie*
15	(Radha Krsna Temple) *Hare Krishna/Prayer to Spiritual Masters*
16	(Hopkin) *Que Sera Sera/Fields of St. Etienne*
17	(Trash) *Golden Slumbers/Carry That Weight/Trash Can*
18	(Hot Chocolate) *Give Peace A Chance/Living Without Tomorrow*
19	(Preston) *Everything's All Right/I Want To Thank You*
20	(Badfinger) *Come & Get It/Rock Of All Ages*
21	(Preston) *All That I've Got/As I Get Older*
22	(Hopkin) *Temma Harbour/Lontano Dagli Occhi*
23	(Lomax) *How The Web Was Woven/Thumbin' A Ride*
24	(Troy) *Ain't That Cute/Vaya Con Dios*
25	(Radha Krsna Temple) *Govinda/Govinda Jai Jai*
26	(Hopkin) *Knock Knock/I'm Going To Fall In Love Again*
27	(NOT USED)
28	(Troy) *Jacob's Ladder/Get Back*
29	(Preston) *My Sweet Lord/Long As I Got My Baby*
30	(Hopkin) *Think About Your Children/Heritage*
31	(Badfinger) *No Matter What/Better Days*
32	(Taylor) *Carolina In My Mind/Something's Wrong*
33	(R. Spector) *Try Some Buy Some/Tandoori Chicken*
34	(Hopkin) *Let My Name Be Sorrow/Kew Gardens*
35	(NOT USED)
36	(B. Elliott) *God Save Us/Do The Oz*
37	(Shankar) *Joi Bangla/Oh Bhaugowan/Raga Mishra—Jhinjhoti*
38	(Y. Ono) *Mrs. Lennon/Midsummer New York*
39	(Hopkin) *Water Paper & Clay/Jefferson*
40	(Badfinger) *Day After Day/Sweet Tuesday Morning*
41	(Y. Ono) *Mind Train/Listen The Snow Is Falling*
42	(Badfinger) *Baby Blue/Flying*
43	(Hodge) *We're On Our Way/Supersoul*
44	(Sundown Playboys) *Sat. Night Special/Valse De Soleil Coucher*
45	(Elephant's Memory) *Power Boogie/Liberation Special*
46	(Van Eaton) *Warm Woman/More Than Words*
47	(Y. Ono) *Death Of Samantha/Yang Yang*
48	(Y. Ono) *Run Run Run/Men Men Men*
49	(Badfinger) *Apple Of My Eye/Blind Owl*
1001	(John) *Cold Turkey/Don't Worry Kyoko*
1002	(John--withdrawn) *You Know My Name/What's The News Maryjane*
1003	(John) *Instant Karma!/Who Has Seen The Wind*
R 5722	*Hey Jude/Revolution*
R 5777	*Get Back/Don't Let Me Down*
R 5786	*Ballad Of John & Yoko/Old Brown Shoe*
R 5814	*Something/Come Together*
R 5833	*Let It Be/You Know My Name*
R 5884	(George) *My Sweet Lord/What Is Life*
R 5889	(Paul) *Another Day/Oh Woman Oh Why*
R 5892	(John) *Power To The People/Open Your Box*
R 5898	(Ringo) *It Don't Come Easy/Early 1970*
R 5912	(George) *Bangla Desh/Deep Blue*
R 5914	(Paul) *Back Seat Of My Car/Heart Of The Country*
R 5932	(Paul--withdrawn) *Love Is Strange/I Am Your Singer*
R 5936	(Paul) *Give Ireland Back To The Irish/Instrumental*
R 5944	(Ringo) *Back Off Boogaloo/Blindman*
R 5949	(Paul) *Mary Had A Little Lamb/Little Woman Love*

R 5953   (John) *Woman Is The Nigger/Sisters O Sisters*
R 5970   (John) *Happy Xmas/Listen The Snow Is Falling*
R 5973   (Paul) *Hi Hi Hi/C Moon*
R 5985   (Paul) *My Love/The Mess*
R 5987   (Paul) *Live & Let Die/I Lie Around*
R 5988   (George) *Give Me Love/Miss O'Dell*
R 5992   (Ringo) *Photograph/Down And Out*
R 5993   (Paul) *Helen Wheels/Country Dreamer*
R 5994   (John) *Mind Games/Meat City*
R 5995   (Ringo) *You're Sixteen/Devil Woman*
R 5996   (Paul) *Jet/Let Me Roll It*
R 5997   (Paul) *Band On The Run/Zoo Gang*
R 5998   (John) *Whatever Gets You Thru The Night/Beef Jerky*
R 5999   (Paul) *Junior's Farm/Sally G*
R 6000   (Ringo) *Only You/Call Me*
R 6001   (George--withdrawn) *Dark Horse/I Don't Care Anymore*
R 6001   (George) *Dark Horse/Hari's On Tour*
R 6002   (George) *Ding Dong/I Don't Care Anymore*
R 6003   (John) *No. 9 Dream/What You Got*
R 6004   (Ringo) *Snookeroo/Oo-Wee*
R 6005   (John) *Stand By Me/Move Over Ms. L*
R 6007   (George) *You/World Of Stone*
R 6009   (John) *Imagine/Working Class Hero*
R 6011   (Ringo) *Oh My My/No No Song*
R 6012   (George) *This Guitar/Maya Love*

NOTE: Paul's releases on the Capitol label and new EMI couplings of Beatle catalogue material (as singles) continue to be released in the R-6000 Parlophone numbering series. These include:

R 6006   (Paul) *Listen To What The Man Said/Love In Song*
R 6008   (Paul) *Letting Go/You Gave Me The Answer*
R 6010   (Paul) *Venus And Mars Rock Show/Magneto And Titanium Man*
R 6013   *Yesterday/I Should Have Known Better*
R 6014   (Paul) *Silly Love Songs/Cook Of The House*
R 6015   (Paul) *Let 'Em In/Beware My Love*
R 6016   *Back In The U.S.S.R./Twist And Shout*
R 6017   (Paul) *Maybe I'm Amazed/Soily*

UK Albums

All Selections by the Beatles unless otherwise noted.
(LP Letter Prefix)

(SAPCOR) Series
1   (George) **Wonderwall Music**
2   (John) **Two Virgins**
3   (Taylor) **James Taylor**
4   (Modern Jazz Quartet) **Under The Jasmine Tree**
5   (Hopkin) **Postcard**
6   (Lomax) **Is This What You Want**
7   (Delaney & Bonnie -- withdrawn) **The Original--Accept No Substitute**
8   (Iveys--Foreign Only) **Maybe Tomorrow**
9   (Preston) **That's The Way God Planned It**
10   (Modern Jazz Quartet) **Space**
11   (John) **Wedding Album**
12   (Badfinger) **Magic Christian Music**
13   (Troy) **Doris Troy**
14   (Preston) **Encouraging Words**
15   (Tavener) **The Whale**

16   (Badfinger) **No Dice**
17   (Y. Ono) **Plastic Ono Band**
18   (Radha Krsna Temple) **Radha Krsna Temple**
19   (Badfinger) **Straight Up**
20   (Tavener) **Celtic Requiem**
21   (Hopkin) **Earth Song -- Ocean Song**
22   (Elephant's Memory) **Elephant's Memory**
23   (Hopkin) **Those Were The Days**
24   (P. Spector) **Christmas Album**
25   (Van Eaton) **Brother**
26   (Y. Ono) **Feeling The Space**
27   (Badfinger) **Ass**

(ZAPPLE) Series
1   (John) **Life With The Lions**
2   (George) **Electronic Music**
3   (Brautigan--withdrawn) **Listening To Richard Brautigan**

(SAPTU) Series
101/102 (Y. Ono) **Fly**

(PCTC) Series
251   (Paul) **Red Rose Speedway**
252   (Ringo) **"Ringo"**
253   (John) **Walls And Bridges**

(STCH) Series
639   (George) **All Things Must Pass**

(PCSP) Series
716   (John) **Sometime In New York City**
717   **The Beatles, 1962--1966**
718   **The Beatles, 1967--1970**

(SAPDO) Series
1001 (Y. Ono) **Approximately Infinite Universe**
1002 (Shankar) **In Concert 1972**

(CORE) Series
2001 (John) **Live Peace In Toronto 1969**

(LYN) Series
2153 (Fan Club) **From Then To You**

(STCX) Series
3385 (George) **Concert For Bangla Desh**

(PCS) Series
7067/7068 **The Beatles**
7070 **Yellow Submarine**
7088 **Abbey Road**
7096 **Let It Be**
7101 (Ringo) **Sentimental Journey**
7102 (Paul) **McCartney**
7124 (John) **Plastic Ono Band**
7142 (Paul) **Wild Life**
7165 (John) **Mind Games**
7168 (Ringo) **Goodnight Vienna**
7169 (John) **Rock 'n' Roll**
7170 (Ringo) **Blast From Your Past**
7173 (John) **Shaved Fish**

197

(PAS) Series
10002 (Ringo) **Beaucoups Of Blues**
10003 (Paul) **Ram**
10004 (John) **Imagine**
10006 (George) **Living In The Material World**
10007 (Paul) **Band On The Run**
10008 (George) **Dark Horse**
10009 (George) **Extra Texture**

Dark Horse &
Ring O' Records

It's too soon to gain a proper focus on either Dark Horse or Ring O' records. They're both too new and, unlike Apple, both still alive and functioning. Several things are apparent, though. It's clear that both George and Ringo were determined to learn from the mistakes of Apple. They kept the ambitions of their new companies modest. They tried to avoid the super-star-association-stigma which generally results in publicity, but only for the ex-Beatle, not the new artist. At first, for example, George didn't even record for his new label; Ringo still doesn't for his. They both tried to keep the business associations loose enough so that artists wouldn't be imprisoned by their own new label, and they both signed old friends and talented new performers to their rosters. Thus far, no super-stars have emerged, but several excellent records have resulted.

Dark Horse, begun in 1974 and originally distributed by A&M records, has seen about a half-dozen artists. Of these, George lavished his personal attention (as producer) on only two: Ravi Shankar and Splinter. Implicit in the A&M/Harrison dispute in 1976, which resulted in Warner Brothers taking over the distribution of Dark Horse product late in 1976, seemed to be A&M's disappointment that George didn't take a more active role in each of the Dark Horse recordings. From the company's promotional point of view, it was a real complaint. Without the "(Beatle) George Harrison" hook, the promotion of the new product (like Jiva) was that much harder. On the other hand, established professionals like the members of Stairsteps and Attitudes hardly needed George Harrison to produce their music, or to introduce them to the public, for that matter. Still, after two years A&M found itself with a few maybe hits, a lot of records that weren't moving, and the prospect of several years' wait before the artists finally cracked the market. The shift to Warner Brothers seemed to satisfy all concerned. The larger hit-making machinery of Warners could churn out an instant hit (33 1/3), or take its time building a following for an act (Attitudes, Stairsteps). As part of the A&M/Warners settlement, all of the A&M Dark Horse albums and singles were taken out of print (becoming instant collector's items). By the fall of 1977, however, new record releases by Attitudes, Keni Burke (from Stairsteps) and Splinter had established a basic catalogue of Warners' own Dark Horse material. Given the rare chance to start fresh again so soon, and with the strong talent intact from the first go-'round, Dark Horse may yet prove to be that elusive hit label the individual Beatles have attempted for years.

Less ambitious but certainly no less interesting is Ringo's own label, Ring O'. The focus from its debut in 1975 was on one-shot, off-beat recordings: first releases included a synthesizer-version of Ringo's **"Ringo"** LP, a disco-rocker, a Christmas/dance novelty disc, and a rock 'n' roll record. Quite a mixed bag, and one which Capitol (the U.S. distributor for the first few discs) and Polydor (the rest of the world) found difficult to promote. Ringo let the label lie dormant in 1976 while he sorted out his other business affairs and career interests, which included signing with Polydor/Atlantic in 1976. In mid-1977, Ringo decided to reactivate the label, and place an emphasis on developing a stable of five or six artists over several years. Graham Bonnet relaunced Ring O' Records in Britain (there's no new American distributor yet) in June 1977 with the classic *It's All Over Now, Baby Blue*. Promotional efforts promised to be more coordinated, with Polydor handling both Ringo and Ring O' worldwide. With Ringo Starr's affection (and nose) for hit singles, his label holds the potential for some real surprises.

Dark Horse Records

Attitudes. On his **Living In The Material World** LP package, George took a quick jab at Paul McCartney's Fan Club promo on **Red Rose Speedway** ("for more information on the Wings' Fun Club send a stamped self-addressed envelope. . .") by inserting his own plug for a Jim Keltner Fan Club ("send a stamped undressed elephant . . ."). Apparently no pachyderms arrived, but three other famous musicians did. The four joined forces to form Attitudes: Jim Keltner (drums, percussion, backing vocals); Paul Stallworth (bass, lead vocals); Danny "Kootch" Kortchmar (guitars, lead vocals); and David Foster (keyboards, synthesizer, backing vocals). Signed to the Dark Horse stable, they released their first single, the upbeat and funky *Ain't Love Enough*, in late 1975, and the follow-up album **Attitudes** in early 1976. Their single for the summer of 1976, *Sweet Summer Music*, even floated for awhile in the lower levels of the charts. Undoubtedly one of the most commercial bands on Dark Horse, Attitudes released the first LP (after George's own **33 1/3**) following the Dark Horse move to Warner Brothers distribution. Called **Good News**, it featured Ringo, Booker T. Jones and the Tower of Power Horn section on the title track, the *Sweet Summer Music* "hit" from 1976, and the usual almost democratic exchange of funky riffs. Warners even reissued the *Sweet Summer Music* track as a single for the summer of 1977.

DEC 9, 1975 (US) Dark Horse DH 10004
FEB 13, 1976 (UK) Dark Horse AMS 5504
by Attitudes Prod: Lee Kiefer and Attitudes
A: Ain't Love Enough---David Foster—Brenda Gordon Russell—Brian
    Russell---*3:05*
*B: The Whole World's Crazy---Paul Stallworth---*4:21*

FEB   6, 1976 (US) Dark Horse SP 22008 (LP)
MAR 19, 1976 (UK) Dark Horse AMLH 22008 (LP)
by Attitudes
ATTITUDES Prod: Lee Kiefer and Attitudes
side one
  AIN'T LOVE ENOUGH---David Foster—Brenda Gordon Russell—
    Brian Russell---*3:14*
  Street Scene--Danny Kortchmar---*3:29*
  A Moment--David Foster—Jim Keltner—Danny Kortchmar—Paul
    Stallworth---*0:55*
  You And I Are So In Love---B. J. Cooke—E. Mercury---*3:59*
  Squank--David Foster—Jim Keltner—Danny Kortchmar—Paul
    Stallworth---*4:23*
side two
  Lend A Hand---Paul Stallworth---*3:02*
  Chump Change Romeo---Danny Kortchmar---*2:28*
  First Ballad---David Foster—Jim Keltner—Danny Kortchmar—Paul
    Stallworth---*4:00*
  Honey Don't Leave L.A.---Danny Kortchmar---*3:43*
  In The Flow Of Love---Gilbert Bottiglier—Chuck Higgins Jr.—Paul
    Stallworth---*3:10*

MAY 31, 1976 (US) Dark Horse DH 10008
by Attitudes Prod: Lee Kiefer and Attitudes
A: *HONEY DON'T LEAVE L.A.*---Danny Kortchmar---*3:12*
B: *LEND A HAND*---Paul Stallworth---*3:02*

JUL 23, 1976 (US) Dark Horse DH 10011
AUG 20, 1976 (UK) Dark Horse AMS 5508
by Attitudes Prod: Attitudes and Jay Lewis (A side); Attitudes and
  Lee Kiefer (B side)
A: *Sweet Summer Music*---Gilbert Bottiglier—Chuck Higgins Jr.—
    Paul Stallworth---*3:39*
*B: *If We Want To*--David Foster—Jim Keltner—Danny Kortchmar—
    Paul Stallworth---*3:20*

MAY   5, 1977 (US) Dark Horse DH 3021 (LP)
JUN   3, 1977 (UK) Dark Horse K 56385 (LP)
by Attitudes
GOOD NEWS Prod: Jay Lewis and Attitudes
side one
  Being Here With You---David Foster—Jim Keltner—Danny
    Kortchmar—Paul Stallworth---*3:23*

202

Drink My Water—Brenda Gordon Russell–Brian Russell—*3:15*
SWEET SUMMER MUSIC—Gilbert Bottiglier–Chuck Higgins Jr.–
    Paul Stallworth—*3:39*
Let's Talk Turkey—Danny Kortchmar—*2:55*
Foster's Frees—David Foster—*2:10*
Turning In Space—Edward Brown–Chuck Higgins Jr.–Paul
    Stallworth—*3:18*
side two
Change—Paul Stallworth—*4:10*
In A Stranger's Arms—Danny Kortchmar—*3:58*
Manual Dexterity—Danny Kortchmar—*3:20*
Promise Me The Moon—Danny Kortchmar—*3:37*
Good News—Paul Stallworth—*3:45*

JUN 13, 1977 (US) Dark Horse DRC 8404
by Attitudes Prod: Jay Lewis and Attitudes
A: *SWEET SUMMER MUSIC*—Gilbert Bottiglier–Chuck Higgins
    Jr.–Paul Stallworth—*3:39*
B: *BEING HERE WITH YOU*—David Foster–Jim Keltner–Danny
    Kortchmar–Paul Stallworth—*3:25*

SEP 6, 1977 (US) Dark Horse DRC 8452
by Attitudes Prod: Jay Lewis and Attitudes
A: *IN A STRANGER'S ARMS*—Danny Kortchmar—*3:58*
B: *GOOD NEWS*—Paul Stallworth—*3:45*

Jiva. Pronounced GEE-VAH. The first American act signed to the
new label, Jiva consisted of: Michael Lanning (guitar, lead vocals),
James Strauss (bass, vocals), Thomas Hilton (guitar, vocals) and
Michael Reed (drums, percussion). Backed by Gary Wright on keyboards, they released their one and only Dark Horse album in October of 1975, and watched it sink into oblivion. The four played the
basic L.A. formula of white funk no worse than but certainly in-
distinguishable from, dozens of other bands. Their single from the
album, *Something's Goin' On Inside L.A.*, was the semi-obligatory
Beatle-inspired song (with allusions to Ringo's *Only You* and various
complicated business deals), though George appeared to have no
personal involvement in the actual production of their record. By
late 1976, Jiva had split from Dark Horse and was last seen backing
Donovan in concert.

OCT 6, 1975 (US) Dark Horse SP 22003 (LP)
OCT 31, 1975 (UK) Dark Horse AMLH 22003 (LP)
by Jiva
JIVA Prod: Stewart Levine
side one
  Something's Goin' On Inside L.A.—Michael Lanning—James
    Strauss—Thomas Hilton—*4:07*
  The Closer I Get—Michael Lanning—James Strauss—Thomas Hilton—
    3:27
  Love Is A Treasure—Michael Lanning—James Strauss—Thomas
    Hilton—*4:06*
  Take My Love—Michael Lanning—James Strauss—Thomas Hilton—
    4:06
  Hey Brother—Michael Lanning—James Strauss—Thomas Hilton—
    3:00
side two
  World Of Love—Michael Lanning—James Strauss—Thomas
    Hilton—*3:29*
  What You're Waiting For—Michael Lanning—James Strauss—
    Thomas Hilton—*3:36*
  It's Time You Know—Michael Lanning—James Strauss—Thomas
    Hilton—*3:22*
  Don't Be Sad—Michael Lanning—James Strauss—Thomas Hilton—
    3:15
  All Is Well—Michael Lanning—James Strauss—Thomas Hilton—*3:45*

FEB 11, 1976 (US) Dark Horse DH 10006
by Jiva Prod: Stewart Levine
A: SOMETHING'S GOIN' ON INSIDE L.A.—Michael Lanning—
    James Strauss—Thomas Hilton—*4:07*
B: TAKE MY LOVE—Michael Lanning—James Strauss—Thomas
    Hilton—*4:06*

Henry McCullough. Formerly of the Grease Band. Formerly of
Wings. Henry McCullough has shifted from one band to another,
and appeared on dozens of records over the years. He relaxed for a
bit back in 1975 and cut a solo disc for Dark Horse. It featured 9
McCullough compositions plus the old Hank Williams standard *Mind
Your Own Business*. The basic performers on the LP included Henry
on vocals and guitar; Alan Spenner, Charlie Harrison and Jim Lever-
ton on bass; Neil Hubbard on guitar: Bruce Rowland, Steve Chapman
and John Halsey on drums; and Mick Weaver and Tim Hinkley on
piano and organ. The disc didn't click, and so Henry moved on. In
early 1977 Roy Harper released a new LP, **One Of Those Days In**

England, and took his newly formed band from the album sessions, including Henry and friend John Halsey, on the road in England.

OCT 20, 1975 (US) Dark Horse SP 22005 (LP)
OCT 24, 1975 (UK) Dark Horse AMLH 22005 (LP)
by Henry McCullough
MIND YOUR OWN BUSINESS Prod: Henry McCullough and John
  Jansen
side one
  You'd Better Run—Henry McCullough—*4:13*
  Sing Me A Song—Henry McCullough—*3:25*
  I Can Drive A Car—Henry McCullough—*4:41*
  Baby What You Do To Me—Henry McCullough—*5:33*
  Country Irish Rose—Henry McCullough—*3:18*
side two
  Lord Knows—Henry McCullough—*4:08*
  Down The Mine—Henry McCullough—*6:07*
  Oil In My Lamp—Henry McCullough—*2:21*
  Mind Your Own Business—Hank Williams—*3:55*
  I'm In Heaven—Henry McCullough—*1:32*

Ravi Shankar. George's first signing to Dark Horse records was, naturally enough, old friend Ravi Shankar. As with Apple (see "Apple"), Ravi used the opportunity and artistic freedom provided by such an association to pursue some special projects. The first resulted in the **Shankar Family And Friends LP**, a surprising combination of Indian, classical, ballet and pop styles. They meshed into Shankar's most accessible—yes, even commercial—offering, produced by George himself. One track, *I Am Missing You*, was even an obvious choice for a single! It featured the very distinctive voice of Lakshmi Shankar, Ravi's sister-in-law (the title of the LP was quite accurate!). Shankar Family & Friends drew heavily from this LP when they performed with Harrison on his 1974 concert tour. Ravi's second Dark Horse album, released in 1976, was a more traditional celebration of Indian music called **Music Festival From India**. It featured extensive liner notes explaining the different Indian instruments, styles and technique. George also produced this LP, though this time there was no single.

SEP 13, 1974 (UK) Dark Horse AMS 7133
NOV 6, 1974 (US) Dark Horse DH 10001
by Ravi Shankar Family & Friends Prod: George Harrison
A: I Am Missing You—Ravi Shankar—*3:40*
B: Lust—Ravi Shankar—*3:12*

SEP 20, 1974 (UK) Dark Horse AMLH 22002 (LP)
OCT 7, 1974 (US) Dark Horse SP 22002 (LP)
by Ravi Shankar Family & Friends
SHANKAR FAMILY & FRIENDS Prod: George Harrison
side one
  I Am Missing You—Ravi Shankar—*3:40*
  Kahan Gayelava Shyam Salone—Ravi Shankar—*3:15*
  Supane Me Aye Preetam Sainya—Ravi Shankar—*4:44*
  I Am Missing You (reprise)—Ravi Shankar—*3:56*
  Jaya Jagadish Hare—P.D.—*4:50*
side two: *Dream, Nightmare & Dawn (Music For A Ballet)*—Ravi
  Shankar—*29:13*
  Overture—Ravi Shankar—*2:28*
  Part One: Dream—*7:02*
    Festivity & Joy—Ravi Shankar—*3:52*
    Love-Dance Ecstasy—Ravi Shankar—*3:10*
  Part Two: Nightmare—*12:15*
    Lust—Ravi Shankar—*3:12*
    Dispute & Violence—Ravi Shankar—*3:05*
    Disillusionment & Frustration—Ravi Shankar—*2:51*
    Despair & Sorrow—Ravi Shankar—*3:07*
  Part Three: Dawn—*7:28*
    Awakening—Ravi Shankar—*3:07*
    Peace & Hope—Ravi Shankar—*4:21*

FEB 6, 1976 (US) Dark Horse SP 22007 (LP)
MAR 19, 1976 (UK) Dark Horse AMLH 22007 (LP)
by Ravi Shankar
RAVI SHANKAR'S MUSIC FESTIVAL FROM INDIA Prod: George
  Harrison
side one
  Vandana—Ravi Shankar—*2:35*
  Dhamar—Ravi Shankar—*5:20*
  Tarana—Ravi Shankar—*3:50*
  Chaturang—Ravi Shankar—*2:00*
  Raga Jait—Ravi Shankar—*9:41*
side two
  Kajri—Ravi Shankar—*4:45*
  Bhajan—Ravi Shankar—*3:50*
  Naderdani—Ravi Shankar—*4:40*
  Dehati—Ravi Shankar—*10:04*

Splinter. Bob Purvis and Bill Elliott grew up in Newcastle, England,
on a heavy dose of Beatles music. At the tender age of six Purvis

blithely told his mom that he had composed a song called *Love Me Do* on his brand new guitar. The two kicked around in various local rock groups before coming to London to attempt to crack the market. Elliott found himself snatched up by John Lennon to sing lead on the song *God Save Us* (see "Apple"), however the single slipped into instant obscurity. Elliott and Purvis soon fell under the watchful eye of Mal Evans. It was while staying at his house that Bob Purvis wrote the song *Lonely Man* with Mal Evans. Mal then suggested to George Harrison that, performed by the right people (Bill Elliott and Bob Purvis, for instance), *Lonely Man* would make an excellent contribution to the film *Little Malcolm & His Struggle Against The Eunuchs*, for which George was executive producer. Harrison then gathered some of his super-star friends into the studio (Billy Preston, Jim Keltner, Bill Dickinson, John Taylor) to record *Lonely Man* as a possible hit single. It turned into an album, in fact, into the first album release on Dark Horse records. **The Place That I Love** featured 9 original Elliott and Purvis compositions as well as an impressive list of backing musicians including George (using such pseudonyms as P. Roducer and the usual Hari Georgeson), *Lonely Man*'s Billy Preston and Jim Keltner, Klaus Voorman, Gary Wright, and Willie Weeks. The first single, *Costafine Town*, sold moderatley well (reaching no. 77 in America), but the follow-up, a remixed version of *China Light*, failed to make the charts. Splinter's second LP, released a year later, finally included *Lonely Man*, but this was the only Harrison-produced cut. Tom Scott took over the producing reins for the rest of the LP, aided by Earl Palmer (drums), Bill Dickinson (bass), Chris Spedding and Robert Wachtel (guitars) and John Taylor (keyboards) with Scott himself on horns, synthesizer, steel drums and percussion. Around the time Warners took over distribution of Dark Horse, two singles were released in Japan. The first, on A&M/Dark Horse, featured *Lonely Man* sung in Japanese; the second, on Warner/Dark Horse, featured two previously unreleased tracks, *White Shoeleather* and *Love Is Not Enough*. They rerecorded *Love Is Not Enough* for their latest album on Warner/Dark Horse, **Two Man Band**. George once again took an active role in the recording, playing guitar and acting as executive producer (with Dennis Morgan). Norbert Putnam, who also doubled on bass at the sessions, was the actual session producer. The first single issued from the album was a Parker McGee tune, *Round And Round*. To support their releases, Elliott and Purvis have embarked on some low-key personal appearance tours (just the 2 of them, guitars in hand), but have yet to set up a full-fledged concert schedule.

SEP 13, 1974 (UK) Dark Horse AMS 7135
NOV 7, 1974 (US) Dark Horse DH 10002
by Splinter Prod: George Harrison
A: *Costafine Town*—Robert J. Purvis—William Elliott—*3:10*
B: *Elly-May*—Robert J. Purvis—*2:43*

SEP 20, 1974 (UK) Dark Horse AMLH 22001 (LP)
SEP 25, 1974 (US) Dark Horse SP 22001 (LP)
by Splinter
THE PLACE I LOVE Prod: George Harrison
side one
  Gravy Train—Robert J. Purvis—*4:50*
  Drink All Day (Got To Find Your Own Way Home)—Robert J.
   Purvis—*3:20*
  China Light—Robert J. Purvis—William Elliott—*4:35*
  Somebody's City—Robert J. Purvis—*5:20*
side two
  Costafine Town—Robert J. Purvis—William Elliott—*3:10*
  The Place I Love—Robert J. Purvis—*4:25*
  Situation Vacant—Robert J. Purvis—*4:00*
  Elly-May—Robert J. Purvis—*2:43*
  Haven't Got Time—Robert J. Purvis—*3:55*

FEB 7, 1975 (UK) Dark Horse AMS 5501
by Splinter Prod: George Harrison
A: *DRINK ALL DAY (GOT TO FIND YOUR OWN WAY HOME)*
   —Robert J. Purvis—3:20
B: *HAVEN'T GOT TIME*—Robert J. Purvis—*3:55*

FEB 21, 1975 (UK) Dark Horse AMS 5502
by Splinter Prod: George Harrison
A: *CHINA LIGHT*—Robert J. Purvis—William Elliott—*3:29*
B: *DRINK ALL DAY (GOT TO FIND YOUR OWN WAY HOME)*
   —Robert J. Purvis—3:20

MAR 7, 1975 (US) Dark Horse DH 10003
by Splinter Prod: George Harrison
A: *CHINA LIGHT*—Robert J. Purvis—William Elliott—*3:29*
B: *HAVEN'T GOT TIME*—Robert J. Purvis—*3:55*

OCT   6, 1975 (US) Dark Horse SP 22006 (LP)
OCT 24, 1975 (UK) Dark Horse AMLH 22006 (LP)
by Splinter
HARDER TO LIVE Prod: Tom Scott except † George Harrison and
  Tom Scott
side one
  Please Help Me--Robert J. Purvis--*2:37*
  Sixty Miles Too Far---Robert J. Purvis---*4:06*
  Harder To Live--Robert J. Purvis--*3:23*
  Half Way There--Robert J. Purvis--*2:57*
  Which Way Will I Get Home---Robert J. Purvis---*3:56*
side two
  Berkley House Hotel--Robert J. Purvis--*3:21*
  After Five Years---Robert J. Purvis---*3:08*
  Green Line Bus---Robert J. Purvis---*4:01*
  †Lonely Man---Robert J. Purvis--Mal Evans---*5:34*
  What Is It (If You Never Ever Tried It Yourself)--Robert J. Purvis--
    William Elliott--*3:43*

NOV   7, 1975 (UK) Dark Horse AMS 5503
by Splinter Prod: Tom Scott
A: WHICH WAY WILL I GET HOME--Robert J. Purvis--*3:56*
B: GREEN LINE BUS--Robert J. Purvis--*4:01*

FEB   9, 1976 (US) Dark Horse DH 10007
by Splinter Prod: Tom Scott
A: WHICH WAY WILL I GET HOME---Robert J. Purvis---*3:56*
B: WHAT IS IT (IF YOU NEVER EVER TRIED IT YOURSELF)---
    Robert J. Purvis--William Elliott---*3:43*

MAY 21, 1976 (UK) Dark Horse AMS 5506
by Splinter Prod: Tom Scott
A: HALF WAY THERE---Robert J. Purvis---*2:57*
B: WHAT IS IT (IF YOU NEVER EVER TRIED IT YOURSELF)---
    Robert J. Purvis--William Elliott---*3:43*

JUL 16, 1976 (US) Dark Horse DH 10010
by Splinter Prod: Tom Scott
A: AFTER FIVE YEARS---Robert J. Purvis---*3:08*
B: HALF WAY THERE---Robert J. Purvis---*2:57*

OCTOBER 1976 (JAPAN) Dark Horse CM 2006
by Splinter Prod: George Harrison and Tom Scott
*A: *Lonely Man (in Japanese)*—M. Nakamura—Robert J. Purvis—
    Mal Evans—*4:15*
B: *LONELY MAN*—Robert J. Purvis—Mal Evans—*4:15*

NOVEMBER 1976 (JAPAN) Dark Horse (Warner-Pioneer) P 77D
by Splinter
*A: *Love Is Not Enough (version one)*—Robert J. Purvis—*3:29*
*B: *White Shoeleather*—Robert J. Purvis—William Elliott—*3:27*

SEP 6, 1977 (US) Dark Horse DRC 8439
SEP 16, 1977 (UK) Dark Horse K 17009
by Splinter Prod: Norbert Putnam
A: *Round And Round*—Parker McGee—*3:04*
*B: *I'll Bend For You*—Robert J. Purvis—*3:48*

OCT 3, 1977 (US) Dark Horse DH 3073 (LP)
OCT 7, 1977 (UK) Dark Horse K 56403 (LP)
by Splinter
TWO MAN BAND Executive Producers: George Harrison
  and Dennis Morgan; Prod: Norbert Putnam
side one
  Little Girl—Robert J. Purvis—William Elliott—*3:14*
  Round And Round—Parker McGee—*3:13*
  Baby Love—Robert J. Purvis—*3:34*
  I Apologize—Robert J. Purvis—*4:33*
  Black Friday—Robert J. Purvis—*2:59*
side two
  New York City (Who Am I)—Robert J. Purvis—*3:49*
  I Need Your Love—Robert J. Purvis—*2:58*
  Motions Of Love—Parker McGee—*3:26*
  Silver—Robert J. Purvis—*3:15*
  Love Is Not Enough (version two)—Robert J. Purvis—*4:02*

Stairsteps. Undoubtedly, one of the most viable groups on Dark Horse. In 1975 the former Five Stairsteps, who hit top ten in 1970 with *O-o-h Child*, fell into the care of Billy Preston, who helped them produce their first Dark Horse LP. The multi-talented Kenny Burke, Dennis Burke, Clarence Burke Jr., and James Burke each shared the vocals, guitar work, writing and production on the record. Several singles were released and *From Us To You* was a genuine hit on the soul charts. Billy Preston brought the T.O.N.T.O. keyboard system, programmed by Robert Margouleff and Malcolm Cecil, to the album and played it throughout. Alvin Taylor joined in on drums, Ricardo Marrero on percussion, Steve Beckmeier on additional guitars, and Ivory Davis on some background vocals. With the shift to Warner Brothers came the promotion of Kenny (Keni) Burke as the lead figure from the group, with the release of his first solo album.

DEC 3, 1975 (US) Dark Horse DH 10005
JAN 30, 1976 (UK) Dark Horse AMS 5505
by Stairsteps Prod: Billy Preston, Bob Margouleff and Stairsteps
A: From Us To You—Clarence Burke Jr.—Kenneth Burke—*3:00*
B: Time—Clarence Burke Jr.—Syreeta Wright—*3:48*

FEB 6, 1976 (US) Dark Horse SP 22004 (LP)
MAR 19, 1976 (UK) Dark Horse AMLH 22004 (LP)
by Stairsteps
2ND RESURRECTION Prod: Billy Preston, Robert Margouleff and
  Stairsteps
side one
FROM US TO YOU—Clarence Burke Jr.—Kenneth Burke—*3:39*
Pasado—Clarence Burke Jr.—James Burke—*3:09*
Theme Of Angels—James Burke—*3:19*
Lifting 2nd Resurrection—Clarence Burke Jr.—Dennis Burke—*3:45*
TIME—Clarence Burke Jr.—Syreeta Wright—*3:48*
side two
Throwin' Stones Atcha—Clarence Burke Jr.—*3:04*
Far East—Clarence Burke Jr.—*1:06*
In The Beginning—Clarence Burke Jr.—*2:53*
Tell Me Why—Kenneth Burke—*4:31*
Salaam—Kenneth Burke—*4:34*

MAY 21, 1976 (UK) Dark Horse AMS 5507
by Stairsteps Prod: Billy Preston, Robert Margouleff and Stairsteps
A: PASADO—Clarence Burke Jr.—James Burke—*3:09*
B: THROWIN' STONES ATCHA—Clarence Burke Jr.—*3:04*

JUN 14, 1976 (US) Dark Horse DH 10009
by Stairsteps Prod: Billy Preston, Robert Margouleff and Stairsteps
A: TELL ME WHY---Kenneth Burke---*3:59*
B: SALAAM---Kenneth Burke---*3:58*

AUG 16, 1977 (US) Dark Horse DH 3022 (LP)
by Keni Burke
KENI BURKE Prod: Keni Burke
side one
  Keep On Singing---Keni Burke–Day Askey---*4:40*
  You Are All Mine---Keni Burke–Day Askey---*3:02*
  Day---Keni Burke---*2:48*
  It's The Last Time---Keni Burke–Day Askey---*4:06*
  Shuffle---Keni Burke–Day Askey---*3:39*
side two
  Give All That You Can Give---Keni Burke–Ronnie Vann---*4:00*
  Tell Me That You Love Me---Keni Burke–Ronnie Vann---*4:03*
  Something New (Like A Sweet Melody)---Keni Burke–Ronnie
   Vann---*4:23*
  From Me To You---Keni Burke---*4:08*

OCT 11, 1977 (US) Dark Horse DRC 8474
by Keni Burke Prod: Keni Burke
A: SHUFFLE---Keni Burke–Day Askey---*3:39*
B: FROM ME TO YOU---Keni Burke---*4:08*

Ring O' Records

Colonel Doug Bogie. In an interview years ago, Ringo said that when he just wanted to relax and have a good time, one of his favorite performers was a local British entertainer, Doug Bogie. It took just one listen to the Colonel's only disc for Ring O' to see why! The record contained two classic tunes: *Cokey Cokey* and *Away In A Manger*. The *Cokey Cokey* was that popular dance favorite (dating back over a quarter of a centruy) which kept couples on their toes waiting for the next set of instructions: Left foot! Right foot! In! Out! In! Out! A great disco number! The flip was, honest to god, the Christmas hymn *Away In A Manger*. If that wasn't enough, the Colonel was even named after that famous tune, the *Colonel Bogey March*--whistled by the men in *Bridge On The River Kwai*– or perhaps it was the other way around. In any case, despite such obvious qualities, the record wasn't released on Ring O' in America, but was picked up instead by ABC, which released it as a novelty Christmas disc. Some people at ABC contended the disc was Ringo himself; indeed, Ringo may well have been a party to the melee in the studio, but he certainly wasn't doing the vocals. No, there's only one Colonel Bogie.

NOV 21, 1975 (UK) Ring O' 2017 104
DEC   8, 1975 (US) ABC 12148
by Colonel (Doug Bogie) Prod: Doug Bogie
*A: *Cokey Cokey*---Jimmy Kennedy---*3:18*
*B: *Away In A Manger*---Traditional arr. Doug Bogie---*3:54*

Graham Bonnet. At the tender age of 14, singer Graham Bonnet auditioned for a position in a band that featured one Ringo Starr (in his pre-Beatle days) on drums. In 1977, Bonnet finally "passed the audition" and was signed as the first new artist on Ringo's revitalized Ring O' label. As a singer-interpreter (*not* singer-*songwriter*) dependent on choosing the right material, Bonnet had managed one minor hit in the 60's with the Marbles (a Bee Gee's tune, *Only One Woman*). For his debut disc on Ring O', he chose the Bob Dylan classic *It's All Over Now, Baby Blue*, and was backed by musicians Dave Markee (bass), Micky Moody (guitar) and Mike Giles (drums). Pip Williams produced this disc. A follow-up single was issued barely two months later, as if to emphasize the label's new commitment to promoting its artists. Both singles appeared on Bonnet's first album, released in September.

JUN 3, 1977 (UK) Ring O' 2017 105
by Graham Bonnet Prod: Pip Williams
**A: It's All Over Now, Baby Blue*---Bob Dylan---*4:11*
**B: Heroes On My Picture Wall*---Williams—Hutchins---*3:37*

AUG 12, 1977 (UK) Ring O' 2017 106
by Graham Bonnet Prod: Pip Williams
**A: Danny*---Weisman—Wise---*3:18*
**B: Rock Island Line*---Traditional arr. Micky Moody---*1:59*
     From the forthcoming Graham Bonnet album **Graham Bonnet
     Ring O' 2320 103

Carl Grossman. Song writer Carl Grossman was signed to Ring O' records in 1975, and by the end of the year released his first single (in Britain only): *I've Had It/C'mon And Roll*. Both sides were upbeat pop rockers, though *I've Had It* seemed to borrow heavily from Fanny's tune of the same name. The next year, Grossman dug into his files and came up with the song *A Dose Of Rock 'n' Roll* for Ringo's **Rotogravure** LP. The track also served as Ringo's first hit single for Atlantic.

NOV 14, 1975 (UK) Ring O' 2017 103
by Carl Grossman Prod: Pete Gage
A: I've Had It---Carl Grossman---*3:05*
B: C'mon And Roll---Carl Grossman---*2:07*

David Hentschel. The first album release on Ring O' records was an instrumental synthesizer version of, appropriately enough, the tracks on Ringo's **"Ringo"** LP. It was produced and performed by David Hentschel, one of the first artists signed to the new label. Hentschel had worked at Trident Studios in London for several years as a studio engineer. He worked with people such as Paul McCartney, Mama Cass, Nilsson, Genesis, the Nice and Ralph McTell. When Trident bought a synthesizer for the studio in 1973, David began to experiment with it, and his synthesizer work soon turned up on albums by Carly Simon, Jim Webb, Rick Wakeman and Elton John (he was

214

nominated for a Grammy for his work on **Goodbye Yellow Brick Road**). Elton's producer, Gus Dudgeon, introduced Hentschel to John Gilbert, who became his manager. Gilbert played some of David's tapes for Ringo, who then commissioned Hentschel to do the synthesizer version of **"Ringo"**.

FEB 17, 1975 (US) Ring O' 4030
MAR 21, 1975 (UK) Ring O' 2017 101
by David Hentschel Prod: David Hentschel and John Gilbert
A: *Oh My My*---Starkey—Vini Poncia---*3:20*
B: *Devil Woman*---Starkey—Vini Poncia---*3:30*

FEB 17, 1975 (US) Ring O' ST 11372 (LP)
APR 18, 1975 (UK) Ring O' 2320-101 (LP)
by David Hentschel
STA*RTLING MUSIC Prod: David Hentschel and John Gilbert
side one
  Devil Woman---Starkey—Vini Poncia---*3:30*
  Six O' Clock---McCartney---*4:21*
  Step Lightly---Starkey---*3:39*
  Oh My My---Starkey—Vini Poncia---*3:20*
  You're Sixteen (I)---Richard Sherman—Robert Sherman---*2:35*
  You're Sixteen (II)---Richard Sherman—Robert Sherman---*0:30*
side two
  Photograph---Starkey—Harrison---*7:48*
  Have You Seen My Baby---Randy Newman---*5:02*
  I'm The Greatest---Lennon---*3:40*
  Sunshine Life For Me (Sail Away Raymond)---Harrison---*2:56*
  You And Me (Babe)---Harrison—Mal Evans---*4:03*

Bobby Keys. A natural. Bobby Keys had built quite a reputation as *the* horn man in rock music of the late 60's, doing extensive session work with such artists as Delaney and Bonnie. Bobby and Ringo had worked together on a number of projects over the years, including Bobby's 1972 super-star solo LP, released only in England. (George Harrison, Eric Clapton, Dave Mason and Nicky Hopkins were some of the other stars appearing on the LP.) Soon after he set up his new label in 1975, Ringo signed Bobby Keys and turned him loose in the studio. With Trevor Lawrence producing, Bobby came up with the appropriately-named disco tune, *Gimmie The Key* (if you know the title you know all the lyrics!). The record featured Bobby (on horns and vibrashap), Steve Maddeo and Trevor Lawrence (also on horns, with all three doing the vocal chant), Spider Webb (drums), Jesse Ed Davis (guitar), Larry Von Nash (keyboards), and Reggie

McBride (bass). An elongated version of the song was even released to the discos (Ring O' SPRO 8193 running 3:54), but the record didn't launch Bobby's career as a solo act, so he returned to his very lucrative session work.

AUG 25, 1975 (US) Ring O' 4129
SEP 5, 1975 (UK) Ring O' 2017 102
by Bobby Keys Prod: Trevor Lawrence
*A: *Gimmie The Key*—Bobby Keys—Trevor Lawrence—*2:34*
*B: *Honky Tonk (Parts 1 & 2)*—Billy Butler—William Doggett—
   Clifford Scott—Shep Shepherd—*3:20*

Dark Horse By The Numbers

A&M Albums. British Prefix: AMLH

American Prefix: SP

22001	(Splinter) **The Place I Love**
22002	**Shankar Family & Friends**
22003	**Jiva**
22004	(Stairsteps) **2nd Resurrection**
22005	(Henry McCullough) **Mind Your Own Business**
22006	(Splinter) **Harder To Live**
22007	(Shankar) **Music Festival In India**
22008	**Attitudes**

Warner Albums. British (K)/American (DH)

56319/3005	(Harrison) **33 1/3**
56385/3021	(Attitudes) **Good News**
/3022	(Burke) **Keni Burke**
/3023	(Splinter) **Two Man Band**

A&M Singles. British (AMS)/American (DH)

7133/10001	(Shankar) *I Am Missing You/Lust*
7135/10002	(Splinter) *Costafine Town/Elly–May*
5501/ ----	(Splinter) *Drink All Day/Haven't Got Time*
5502/ ----	(Splinter) *China Light/Drink All Day*
---- /10003	(Splinter) *China Light/Haven't Got Time*
5503/ ----	(Splinter) *Which Way Will I Get Home/Green Line Bus*
5504/10004	(Attitudes) *Ain't Live Enough/Whole World's Crazy*
5505/10005	(Stairsteps) *From Us To You/Time*
---- /10006	(Jiva) *Something Goin' On Inside L.A./Take My Love*
5506/ ----	(Splinter) *Halfway There/What Is It*
---- /10007	(Splinter) *Which Way Will I Get Home/What Is It*
5507/ ----	(Stairsteps) *Psado/Throwin' Stones Atcha*
---- /10008	(Attitudes) *Honey Don't Leave L.A./Lend A Hand*
---- /10009	(Stairsteps) *Tell Me Why/Salaam*
---- /10010	(Splinter) *After Five Years/Halfway There*
5508/10011	(Attitudes) *Sweet Summer Music/If We Want To*

Warner Singles. British (K)/American (DRC)

16856/8294	(Harrison) *This Song/Learning How To Love You*
---- /8313	(Harrison) *Crackerbox Palace/Learning How To Love You*
16896/ ----	(Harrison) *True Love/Pure Smokey*
---- /8404	(Attitudes) *Sweet Summer Music/Being Here With You*
16967/ ----	(Harrison) *It's What You Value/Woman Don't Cry For Me*
17009/8439	(Splinter) *Round And Round/I'll Bend For You*
/8452	(Attitudes) *In A Stranger's Arms/Good News*
/8474	(Keni Burke) *Shuffle/From Me To You*

Ring O' By The Numbers

Singles. American/British

4030/2017101	(Hentschel) *Oh My My/Devil Woman*
4129/2017102	(Keys) *Gimmie The Key/Honky Tonk*
---- /2017103	(Grossman) *I've Had It/C'mon And Roll*
---- /2017104	(Colonel) *Cokey Cokey/Away In A Manger*
---- /2017105	(Bonnet) *It's All Over Now, Baby Blue/Heroes On My Picture Wall*
/2017106	(Bonnet) *Danny/Rock Island Line*

Albums. American/British

11372/2320 101	(Hentschel) **Sta*rtling Music**

Penny Lane/
   Strawberry Fields Forever

Capitol 5810 (45)

Not For You!

All record companies treat radio stations differently than they do the general public. They provide them, free of charge, with all of their latest releases in the hope that their records will get airplay. Almost all singles have equivalent "DJ copies" which generally consist of the A (hit) side presented on both sides of the disc, one side in stereo, one side in mono. Aside from this, record companies regularly issue special promotional items, trying to capture the attention of the always harried DJs. Of this latter category, a number of Beatle-related items have gained fairly wide distribution via collectors. The following are some of the major items of this sort.

Penny Lane by The Beatles Capitol P 5810 (February 1967)

The DJ copies of *Penny Lane* differed from the subsequent commercial release by the inclusion of an extra bit of trumpet solo mixed in at the very end of the song. This version was never released as a part of any commercial issuing.

Jet by Wings Apple PRO 6827 (January 1974)
Band On The Run by Wings Apple PRO 6825 (April 1974)
Silly Love Songs by Wings Capitol SPRO 8365 (April 1976)
Let 'Em In by Wings Capitol SPRO 8424 (June 1976)

Each of these songs ran over four minutes, so special DJ cut-downs were issued to stations when the tracks were released as singles. The editing on *Jet* was quite good and tightened the song considerably, no doubt contributing to its top-forty popularity. The other three-cut-downs involved much simpler editing: merely removing a verse. All the commercial copies of these singles retained the original album length running time.

Letting Go by Wings Capitol PRO 8225 (September 1975)

The store copies of this single contained the edited version of this LP track from **Venus and Mars**. However, the mono side of the DJ single contained a new mix of the song, hotter and tighter for top-forty play. It still failed to generate enough interest and the disc died at 39.

Helter Skelter by The Beatles Capitol P-4274 (April 30, 1976)

The intense interest in the Charles Manson murders was rekindled by all the publicity surrounding a two-part television dramatization of the bizarre events, broadcast on CBS, which garnered top ratings across the country. Capitol was just preparing to launch a massive Beatle campaign, spearheaded by a new single and album package. The temptation to issue *Helter Skelter* as that single was quite strong (Manson seemed quite affected by the track and stated that he took the imagery in the song as a blueprint for a black/white race war), but instead the company issued a special limited edition DJ single "to meet programming demands." The disc identified the song as being from the *White Album*, and instantly became a collector's item. Later, *Helter Skelter was* included as the B-side of *Got To Get You Into My Life*, but both tracks were identified as being from the **Rock 'n' Roll Music** repackage. "Helter Skelter," by the way, is the English term for a children's slide (or a spiral slide found in English amusement parks or fairgrounds.)

Balanced For Broadcast--Excerpts From Great New Releases From The Sound Capitol Of The World

    (LP) Capitol PRO 2537 (February 1964)

      includes the Beatles' *This Boy/It Won't Be Long*

    (LP) Capitol PRO 2685 (August 1964)

      includes Peter & Gordon's *A World Without Love*

    (LP) Capitol SPRO 5003 (April 1970)

      includes the Beatles' *Here Comes The Sun*

The Greatest Music Ever Sold (LP) Capitol SPRO 8511/8512 (November 1976)

      includes the Beatles' *Got To Get You Into My Life/Eleanor Rigby/Ob-La-Di, Ob-La-Da*; John's *Imagine*; and Ringo's *You're Sixteen*

Season's Best (2 LPs) WEA SMP 2 (October 1976)

      includes Ringo's *A Dose of Rock 'n' Roll*

These modestly-titled sampler packages were assembled to help radio stations sort through the hundreds of records released each month. (Warner Brothers does the same thing for the general record public with its mail-order loss-leaders.) The Capitol **Balanced For Broadcast** series was a monthly sampler of new Capitol releases. **The Greatest Music Ever Sold** was issued to hype the winter 1976 campaign for Capitol's *Greatest Hits* packages, and **Season's Greetings** called attention to the different Warner-Elektra-Atlantic releases made available just in time for Christmas. Actually, the Beatles rarely appeared on such packages–a provision in their contract specifically limited their inclusion on any sort of "various artists" consumer package. Their own records usually received enough attention at radio stations anyway, so extra hype was unnecessary.

1966 Grammy Award Winners (LP) XTV 123942
includes the Beatles' *Eleanor Rigby*
To help radio stations showcase the Grammy-winning songs of that year, a special LP assembled the winners from the different record labels.

Gerry Goffin & Carole King: Solid Gold (LP) Screen-Gems—
Columbia Music CPL 713
includes the Beatles' *Chains*
Drawing from many different labels, this package showcased different cover versions of Goffin & King songs. Song writers (and their publishing companies!), of course, receive royalties when their songs are performed on the air--by *anybody*.

Special Capitol Open End Interview (7 inch 33 1/3 disc)
Highlights From "Meet The Beatles" Capitol PRO 2548 (January 1964)
includes *Interview* & *I Want To Hold Your Hand* b/w *This Boy* & *It Won't Be Long*
Highlights from "The Beatles' Second Album" Capitol PRO 2598 (April 1964)
includes *Interview* & *Roll Over Beethoven* b/w *Please Mr. Postman* & *Thank You Girl*
"Band On The Run" Open End Interview (LP) (December 1973)
Just ask the right question and the answer will lead right into a song from the latest LP! The comments on the special Capitol discs put out in 1964 lasted only about three minutes, and easily slipped into a station's programming. McCartney's interview, however, ran well over half an hour (depending on how much the DJ ad-libbed from the script), introducing cuts from the new LP. The interview is conspicuous in its failure to elaborate much on the newsworthy events at the time (e.g., the fact that two Wings had taken flight), and Paul's invitation to "come out and see the band when we're in your town" seemed patently absurd. It's doubtful that many stations used this obviously canned "live" interview.

George Harrison Interview Record (LP) Dark Horse (August 1974)
A Personal Music Dialogue With George Harrison At 33 1/3 (LP)
Dark Horse PRO 649 (November 1976)
Dark Horse put together two special interview records with

George Harrison. Neither made any pretense that George was actually in X-radio station's studio, but merely presented an already completed interview for broadcast on any station. Chuck Cassell conducted the first interview in Los Angeles, questioning George on matters ranging from the group Splinter through Ravi Shankar and Friends, and on to spiritualism. Excerpts from both Splinter's and Shankar's first albums were included on the record (George was not yet on Dark Horse). *Radio And Records* editor Mike Harrison conducted the discussion on 33 1/3, George's first album on Dark Horse. This disc was very well layed out--none of the actual songs are included, they were to be inserted from the 33 1/3 disc itself, so the actual interview lasts nearly an hour.

Hear The Beatles Tell All (LP) Vee Jay VJPRO 202 (Fall 1964)

Vee Jay put together a special interview album, recorded during the Beatles' tour of America in August of 1964. It contained two complete interviews, with background music and editing by Lou Adler. Side one, Jim Steck's interview with John Lennon, was one of the most intelligent of that time. Side two, in which Dave Hull interviewed all four Beatles, was less revealing and closer to the average of that era.

Earth News Interviews
Allan Williams July 1975
George Harrison for the week of December 15, 1975
John Lennon for the week of January 26, 1976
Paul McCartney for the week of July 12, 1976

These interviews, provided for a charge through the Earth News Service, were broken into short bits to be distributed throughout the day (and week). During his interviews, Allan Williams gave selections from the as-of-then-unreleased Hamburg tapes their first public airing. Other excerpts from the tapes opened segments of the Harrison and McCartney interviews, though among the cuts used were the non-Beatle vocals on *Hallelujah, I Love Her So* and *Be-Bop-A-Lula*.

Get Off: Anti-Drug Public Service Announcements (2 LPs)

While in Los Angeles working on his **"Ringo"** LP, Ringo cut a thirty second anti-drug public service announcement for this "hands across the water" package of anti-drug spots. His famous drumbeat passage from **Abbey Road** provided the musical backdrop to his no-nonsense message ("Don't take dangerous drugs!").

The Beatles Introduce New Songs Capitol PRO 2720 (September 1964)

Side one included John Lennon's introduction of Cilla Black's song *It's For You*, then the song itself, Paul McCartney's introduction of Peter & Gordon's *I Don't Want To See You Again*, and the song. Both, of course, were Lennon/McCartney compositions, and they both appeared on the B-side sans introductions.

John Lennon On Ronnie Hawkins Cotillion PR 104/105 (Early 1970)

In December of 1969, John stayed with Ronnie Hawkins at his farm house outside Toronto, Canada, while signing each of his three thousand erotic lithographs. Ronnie played his soon-to-be-released LP for John, who liked it. They cut a special promo disc for radio stations to "drop-in" before playing the single, *Down In The Alley*, from the **Ronnie Hawkins** LP. The "Short Rap" preceding the song was just that — five seconds! The "Long Rap" on the flip side, though, ran nearly a minute and a half, since the song didn't follow it.

An Introduction To Roy Harper (LP) Chrysalis PRO 620 (February 1976)
 includes 2 raps by Paul McCartney

To promote his new album **(When An Old Cricketer Leaves The Crease)**, Chrysalis distributed a special dj record featuring an interview with Roy Harper, similar to the first Dark Horse interview disc with George Harrison. Excerpts from the new LP were also included, as well as comments by other musicians, including two tracks by Paul McCartney. In 1977, Paul appeared on Harper's **One Of Those Days In England** LP.

Brung To Ewe By Hal Smith (LP) Apple SPRO 6210 (Spring 1971)

A very strange collection of fifteen short skits featuring Paul and Linda, which were to be used to promote their new album **Ram**. The only recurrent themes are Paul singing *Now Hear This Song Of Mine*, and the repeated recorded bleat from some poor sheep. The production and mixing are rather poor, and it is very doubtful that these spots helped the album's sales very much.

Dialogue From the Film "Let It Be" United Artists (May 1970)

To promote its *Let It Be* film, United Artists issued a special single containing dialogue excerpts from the film. For obvious reasons, of course, no music was included on the disc.

Mike McGear Limited Edition (LP) Warner Brothers (1974)
 Simply Love You/Givin' Grease A Ride/The Man Who Found God On The Moon/Sea Breezes/Rainbow Lady/Leave It
 Warners issued a limited edition (500 copies--each numbered

and then autographed by Mike) of tracks from Mike McGear's forth-coming LP, *McGear, produced by Paul McCartney. The records were given to radio stations by Mike as he made an extensive interview tour of the U.S.

KFWBeatles/You Can't Do That RB 2637/2638 (June 5, 1964)
Los Angeles radio station KFWB and a local music store, Music City, issued (with Capitol's permission) a special promotional item available only through them. The A-side contained an interview conducted with the Beatles, and the B-side was, in fact, the flip of their recent hit single *Can't Buy Me Love*. One of the rare, legitimate local repackagings.

From "Meet The Beatles" (EP) Capitol SXA 2047 (January 1964)
includes *It Won't Be Long/This Boy/All My Loving* b/w *Don't Bother Me/All I've Got To Do/I Wanna Be Your Man*
From "The Beatles' Second Album" (EP) Capitol SXA 2080 (April 1964)
includes *Thank You Girl/Devil In Her Heart/Money* b/w *Long Tall Sally/I Call Your Name/Please Mr. Postman*
From "Something New" (EP) Capitol SXA 2108 (July 1964)
includes *I'll Cry Instead/And I Love Her/Slow Down* b/w *If I Fell/ Tell Me Why/Matchbox*
Three special juke box EPs were issued by Capitol to coincide with the release of these 1964 LPs. Each cardboard sleeve reproduced the original album cover.

Maybe I'm Amazed (12 inch single) Capitol PRO 8574 (February 7, 1977)
Seaside Woman (12 inch single) Epic ASF 361 (June 1977)
The growth of discos created a demand both for extended versions of popular disco hits and for higher quality pressings of tracks not yet on an LP. Thus, the 12-inch single became quite popular. Always on the lookout for another way to catch a DJ's attention, companies increased their production of these discs for radio station use. For one thing, a 12-inch single sent to a station *literally* stood out from all the other singles. Besides, this allowed both the mono and stereo, full-length and cut-down versions (a total of 4) to be included on one disc. And so it was with *Maybe I'm Amazed*. For Linda's debut disc on Epic, that company also issued a 12-inch version of *Seaside Woman* (full length stereo on *both* sides), perhaps *in lieu* of an album.

LIVE
AND
IN COLOR

"And Loved Here In America . . . "

The Beatles appeared "live on stage" literally hundreds upon hundreds of times since John and Paul first met on June 15, 1956. They made their first appearance together at a church hall in Woolton, Liverpool on that day, and played on and off together for years as part of John's band, the Quarrymen. In August of 1958, George Harrison joined them for the opening of the Casbah Club, run by drummer Pete Best's mother, and stayed on to play there and at other small clubs in and around Liverpool. This went on for years, till they finally got a few breaks in 1960 that started them on their long road to stardom. It would be pointless, not to mention impossible, to note each live appearance in their formative years, and even into the early 60's, but a *reasonably complete* guide to their touring careers has been surprisingly absent from Beatle literature for all these years. The best hagiography to date was printed in Richard DiLello's *Longest Cocktail Party*, though even that one missed several major appearances and, more importantly, ended in 1966, thus leaving subsequent accounts of the individual post-Beatle tours widely scattered in different sources.

The following, then, is a guide to the tours and major performances by the individual Beatles from 1960 through 1977.

1960

The Beatles' audition before big-time promoter Larry Parnes led to their first fully professional gig, a two-week tour round the north of Scotland, as the Silver Beatles, backing singer Johnny Gentle. In the late summer, the Beatles journeyed to Hamburg with then-manager Allan Williams and new drummer Pete Best to open club owner Bruno Koschmeider's new venue, the Indra. After two months, their raucous rock show finally proved too much for the neighborhood. The Indra was closed and they were moved to Koschmeider's main club, the Kaiserkeller. There they alternated with Rory Storme and the Hurricanes, seven days a week, from seven in the evening until two in the morning. The German audiences loved loud, aggressive rock music and constantly urged the performing groups to *mak show*. When the Beatles shifted to the competing Top Ten Club in December, the German authorities suddenly found a number of reasons to ask them to leave the country (for one, George was under age). On their return home, they discovered that the seasoning in Hamburg had turned them into a powerhouse band. At their "Welcome Home Concert" at Litherland Town Hall they simply overpowered the audience.

Spring................................Two-week Tour round the north of Scotland, asbacking group behind Johnny Gentle; the Silver Beatles were John, Paul, George, Stu Sutcliffe and Thomas Moore (drums).
AUG-DEC.........................Hamburg, Germany, Indra (2 months)
Hamburg, Germany, Kaiserkeller (2 months)
Hamburg, Germany, Top Ten Club (1 day)
DEC 27..............................Litherland Town Hall

1961

Throughout the year, the Beatles marked time in Liverpool, appearing at a number of local halls including the Casbah, Hambledon Hall, Grosvenor Ballroom and finally, the Cavern Club. They began at the Cavern by guesting for the Swinging Blue Jeans early in the year, but soon had their own "host night" at the club. They were practically a resident band of the club, and it was, of course, at one of their lunchtime sessions that Brian Epstein first heard them perform. During their second trip to Hamburg, Stu Sutcliffe left the group, reducing it to John, Paul, George and Pete Best.

APR-JUL...........................Hamburg, Germany, Top Ten Club
Spring-Winter....................Liverpool, Cavern Club

1962

For most of the year, the Beatles were scheduled for odd bookings at places like the Casbah (not after August!), New Brighton Tower, Norwich Memorial Hall, Majestic Ballroom and the like, while also remaining a permanent fixture at the Cavern Club. They made three more trips to Hamburg, to the newly opened Star Club. It was on the fifth and final trip that Ted "Kingsize" Taylor recorded them on stage. By mid--August they had dumped drummer Pete Best and taken on Ringo Starr, bringing the group to its final, permanent line--up. They also signed a record contract with Parlophone, and their bookings began to reflect both their own increased stature, and the continued growth of successful Epstein--managed Merseyside groups.

APR 23-JUN 4 ....Hamburg, Germany, Star Club
JUN 9...............................Liverpool, Cavern Club
                              Welcome Home Show
JUN 21.............................New Brighton, Tower Ballroom
                              The Beatles on the bill w/Bruce Channel
JUL 1..............................Liverpool, Cavern Club
                              The Beatles w/Gene Vincent
AUG 1.............................Liverpool, Cavern Club
                              The Beatles w/Gerry & The Pacemakers
OCT 12............................New Brighton, Tower Ballroom
                              The Beatles on the bill w/Little Richard, Billy J. Kramer, the Undertakers and Rory Storme
NOV 1--14........................Hamburg, Germany, Star Club
DEC 10............................Peterborough, Embassy Theater
                              The Beatles on the bill w/Frank Ifield, Ted Taylor and Julie Grant
DEC 18--JAN 1.................Hamburg, Germany, Star Club
                              Ted "Kingsize" Taylor records the Beatles on stage.

1963

As *Please Please Me* topped the British charts, Brian Epstein's promotion of the Beatles began in earnest. For almost the entire year, they were signed up with promoter Arthur Howes for a series of "package tours" of Britain. "Package tours" were just that -- one or two main headliners and as many as six or seven supporting acts, each performing no more than 8/10 songs, *twice* a night (6:30 and 8:45, for example), in a different city practically every night. The Beatles started by backing young singing sensation, Helen Shapiro, but by the middle of the Chris Montez/Tommy Roe tour they had, in fact, if not in billing, become the headliners. Already, the emotional strains of "Beatlemania" were infecting the concerts. In between the package tours, the Beatles appeared in an endless stream of individual performances, including the *New Musical Express* Poll Winner's Concert, *Sunday Night At The London Palladium* (topping

the bill), and the prestigious Royal Variety Show, which also in--
cluded Tommy Steele, Wilfred Bramwell, and Marlene Dietrich.
The press coverage of the wild mobs outside the theatre for the
London Palladium performance marked the beginning of the never-
ending news analysis of Beatlemania. (TV news crews filmed the
November 16 Bournemouth Concert giving Americans a taste of
Beatlemania in 1963). The group made its final appearance at the
Cavern Club in August, and closed the year with a special Christmas
show.

January..............................Short Tour of Scotland

HELEN SHAPIRO TOUR w/The Beatles, Danny Williams, Kenny Lynch,
  The Honeys, The Kestrels, Dave Allen and Red Price Band
FEB 2...............................Bradford, Gaumont
FEB 5...............................Doncaster, Gaumont
FEB 6...............................Bedford, Granada
FEB 7...............................Wakefield, ABC
FEB 8...............................Carlisle, ABC
FEB 9...............................Sunderland, Odeon
FEB 10.............................Peterborough, Embassy
FEB 23.............................Mansfield, Granada
FEB 24.............................Coventry, Coventry Theater
FEB 26.............................Taunton, Odeon
FEB 27.............................York, Rialto
FEB 28.............................Shrewsbury, Granada
MAR 1..............................Southport, Odeon
MAR 2..............................Sheffield, City Hall
MAR 3..............................Hanley, Gaumont

CHRIS MONTEZ & TOMMY ROE TOUR w/The Beatles, The Viscounts,
  Debbie Lee, Tony Marsh and Terry Young Six
MAR 9..............................East Ham, Granada
MAR 10............................Birmingham, Hippodrome
MAR 12............................Bedford, Granada
MAR 13............................York, Rialto
MAR 14............................Wolverhampton, Gaumont
MAR 15............................Bristol, Colston Hall
MAR 16............................Sheffield, City Hall
MAR 17............................Peterborough, Embassy
MAR 18............................Gloucester, ABC
MAR 19............................Cambridge, ABC
MAR 20............................Rumford, Ritz
MAR 21............................Croydon, ABC
MAR 22............................Doncaster, Gaumont
MAR 23............................New Castle, City Hall
MAR 24............................Liverpool, Empire
MAR 26............................Mansfield, Granada

```
MAR 27............................Northampton, ABC
MAR 28............................Exeter, ABC
MAR 29............................Lewisham, Odeon
MAR 30............................Portsmouth, Guildhall
MAR 31............................Leicester, De Montfort Hall

APR 21............................Wembley, Empire Pool
                                  New Musical Express Poll Winner's Concert

MAY 9.............................London, Royal Albert Hall
MAY 11............................Nelson, Imperial Ballroom
MAY 14............................Sunderland, Rank
MAY 15............................Chester Royalty
```

THE BEATLES' TOUR w/Roy Orbison, Gerry & The Pacemakers and David Macbeth, Louise Cordet, Erkey Grant, Ian Crawford, Terry Young Six and Tony Marsh

```
MAY 18............................Slough, Granada
MAY 19............................Hanley, Gaumont
MAY 20............................Southampton, Gaumont
MAY 22............................Ipswich, Gaumont
MAY 23............................Nottingham, Odeon
MAY 24............................Walthamstow, Granada
MAY 25............................Sheffield, City Hall
MAY 26............................Liverpool, Empire
MAY 27............................Cardiff, Capitol
MAY 28............................Worcester, Gaumont
MAY 29............................York, Rialto
MAY 30............................Manchester, Odeon
MAY 31............................Southend, Odeon
JUN 1.............................Tooting, Granada
JUN 2.............................Brighton, Hippodrome
JUN 3.............................Woolwich, Granada
JUN 4.............................Birmingham, Town Hall
JUN 5.............................Leeds, Odeon
JUN 7.............................Glasgow, Odeon
JUN 8.............................Newcastle, City Hall
JUN 9.............................King George's Hall

JUN 12............................Liverpool, Grafton Ballroom
                                  Charity Concert: Wayward Society for Pre--
                                  vention of Cruelty to Children
JUN 14............................Liverpool, New Brighton Tower
JUN 16............................Romford, Odeon
                                  The Beatles w/Gerry & the Pacemakers, Billy
                                  J. Kramer
JUN 22............................Abergavenny, Town Hall
JUN 28............................Leeds, Queen's Hall
JUN 30............................Yarmouth, Regal
```

```
JUL 5................................Oldhill, Plaza Ballroom
JUL 7................................Blackpool, ABC
JUL 8--13..........................Margate, Winter Gardens
                                   The Beatles w/Billy J. Kramer
JUL 21..............................Blackpool, Queens
JUL 22--27........................Weston, Super Mare Odeon
                                   The Beatles w/Gerry & the Pacemakers,
                                   Tommy Quickly
JUL 28..............................Great Yarmouth, ABC
AUG 1...............................Southport
AUG 2...............................Liverpool, Grafton Ballroom
                                   The Beatles w/Undertakers, Dennisons, Cas--
                                   cades
AUG 3...............................Liverpool, Cavern Club (final appearance)
                                   The Beatles w/Escorts and Merseybeats
AUG 4...............................Blackpool, Queens
AUG 6--9..........................Jersey, St. Helier Springfield Ballroom
AUG 11.............................Blackpool, ABC
AUG 12--17......................Llandudno, Odeon
                                   The Beatles w/Billy J. Kramer, Tommy Quickly
AUG 18.............................Torquay, Princess Theatre
AUG 19--24......................Bournemouth, Gaumont
                                   The Beatles w/Billy J. Kramer, Tommy Quickly
AUG 25.............................Blackpool, ABC
AUG 26--31......................Southport, Odeon
                                   The Beatles w/Gerry & the Pacemakers,
                                   Tommy Quickly
```

THE BEATLES MINI--TOUR w/Mike Berry

```
SEP 4................................Worcester, Gaumont
SEP 5................................Taunton, Gaumont
SEP 6................................Luton, Odeon
SEP 7................................Croydon, Fairfields
SEP 8................................Blackpool, ABC

SEP 13..............................Preston, Public Hall
SEP 14..............................Nantwich, Memorial Hall
SEP 15..............................London, Royal Albert Hall
OCT 5...............................Glasgow Concert Hall
OCT 6...............................Kirkcaldy Regal
OCT 7...............................Dundee Caird Hall
OCT 13.............................London, Palladium
                                   Broadcast Live on Sunday Night At The
                                   London Palladium
OCT 15.............................Southport, Floral
OCT 18.............................Shrewsbury, Music Hall

OCT 24--29......................Sweden (5 concerts)
```

THE BEATLES' AUTUMN TOUR w/Peter Jay & the Jaywalkers, the
Brook Brothers, Kestrels, Vernons Girls
NOV 1..............................Cheltenham, Odeon
NOV 2..............................Sheffield, City Hall
NOV 3..............................Leeds, Odeon
NOV 4..............................London, Prince Of Wales Theatre
Royal Variety Show
NOV 5..............................Slough, Adelphi
NOV 6..............................Northampton, ABC
NOV 7..............................Dublin, Ireland, Adelphi
NOV 8..............................Belfast, Ireland, ABC
NOV 9..............................East Ham, Granada
NOV 10............................Birmingham, Hippodrome
NOV 13............................Plymouth, ABC
NOV 14............................Exeter, ABC
NOV 15............................Bristol, Colston Hall
NOV 16............................Bournemouth, Winter Gardens
NOV 17............................Coventry, Coventry Theater
NOV 19............................Wolverhampton, Gaumont
NOV 20............................Manchester, Adrwick Apollo
NOV 21............................Carlisle, ABC
NOV 22............................Stockton, Globe
NOV 23............................Newcastle, City Hall
NOV 24............................Hull, ABC
NOV 26............................Cambridge, ABC
NOV 27............................York, Rialto
NOV 28............................Lincoln, ABC
NOV 29............................Huddersfield, ABC
NOV 30............................Sunderland, Empire
DEC 1..............................Leicester, De Montfort Hall
DEC 2..............................London, Grosvenor Hotel *(charity show)*
DEC 3..............................Portsmouth, Guild Hall
DEC 7..............................Liverpool, Empire
DEC 8..............................Lewisham, Odeon
DEC 9..............................Southend, Odeon
DEC 10............................Doncaster, Gaumont
DEC 11............................Scarborough, Futurist
DEC 12............................Nottingham, Odeon
DEC 13............................Southampton, Gaumont

DEC 14............................Wimbledon Palais
Southern England Fan Club Convention

THE BEATLES' CHRISTMAS SHOW w/Rolf Harris, Billy J. Kramer,
Fourmost, Cilla Black, Tommy Quickly, the Barron Knights
DEC 21............................Bradford, Gaumont *(previews)*
DEC 22............................Liverpool, Empire *(previews)*
DEC 24............................Finsbury Park, Astoria *(opening night)*
DEC 26--Jan 11................Finsbury Park, Astoria *(excluding Sundays)*

1964

In 1964, the Beatles began touring the world, and in doing so pioneered many aspects of large–scale performing by rock stars. The crude staging effects seem amateur by today's standards, but were important in developing a foundation for later, more sophis-ticated shows such as Wings' 1976 tour. Despite the difficulties, of course, from their very first concert at the Washington Coliseum, shown in March as a closed–circuit theatre film, the Beatles' con-quest of America ended years of frustration by British performers. All of their foreign ventures, though, didn't set the world on fire. France was noticeably cool to the group, and they missed selling out the Stockholm Ice Stadium (capacity: 8,500) by several thou-sand. On the eve of the world tour in June, Ringo became ill. Drummer Jimmy Nicol from Georgie Fame's Blue Flames replaced him, until Ringo rejoined the group in Melbourne, Australia. The Beatles ended an exhausting year of touring with "Another Beatles Christmas Show."

JAN 16--FEB 4..................Paris, France, Olympia Theater
The Beatles w/Trini Lopez and Sylvie Vartan

THE BEATLES' FIRST VISIT TO AMERICA w/Tommy Roe, Chiffons, Caravelles
FEB 11.............................Washington, DC, Coliseum
FEB 12.............................New York, Carnegie Hall

MAR 30--APR 4.................Liverpool, Empire
APR 26.............................Wembley, Empire Pool
New Musical Express Poll Winner's Concert
APR 29.............................Edinburgh
APR 30.............................Glasgow, Odeon
MAY 31...........................London, Prince Of Wales Theatre

THE BEATLES' WORLD TOUR
JUN 4................................Copenhagen, Denmark, Tivoli Garden
JUN 6................................Blokker, Denmark, Exhibition Hall
JUN 10..............................Hong Kong, Princess Theater
JUN 12--13........................Adelaide, Australia, Centennial Hall
JUN 15..............................Melbourne, Australia, Festival Hall
JUN 18--20........................Sydney, Australia, Sydney Stadium
JUN 22--23........................Wellington, New Zealand
JUN 24--25........................Aukland, New Zealand
JUN 26--27........................Christchurch, New Zealand
JUN 29..............................Brisbane, Australia

JUL 12..............................Brighton, Hippodrome
The Beatles w/Fourmost, Jimmy Nicol

JUL 26............................Blackpool, Opera House
JUL 28--29......................Stockholm, Sweden, Ice Hockey Stadium
AUG 2............................Bournemouth, Gaumont
AUG 16..........................Scarborough, Futuris

THE BEATLES' FIRST AMERICAN TOUR w/Jackie De Shannon,
Righteous Brothers, Bill Black Combo, Exciters
AUG 19..........................San Francisco, Cow Palace
AUG 20..........................Las Vegas, Convention Hall
AUG 21..........................Seattle, Municipal Stadium
AUG 22..........................Vancouver, Empire Stadium
AUG 23..........................Los Angeles, Hollywood Bowl
AUG 26..........................Denver, Red Rock Stadium
AUG 27..........................Cincinnati, Gardens
AUG 28..........................New York, Forest Hills Stadium
AUG 30..........................Atlantic City, Convention Hall
SEP 2............................Philadelphia, Convention Hall
SEP 3............................Indianapolis, State Fair Coliseum
SEP 4............................Milwaukee, Auditorium
SEP 5............................Chicago, International Amphitheater
SEP 6............................Detroit, Olympia Stadium
SEP 7............................Toronto, Maple Leaf Gardens
SEP 8............................Montreal, Forum
SEP 11..........................Jacksonville, Gator Bowl
SEP 12..........................Boston, Boston Gardens
SEP 13..........................Baltimore, Civic Center
SEP 14..........................Pittsburgh, Civic Arena
SEP 15..........................Cleveland, Public Auditorium
SEP 16..........................New Orleans, City Park Stadium
SEP 17..........................Kansas City, Municipal Stadium
SEP 18..........................Dallas, Memorial Coliseum
SEP 20..........................New York City, Paramount Theater *(charity
                                concert)*

THE BEATLES' AUTUMN TOUR w/Mary Wells, Tommy Quickly,
Sounds Incorporated, Michael Haslam, Remo Four, Rustiks, Bob Bain
OCT 9............................Bradford, Gaumont
OCT 10..........................Leicester, De Montfort Hall
OCT 11..........................Birmingham, Odeon
OCT 13..........................Wigan, ABC
OCT 14..........................Manchester Adrwick, Apollo
OCT 15..........................Stockton, Globe
OCT 16..........................Hull, ABC
OCT 19..........................Edinburgh, ABC
OCT 20..........................Dundee, Caird Hall
OCT 21..........................Glasgow, Odeon
OCT 22..........................Leeds, Odeon
OCT 23..........................Kilburn, Gaumont State
OCT 24..........................Walthamstow, Granada
OCT 25..........................Brighton, Hippodrome

```
OCT 28...........................Exeter, ABC
OCT 29...........................Plymouth, ABC
OCT 30...........................Bournemouth, Gaumont
OCT 31...........................Ipswich, Gaumont
NOV 1............................Finsbury Park, Astoria
NOV 2............................Belfast
NOV 4............................Luton, Ritz
NOV 5............................Nottingham, Odeon
NOV 6............................Southampton, Gaumont
NOV 7............................Cardiff, Capitol
NOV 8............................Liverpool, Empire
NOV 9............................Sheffield, City Hall
NOV 10..........................Bristol, Colston Hall
```

ANOTHER BEATLES' CHRISTMAS SHOW w/Freddie & the Dreamers, Yardbirds, Jimmy Savile, Sounds Incorporated, Elkie Brooks, and the Mike Cotton Sound

```
DEC 24...........................Hammersmith, Odeon (opening night)
DEC 26--JAN 16...............Hammersmith, Odeon (excluding Sundays)
```

1965

Busy with many other projects, and increasingly depressed at being held prisoner by the necessary security surrounding a concert tour anyway, the Beatles limited themselves to three quick tours. In fact, the British leg in December was a surprise last minute ad--dition and their last ever tour of Britain. On tour, the huge (over 55,000) Shea Stadium concert in New York was filmed for a TV documentary, and the Hollywood Bowl concert was recorded by Capitol for a possible live album, finally released in 1977 (though actually combining recordings from both the 1965 and 1964 Hollywood Bowl concerts).

```
APR 11...........................Wembley, Empire Pool
                                New Musical Express Poll Winner's Concert
```

THE BEATLES' EUROPEAN TOUR
```
JUN 20...........................Paris, France, Palais des Sports
JUN 22...........................Lyons, France, Palais d'Hiver
JUN 24...........................Milan, Italy, Velodromo Vigonelli
JUN 26...........................Genoa, Italy, Palais des Sports
JUN 27...........................Rome, Italy, Adriana Hotel
JUN 30...........................Nice, France, Palais des Fetes
JUL 2............................Madrid, Spain, Monumental Bullring
JUL 3............................Barcelona, Spain, Barcelona Bullring
```

THE BEATLES' AMERICAN TOUR w/King Curtis Band, Brenda Holl--
oway, Sounds Incorporated
AUG 15--16.......................New York, Shea Stadium
AUG 17...........................Toronto, Maple Leaf Stadium
AUG 18...........................Atlanta, Atlanta Stadium
AUG 19...........................Houston, Sam Houston Coliseum
AUG 20...........................Chicago, Comiskey Park
AUG 21...........................Minneapolis, Metropolitan Stadium
AUG 22...........................Portland, Portland Coliseum
AUG 28...........................San Diego, Balboa Stadium
AUG 29--30.......................Los Angeles, Hollywood Bowl
AUG 31...........................San Francisco, Cow Palace

THE BEATLES' BRITISH TOUR w/The Moody Blues, Paramounts,
Koobas, Beryl Marsden, Steve Aldo
DEC 3............................Glasgow, Odeon
DEC 4............................Newcastle, City Hall
DEC 5............................Liverpool, Empire
DEC 7............................Manchester Adrwick, Apollo
DEC 8............................Sheffield, City Hall
DEC 9............................Birmingham, Odeon
DEC 10...........................Hammersmith, Odeon
DEC 11...........................Finsbury Park, Astoria
DEC 12...........................Cardiff, Capitol

1966

Even though their touring schedule had been reduced to little
more than a month for 1966, it was in many ways the most de--
pressing ever. A film of their 1966 Japanese concert reveals a group
going through the motions, with not much energy behind them.
The incidents on this last tour only added to the normal aggrava-
tion. After performing before their largest concert crowd ever
(100,000) in Manila, the Beatles became involved in an alleged
snubbing of that country's President. The airport send--off the
next day was akin to a lynching party, and the Beatles were rough--
ed up in the escape. No sooner had they touched down in America,
then they were embroiled in a new controversy: John's statement
that the Beatles were more popular than Jesus Christ. Though
Lennon's "apology" soon took the matter from the front pages,
it set the mood for the whole tour. Even pop journalists covering
the tour as a *tour* recognized that the time had come for the Beatles
to move on. The superbowl concerts were going nowhere, and
certainly couldn't keep up with the Beatles' music. The Beatles
made their last appearance together in concert at Candlestick Park
in San Francisco.

Their last British appearance, though, was considerably more upbeat and exciting. It occurred earlier in the year, before any of the touring had begun, at the *New Musical Express* Poll Winner's Concert, a veritable who's who of 60's British rock (Small Faces, Spencer Davis, Roy Orbison, Yardbirds, and Cliff Richard were but a few of the performers). Closing the entire show were perfor--mances by the Who, the Rolling Stones and, finally, the Beatles. Quite a memorable finale. Members of the Beatles would not per--form in concert again until 1969.

MAY 1...............................Wembley, Empire Pool
                        New Musical Express Poll Winner's Concert

BEATLES' TOUR OF GERMANY AND JAPAN w/Cliff Bennett & the Rebel Rousers, Peter & Gordon
JUN 24............................Munich, Germany, Circus Krone
JUN 25............................Essen, Germany, Grugahalle
JUN 26............................Hamburg, Germany, Ernst Merck Halle
JUN 30--JUL 1.................Tokyo, Japan, Martial Arts Hall
JUL 4..............................Manila, Philippines, Araneta Coliseum

BEATLES' AMERICAN TOUR w/The Ronettes and The Cyrkle
AUG 12...........................Chicago, International Amphitheater
AUG 13...........................Detroit, Olympia Stadium
AUG 14...........................Cleveland, Municipal Stadium
AUG 15...........................Washington, DC, Washington Stadium
AUG 16...........................Philadelphia, Philadelphia Stadium
AUG 17...........................Toronto, Maple Leaf Gardens
AUG 18...........................Boston, Suffolk Downs Racetrack
AUG 19...........................Memphis, Memphis Coliseum
AUG 20...........................Cincinnati, Crosley Field
AUG 21...........................St. Louis, Busch Stadium
AUG 23--24.....................New York, Shea Stadium
AUG 25...........................Seattle, Seattle Coliseum
AUG 28...........................Los Angeles, Dodger Stadium
AUG 29...........................San Francisco, Candlestick Park

1969

The Beatles made their last public appearance as a group at their famed roof--top concert, January 30, 1969. Film director Michael Lindsay--Hogg set up his cameras and the Beatles, along with Billy Preston, set up their equipment on the roof of the Apple building. As depicted in the *Let It Be* film, they sang *I've Got A Feeling, One After 909, I Dig A Pony* and *Get Back* – before local police asked them to please cease and desist, which they did, leaving the world to wait for the ever–anticipated reunion concert. By the end of the year, though, both John and George had stepped back on stage.

John and Yoko were, by 1969, inseparable and in the midst of an aggressive public life. Early in the year they took part in an avant garde jazz concert recorded and issued on the Zapple LP **Life With The Lions**. In the fall, John electrified the Toronto Peace Festival by appearing live with his Plastic Ono Band, a spur--of--the--moment group which consisted of Eric Clapton on guitar, Klaus Voorman on bass, Alan White on drums, Yoko Ono on vocals, and John himself on guitar and vocals. This entire concert appearance was issued as the **Live Peace In Toronto** LP.

George Harrison took his cue from friend Eric Clapton, who had joined the Delaney and Bonnie tour of England. After their Royal Albert Hall concert, George went backstage and arranged to join them, too. He played with the group its last weekend in England, and stayed with them for their swing through Scandinavia. He brought the whole entourage to London's Lyceum Gallery for John's UNICEF benefit concert on December 15. The Delaney & Bonnie & Friends Croydon concert was issued as the **Delaney & Bonnie On Tour** LP, while highlights from the Lyceum concert were recorded and issued on **Sometime In New York City**.

MAR 2...............................Cambridge, Lady Mitchell Hall
                                                         John Lennon & Yoko Ono
SEP 13.............................Toronto, Varsity Stadium
                                                         John Lennon and the Plastic Ono Band

DELANEY AND BONNIE & FRIENDS w/Eric Clapton and George Harrison
DEC 5...............................Newcastle, City Hall
DEC 6...............................Liverpool, Empire
DEC 7...............................Croydon, Fairfield Hall
DEC 10--14.......................Tour of Scandinavia

DEC 15.............................London, Lyceum Gallery
                                                         John Lennon and the Plastic Ono Supergroup, featuring George Harrison and Delaney and Bonnie and Friends

1971

John made two concert appearances in 1971. The first was a surprise guest spot with Yoko in the encore to a Frank Zappa show at the Fillmore East in New York, recorded and released on -- what else -- **Sometime In New York City**. The second was at a benefit rally in Ann Arbor, Michigan for imprisoned radical, John Sinclair. Joining John and Yoko on stage was Jerry Rubin (on bongos). George had a far more impressive backup band for his one concert appearance of the year, the Concert for Bangla Desh. Ringo Starr, Bob Dylan, Eric Clapton and others joined in the two shows at Madison Square Garden. A film and a three–record set were issued, preserving the concert from beginning to end.

JUN 6................................New York, Fillmore East
Frank Zappa & The Mothers of Invention, joined by John Lennon and Yoko Ono
AUG 1..............................New York, Madison Square Garden *(2 shows)*
The Special Benefit Concert for Bangla Desh, featuring George Harrison, Ringo Starr, Bob Dylan, Eric Clapton, Billy Preston, Leon Russell, Ravi Shankar and others
DEC 11............................Ann Arbor, Michigan
John Lennon and Yoko Ono join John Sinclair Rally

1972

In the *Let It Be* film, Paul expressed his desire to get back on the road with the Beatles. To avoid all the touring hassles of the past, he suggested they turn up unannounced and just play, charg– ing a nominal fee. The Beatles never tried it, but in February of 1972, Paul did. He took his new band Wings onto the British uni– versity circuit. There, Henry McCullough (guitar), Denny Seiwell (drums), Denny Laine (guitar), the lovely Linda (keyboards), and Paul himself found out if they could play together. For two weeks in February, they'd turn up at a university, ask if they could play there the next day, and set up – sometimes in a gym, sometimes even on a stage. The first "historic" Wings concert, February 9 at Nottingham, included numbers like *Give Ireland Back To The Irish, Blue Moon Of Kentucky, Seaside Woman, Bip Bop, The Mess* and *Lucille*. (Paul would not include Beatle selections in his concerts for several years.) Wings next conducted a summer tour of Europe, building both confidence and a reputation (the dates of this tour were announced in advance). The only recording released from these tours was *The Mess*, the flip side of *My Love*.

Stateside, John held a special benefit concert (dubbed the "One To One" show) for the Willowbrook school for handicapped children. The show featured John and Yoko, backed by the Elephant's Memory band. Stevie Wonder and Sha--Na--Na were among the guest artists.   Highlights from the performance were broadcast on ABC TV on December 14, 1972.

WINGS' UNIVERSITY TOUR

FEB 9	Nottingham University
FEB 10--12	York University
	University at Hull
FEB 14--19	University at Lancaster
	University at Leeds
	Sheffield University
	University at Salford (Manchester)
FEB 21--23	University at Birmingham
	University at Swansea

WINGS' TOUR OF EUROPE

JUL 9	Chateau Vallon, France, Centre Culturale
JUL 12	Juan Les Pins, France
JUL 13	Arles, France, Theatre Antique
JUL 14	Lyon, France
JUL 16	Paris, France, Olympia
JUL 18	Munich, Germany, Circus Krone
JUL 19	Frankfurt, Germany, Offenbach Hall
JUL 21	Zurich, Switzerland, Congress Halle
JUL 22	Montreux, Switzerland, Pavillion
AUG 1	Copenhagen, Denmark, KB Hall
AUG 4	Helsinki, Finland, Maess Hall
AUG 5	Turke, Finland, Idraets
AUG 7	Stockholm, Sweden, Tivoli Gardens
AUG 8	Oerebro, Sweden, Idretis Hall
AUG 9	Oslo, Norway
AUG 10	Gothenburg, Sweden, Scandinavian
AUG 11	Lund, Sweden, Olympean
AUG 13	Odense, Denmark, Flyns Farum
AUG 14	Aarhus, Denmark, Wejlby
AUG 16	Hanover, Germany
AUG 17	Gronnegan, Holland, Evenmanten
AUG 18	Rotterdam, Holland, Doelan
AUG 19	Breda, Holland, Turschip
AUG 20	Amsterdam, Holland, Concert Gerbou
AUG 22	Brussels, Belgium, Circue Royale
AUG 24	Berlin, Germany, Deutschland Halle
AUG 30	New York, Madison Square Garden *(2 shows)* *John Lennon & Yoko Ono w/Elephant's Memory, Stevie Wonder, Sha--Na--Na and others in the "One To One" Concert*

1973

Wings conducted its first scheduled British tour in the spring, following a well--received surprise appearance in a benefit show at London's Hard Rock Cafe. On its British tour, as it had from the very beginning, Wings performed without any warm--up act, as--suming full responsibility for a good show. They drew generally favorable reviews. By the end of the year, though, two Wings (Henry McCullough and Denny Seiwell) had left the group. Paul's future performing plans were set back a bit, then, as he had to search for two new members.

MAR 18.............................London, Hard Rock Cafe
Wings at a benefit show for Release

WINGS' BRITISH TOUR
MAY 11.............................Bristol, Hippodrome
MAY 12.............................Oxford, New Theatre
MAY 13.............................Cardiff, Capitol Theatre
MAY 15.............................Bournemouth, Winter Gardens
MAY 16--17.......................Manchester, Hard Rock
MAY 18.............................Liverpool, Empire
MAY 19.............................Leeds, University
MAY 21.............................Preston, Guildhall
MAY 22--23.......................Edinburgh, Odeon
MAY 24.............................Glasgow, Greens Playhouse
MAY 25--27.......................Hammersmith, Odeon
JUL 4...............................Sheffield, City Hall
JUL 6...............................Birmingham, Odeon
JUL 9...............................Leicester, Odeon
JUL 10..............................Newcastle, City Hall

1974

George Harrison tried his own full--fledged tour of America late in the year, the first ex–Beatle to do so (50 concerts in 27 cities over 7 weeks). He was accompanied by Billy Preston on key--boards, Willie Weeks on bass, Andy Newmark on drums, Robben Ford on guitar, Emil Richards on percussion, Chuck Findley on trumpet and trombone, and Tom Scott on saxes and woodwinds. Unlike Paul, Geroge worked an additional act into the show: Ravi Shankar, who led a group of Indian musicians. Generally, they would come on in the middle of the first half, and close that part of the show. George's strained voice, his dogged refusal to play the part of "Beatle George," and the general arrangement of the show – Harrison was all but lost in an army of musicians, in–

cluding over a dozen Indian performers with Ravi Shankar -- left some fans disappointed. The critics were fairly negative at the opening leg along the west coast, but seemed more receptive midway through the tour, perhaps finding the show better than the first reports led them to expect. Ravi Shankar was taken ill after the Chicago performance and missed several dates.

John Lennon, meanwhile, made good on his promise to Elton John that if the song they had just recorded together got to number one, he'd appear on stage to sing it with Elton. It did and John did. On Thanksgiving day Lennon stepped onto the stage of Madison Square Garden during Elton's concert, and the two of them sang *Whatever Gets You Thru The Night, Lucy In The Sky With Diamonds,* and *I Saw Her Standing There.* That last track was issued as the B–side to Elton John's *Philadelphia Freedom* single.

GEORGE HARRISON'S AMERICAN TOUR w/Ravi Shankar
NOV 2................................Vancouver, Pacific Coliseum
NOV 4................................Seattle, Seattle Center Coliseum
NOV 7................................San Francisco, Cow Palace
NOV 8................................Oakland, Coliseum
NOV 10..............................Long Beach, Arena
NOV 11--12.......................Los Angeles, Forum
NOV 14..............................Phoenix
NOV 16..............................Salt Lake City, Salt Palace
NOV 18..............................Denver, Coliseum
NOV 20..............................St. Louis, Arena
NOV 21..............................Tulsa, Civic Center
NOV 22..............................Fort Worth
NOV 24..............................Houston, Hofheinz Pavilion
NOV 26..............................Baton Rouge, LSU Assembly Center
NOV 27..............................Memphis, Mid--South Coliseum
NOV 28..............................Atlanta, Omni
NOV 30..............................Chicago, Stadium
DEC 2................................Cleveland, Coliseum
DEC 4................................Detroit, Olympia Stadium
DEC 6................................Toronto, Maple Leaf Gardens
DEC 8................................Montreal, Forum
DEC 10..............................Boston, Garden
DEC 11..............................Providence, Civic Center
DEC 13..............................Washington, DC, Capitol Centre
DEC 15..............................Long Island, Nassau Coliseum
DEC 16--17.......................Philadelphia, Spectrum
DEC 19--20.......................New York, Madison Square Garden

NOV 28..............................New York, Madison Square Garden
Elton John w/John Lennon

1975

Paul finally commenced his long--planned world tour, with a new Wings line--up: Paul (bass), Linda (keyboards), Denny Laine (guitar), Jimmy McCulloch (guitar), and Joe English (drums). They first launched a tour of Britain, followed by a swing through Australia. A planned tour through Japan was cancelled due to a visa problem. The group was augmented by a four man horn sec--tion: Tony Dorsey (trombone), Howie Casey (saxophone), Steve Howard (trumpet, flugelhorn) and Thadeus Richard (saxophone). In addition to the expected work--out of Wings' hits, Paul delighted the crowds by comfortably mixing about a half--dozen Beatle tunes into the show.

WINGS' BRITISH TOUR
SEP 9..............................Southampton, Gaumont
SEP 10.............................Bristol, Hippodrome
SEP 11.............................Cardiff, Capitol Theatre
SEP 12.............................Manchester, Free Trade Hall
SEP 13.............................Birmingham, Hippodrome
SEP 15.............................Liverpool, Empire
SEP 16.............................Newcastle, City Hall
SEP 17--18.......................Hammersmith, Odeon
SEP 20.............................Edinburgh, Usher Hall
SEP 21.............................Glasgow, Apollo
SEP 23.............................Dundee, Caird Hall

WINGS' AUSTRALIAN TOUR
NOV 1..............................Perth, Australia, Entertainment Center
NOV 4--5.........................Adelaide, Australia, Apollo Stadium
NOV 7--8.........................Sydney, Australia, Horden Pavilion
NOV 10--11......................Brisbane, Australia, Festival Hall
NOV 13--14......................Melbourne, Australia, Myer Music Bowl

1976

It was all Wings in 1976. Though the American tour was slightly delayed by an injury to Jimmy McCulloch at the end of the swing through Europe, once Wings reached America they could do no wrong. Reviews were ecstatic. After the conquest of America, Wings took one more swing through Europe and then ended the year--long world tour back in England. A massive three--record set was issued from the American tour, containing the en--tire concert, all thirty numbers.

WINGS' EUROPEAN TOUR

MAR 20--21......................Copenhagen, Denmark, Falkoner Theatre
MAR 23...........................Berlin, Germany, Deutschland Halle
MAR 25...........................Rotterdam, Netherlands, Ahoy Sports Stadium
MAR 26...........................Paris, France, Pavillion

WINGS' AMERICAN TOUR

MAY 3...............................Fort Worth, TCCC
MAY 4...............................Houston, Summit
MAY 7--8..........................Detroit, Olympia
MAY 9.............................Toronto, Maple Leaf Garden
MAY 10...........................Cleveland, Richfield Coliseum
MAY 12 & 14....................Philadelphia, Spectrum
MAY 15--16.....................Washington, DC, Capitol Center
MAY 18--19.....................Atlanta, Omni
MAY 21...........................Long Island, Nassau Coliseum
MAY 22...........................Boston, Garden
MAY 24--25.....................New York, Madison Square Garden
MAY 27...........................Cincinnati, River Front Stadium
MAY 29...........................Kansas City, Kemper Arena
MAY 31--JUN 2.................Chicago, Stadium
JUN 4..............................St. Paul, Civic Centre
JUN 7..............................Denver, McNichols Arena
JUN 10............................Seattle, Seattle King Dome
JUN 13--14......................San Francisco, Cow Palace
JUN 16............................San Diego, Sports Arena
JUN 18............................Tuscon, Community Forum
JUN 21--23......................Los Angeles, Forum

WINGS' EUROPEAN TOUR--II

SEP 19.............................Vienna, Austria
SEP 21.............................Zagreb, Yugoslavia
SEP 25.............................Venice, Italy, Piazza San Marco
                                Special UNESCO Benefit Concert
SEP 27.............................Munich, Germany

OCT 19--21......................Wembley, Empire Pool

Yesterday   Parlophone GEP 8948 (EP)

Yesterday/I Should Have Known Better   EMI R 6013 (45)

Top Of The Pops

The following are the weekly chart positions of Beatle and Beatle-related records released in Britain during 1976 and 1977.

The chart positions are taken from *Melody Maker*'s weekly Top 30 Singles and Top 30 Album charts. Both the singles and the albums are included in the same listing.

All records are by the Beatles unless otherwise indicated. The following abbreviations are used to identify the other artists.

DBw--David Bowie
J--John Lennon
P/W--Paul McCartney & Wings
RdS--Rod Stewart
RS--Rolling Stones

For a listing of British and American chart positions before 1976, consult *All Together Now*.

Melody Maker
Charts

1976

	JAN				FEB				MAR
	10	17	24	31	7	14	21	28	6
Shaved Fish (LP)–J	13	16	21	23					
(Rolled Gold (LP)–RS)	10	11	11	10	13	16	23	22	28

NO RECORDS ON CHARTS: March 13, 1976

	MAR		APR				MAY					JUN
	20	27	3	10	17	24	1	8	15	22	29	5
Yesterday	18	11	6	4	10	10	20					
Paperback Writer				25	24	23	30					
Hey Jude				26	20	11	16	28				
Get Back				30								
Silly Love Songs–P/W										17	9	5
Speed Of Sound (LP)–P/W				23	13	5	4	2	2	3	2	
Beatles, 1967-1970 (LP)					22	22	20					

	JUN			JUL					AUG			
	12	19	26	3	10	17	24	31	7	14	21	28
Silly Love Songs–P/W	3	2	3									
Back In The USSR						26	26	18	24	28		
Let 'Em In–P/W										15	9	4
Speed Of Sound (LP)–P/W	3	3	3	3	2	3	6	11	10	15	10	6
Rock 'n' Roll Music (LP)				17	11	11	14	14	16	17	22	22
(Changesonebowie (LP)–DBw)	14	7	6	5	4	2	4	6	5	11	5	11
(Rolled Gold (LP)–RS)	28	29	30									

	SEP				OCT			
	4	11	18	25	2	9	16	23
Let 'Em In–P/W	*1	2	2	11	16	24		
Speed Of Sound (LP)–P/W	7	7	6	6	7	9	18	26
Rock 'n' Roll Music (LP)	18	16						
(Changesonebowie (LP)–DBw)	13	14	22	23				

NO RECORDS ON CHARTS: October 30, 1976–January 15, 1977

1977

	JAN		FEB				MAR		
	22	29	5	12	19	26	5	12	19
Maybe I'm Amazed–P/W							28	20	28
Over America (LP)–P/W	14	10	9	8	12	11	13	19	24

NO RECORDS ON CHARTS: March 26, 1977–April 2, 1977

	APR	
	9	16
Over America (LP)–P/W	30	29

NO RECORDS ON CHARTS: **April 23, 1977–May 14, 1977**

	MAY		**JUN**				**JUL**			
	21	28	4	11	18	25	2	9	16	23
Hollywood Bowl (LP)	23	13	7	5	4	3	4	4	7	8

	JUL	**AUG**				**SEP**
	30	6	13	20	27	3
Hollywood Bowl (LP)	16	21				
(**Best Of** (LP)–RdS)	17		14	14	11	22

The Beatles/1962—1966   Apple PCSP 717 (LP)

The Beatles/1967—1970   Apple PCSP 718 (LP)

Solid Gold

The following Beatle records have been certified by the Record Industry Association of America (R.I.A.A.) as Gold Records and *Platinum Records.

Date Awarded	Title
February 3, 1964	**Meet The Beatles**
February 3, 1964	*I Want To Hold Your Hand*
March 31, 1964	*Can't Buy Me Love*
April 13, 1964	**The Beatles' Second Album**
August 24, 1964	**Something New**
August 25, 1964	*A Hard Day's Night*
December 31, 1964	*I Feel Fine*
December 31, 1964	**Beatles '65**
December 31, 1964	**The Beatles' Story**
July 1, 1965	**Beatles' VI**
August 23, 1965	**Help!**
September 2, 1965	*Help!*
September 16, 1965	*Eight Days A Week*
October 20, 1965	*Yesterday*
December 24, 1965	**Rubber Soul**
January 6, 1966	*We Can Work It Out*
April 1, 1966	*Nowhere Man*
July 8, 1966	**"Yesterday" . . . And Today**
July 14, 1966	*Paperback Writer*
August 22, 1966	**Revolver**
September 12, 1966	*Yellow Submarine*
March 20, 1967	*Penny Lane*
June 15, 1967	**Sgt. Pepper's Lonely Hearts Club Band**
September 11, 1967	*All You Need Is Love*
December 15, 1967	**Magical Mystery Tour**
April 8, 1968	*Lady Madonna*
September 13, 1968	*Hey Jude*
December 6, 1968	**The Beatles**
February 5, 1969	**Yellow Submarine**

May 19, 1969	*Get Back*
July 16, 1969	*The Ballad Of John And Yoko*
October 27, 1969	**Abbey Road**
October 27, 1969	*Something/Come Together*
March 6, 1970	**Hey Jude**
March 17, 1970	**Live Peace In Toronto** (Lennon)
March 17, 1970	*Let It Be*
April 30, 1970	**McCartney** (McCartney)
May 26, 1970	**Let It Be**
December 14, 1970	*Instant Karma!* (Lennon)
December 14, 1970	*My Sweet Lord* (Harrison)
December 17, 1970	**All Things Must Pass** (Harrison)
January 28, 1971	**Plastic Ono Band** (Lennon)
June 9, 1971	**Ram** (McCartney)
August 3, 1971	*It Don't Come Easy* (Starr)
September 21, 1971	*Uncle Albert/Admiral Halsey* (McCartney)
October 1, 1971	**Imagine** (Lennon)
January 4, 1972	**Concert For Bangla Desh** (Harrison)
January 13, 1972	**Wild Life** (McCartney)
April 13, 1973	**The Beatles, 1962--1966**
April 13, 1973	**The Beatles, 1967--1970**
May 25, 1973	**Red Rose Speedway** (McCartney)
June 1, 1973	**Living In The Material World** (Harrison)
July 6, 1973	*My Love* (McCartney)
August 31, 1973	*Live and Let Die* (McCartney)
November 8, 1973	**"Ringo"** (Starr)
November 30, 1973	**Mind Games** (Lennon)
December 7, 1973	**Band On The Run** (McCartney)
December 28, 1973	*Photograph* (Starr)
January 8, 1974	**The Early Beatles**
January 31, 1974	*You're Sixteen* (Starr)
June 4, 1974	*Band On The Run* (McCartney)
October 22, 1974	**Walls And Bridges** (Lennon)
December 9, 1974	**Goodnight Vienna** (Starr)
December 16, 1974	**Dark Horse** (Harrison)
June 2, 1975	**Venus And Mars** (McCartney)
September 5, 1975	*Listen To What The Man Said* (McCartney)
November 11, 1975	**Extra Texture** (Harrison)
March 25, 1976	**Wings At The Speed Of Sound** (McCartney)
May 3, 1976	***Wings At The Speed Of Sound** (McCartney)
June 11, 1976	*Silly Love Songs* (McCartney)
June 14, 1976	**Rock 'n' Roll Music**
June 14, 1976	***Rock 'n' Roll Music**
October 25, 1976	*Let 'Em In* (McCartney)
December 13, 1976	**Wings Over America** (McCartney)
December 20, 1976	***Wings Over America** (McCartney)
January 19, 1977	**33 1/3** (Harrison)
February 15, 1977	**Best Of George Harrison** (Harrison)
May 5, 1977	**Beatles At The Hollywood Bowl**
August 12, 1977	***Beatles At The Hollywood Bowl**

Total Awarded to the Beatles: 41 Gold Records, 2 Platinum
Total Awarded to John Lennon: 6 Gold Records
Total Awarded to Paul McCartney: 15 Gold Records, 2 Platinum
Total Awarded to George Harrison: 8 Gold Records
Total Awarded to Ringo Starr: 5 Gold Records

The Beatles received the following Ivor Novello Awards from the British Music Industry.

October 25, 1964 (for 1963): 5 Awards
Most Outstanding Contribution To Music in 1963.
She Loves You: Most Broadcast Song
She Loves You: Top Selling Record
I Want To Hold Your Hand: 2nd Top Selling Record
All My Loving: 2nd Most Outstanding Song

March 25, 1967 (for 1966): 2 Awards
Michelle: Most Performed Work
Yellow Submarine: Top Selling Single

May 19, 1969 (for 1968): 1 Award
Hey Jude: Top Selling Song in Britain

The Beatles received the following Grammy Awards from the American National Academy of Recording Arts and Sciences.

March 11, 1967 (for 1966): 3 Awards
Michelle: Song of the Year (Composing)
Eleanor Rigby: Best Contemporary Solo Vocal Performance
Revolver: Sleeve Design

March 9, 1968 (for 1967): 4 Awards
Sgt. Pepper: Best Album
Sgt. Pepper: Best Contemporary Album
Sgt. Pepper: Best Album Cover
Sgt. Pepper: Best Engineered Recording

March 1, 1975 (for 1974): 2 Awards
Band On The Run: Best Pop Vocal Performance by a Group
Band On The Run: Best Produced Non–Classical Recording

On April 15, 1971, the Beatles received an Oscar in the Category Best Film Music (Original Song Score) for *Let It Be* (1970).

Got To Get You Into My Life/
Helter Skelter   **Capitol 4274 (45)**

Ob-La-Di, Ob-La-Da/Julia   **Capitol 4347 (45)**

N? 008603

So What Else Is New?

Continued from page 69

570.   SEP 26, 1977 (US) Atlantic SD 19108 (LP)
       SEP 30, 1977 (UK) Polydor 2310 556 (LP)
       by Ringo Starr
       RINGO THE 4TH Prod: Arif Mardin
       side one
           Drowning In The Sea Of Love---Kenny Gamble—Leon Huff
           ---*5:08*
           Tango All Night---Steve Hague—Tom Seufert---*2:55*
           Wings---Starkey—Vini Poncia---*3:24*
           Gave It All Up---Starkey—Vini Poncia---*4:40*
           Out On The Streets---Starkey—Vini Poncia---*4:25*
       side two
           Can She Do It Like She Dances---Steve Duboff—Gerry
           Robinson---*3:12*
           Sneaking Sally Through The Alley---Allan Toussaint---*4:08*
           It's No Secret---Starkey—Vini Poncia---*3:40*
           Gypsies In Flight---Starkey—Vini Poncia---*3:01*
           Simple Love Song---Starkey—Vini Poncia---*2:57*
       Musicians performing on the Ringo Starr album listed above include
       Ringo:*Lead Vocals & Drums*; Dave Spinozza:*Lead Guitar*; Jeff Mironov
       or John Tropea:*Guitars*; Don Grolnick:*Keyboards*; Tony Levin:*Bass*;
       and Steve Gadd:*Drums* for every song except *Gypsies In Flight,*
       Simple Love Song and *Sneaking Sally Through The Alley*. Personnel
       for these individual tracks include:
       on *Gypsies In Flight* Ringo:*Lead Vocals, Snare Drum & Brush*; David
       Bromberg:*Electric Guitar*; Dick Fegy:*Acoustic Guitar*; Hugh McDonald:
       Bass; and Jeff Gutcheon:*Electric Piano*;
       on *Simple Love Song* Ringo:*Lead Vocals & Drums*; Danny Kortchmar
       and Lon Van Eaton:*Guitars*; David Foster:*Piano & Keyboards*; and
       Chuck Rainey:*Bass*;
       and on *Sneaking Sally Through The Alley* Ringo:*Lead Vocals & Drums*;
       Cornell Dupree and Lon Van Eaton:*Guitars*; Richard Tee: *Electric Piano
       & Clavinet*; David Foster:*Clavinet*; Chuck Rainey:*Bass*; Steve Gadd:*Drums*;
       and Nick Marrero:*Percussion*;
       Additional musicians for the album include Ken Bischel:*Synthesizer*;
       Don Brooks:*Harmonica*; Randy Brecker:*Trumpet* (leading a *Brass &
       Reeds* section); Michael Brecker:*Tenor Solos*; and *Background Vocals*
       by Maxine Anderson, Joe Bean, Robin Clark, Jimmy Gilstrap, Debra
       Gray, Duitch Helmer, Brie Howard, David Lasley, Rebecca Louis,
       Arnold McCuller, Melissa Manchester, Lynn Pitney, Vini Poncia, Luther
       Vandross and Marletta Waters, with Bette Midler, Melissa Manchester and
       Vini Poncia alone on *Tango All Night*.

571.   SEP 30, 1977, (US) MCA MCA 3027 (LP)
        SEP 30, 1977 (UK) DJM DJH 20520 (LP)
        by Elton John Prod: Gus Dudgeon
        ELTON JOHN'S GREATEST HITS VOLUME II
        side one
          cut two: *LUCY IN THE SKY WITH DIAMONDS*—L-McC—
          5:59
            John: Guitars and Backing Vocal

572.   OCT 3, 1977 (US) Dark Horse DH 3073
        OCT 7, 1977 (UK) Dark Horse K 56403
        Recorded: Mid 1977
        by Splinter
        TWO MAN BAND Executive Producers: George Harrison and
          Dennis Morgan; Prod: Norbert Putman
          George: Guitar
        side one
          Little Girl—Robert J. Purvis—William Elliott—*3:14*
          Round And Round—Parker McGee—*3:13*
          Baby Love—Robert J. Purvis—*3:34*
          I Apologize—Robert J. Purvis—*4:33*
          Black Friday—Robert J. Purvis—*2:59*
        side two
          New York City (Who Am I)—Robert J. Purvis—*3:49*
          I Need Your Love—Robert J. Purvis—*2:58*
          Motions Of Love—Parker McGee—*3:26*
          Silver—Robert J. Purvis—*3:15*
          Love Is Not Enough—Robert J. Purvis—*4:02*
        Musicians performing on the Splinter album listed above include the
        two members of Splinter, Bob Purvis and Bill Elliott:*Vocals;* joined by
        George Harrison, Steve Gibson and Parker McGee:*Guitars;* Norbert Putnam:
        Bass; Kenny Buttrey:*Drums and Percussion;* and Rod Argent:*Synthesizer.*

573　OCT 21, 1977 (US) Capitol SKBL 11711 (2 LPs)
by The Beatles
LOVE SONGS Prod: George Martin; † George Martin
(January 1969) and Phil Spector (March 1970)
side one
  YESTERDAY—2:04
  I'LL FOLLOW THE SUN—1:46
  *I NEED YOU—*Harrison*—2:28*
  GIRL—2:26
  IN MY LIFE—2:23
  *WORDS OF LOVE—*Buddy Holly*—2:10*
  HERE, THERE AND EVERYWHERE—2:29
side two
  *SOMETHING—*Harrison*—2:59*
  AND I LOVE HER—2:27
  IF I FELL—2:16
  I'LL BE BACK—2:22
  TELL ME WHAT YOU SEE—2:35
  YES IT IS—2:40
side three
  MICHELLE—2:42
  IT'S ONLY LOVE—1:53
  YOU'RE GONNA LOSE THAT GIRL—2:18
  EVERY LITTLE THING—2:01
  FOR NO ONE—2:03
  SHE'S LEAVING HOME—3:24
side four
  †THE LONG AND WINDING ROAD—3:40
  THIS BOY—2:11
  NORWEGIAN WOOD (THIS BIRD HAS FLOWN)—2:00
  YOU'VE GOT TO HIDE YOUR LOVE AWAY—2:08
  I WILL—1:46
  P.S. I LOVE YOU—2:02

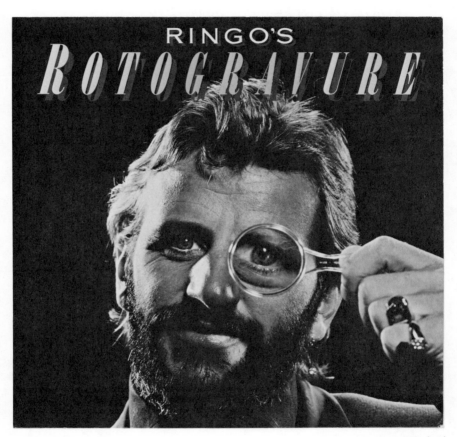

Ringo's Rotogravure   Atlantic SD 18193 (LP)

INDEX

This index serves both *All Together Now* and *The Beatles Again*. It incorporates, in one alphabetical listing, references to all the songs, records and artists with which the Beatles have been associated as producers, writers or performers, since 1961. The purpose of this index is to key the reader to each appearance by these Beatle-related records in the continuing chronological listing begun in *All Together Now* and brought up-to-date in *The Beatles Again*. Thus, most of the numbers in this index are *entry numbers*, not page numbers. (For a complete explanation of the chronological entries, see the *Nuts and Bolts* section at the beginning of this book.) Entry numbers 500 and below refer to entries appearing in *All Together Now*, while entries above 500 appear in *The Beatles Again*.

Additionally, this index also lists: some important studio outtakes, artists from the *Pandemonium Shadow Show/Aerial Ballet* sections, a handful of important bootleg records, and other Apple, Dark Horse and Ring O' artists (but not *all* their records). As these items are not part of the chronological sequence of numbered entries, the numbers following each refer to *page numbers* in either *All Together Now* or *The Beatles Again*. Page numbers below 225 refer to appearances in *The Beatles Again*; numbers above 225 refer to appearances in *All Together Now*. All page numbers are set in **boldface** type.

All selections in this index are by *The Beatles* as a group unless otherwise noted. (Still, for the sake of clarification on some obscure album titles, a *B* is included for emphasis in identification).

Solo efforts by the individual Beatles (*Harrison, Starr, McCartney*, or *Lennon*) are identified with an *H, S, M*, or *L*.

Instances in which the Beatles worked with or *for other* artists are denoted by *FO*; that is: *BFO, HFO, LFO, MFO, SFO*. Practically speaking, this identification system is an extension of the individual indexes/musician credit sections in the "Album & Song Title Index" of *All Together Now* (Beatles, Beatles For Others, Lennon, Lennon For Others, etc.).

The names of albums and EPs appear in **boldface** type, followed by an *LP* or *EP* identification and the particular Beatle association

(*B, BFO, H, HFO, L, LFO, M, MFO, S, SFO*) on the cuts involved. The names of artists also appear in **boldface** type. These are followed by a quick identification of the artist's Beatle connection, either directly with the Beatles (*B, H, L, M, S*) or as part of a special interest section: Apple (*ap*), Dark Horse (*dh*), Ring O' (*ro*), Friends, Relatives and Total Strangers (*frs*) or No, You're Wrong (*nyw*). Studio outtakes are indicated by (*ot*), particular bootleg records by (*boot*), and special disc jockey records by (*dj*).

If alternate versions of the same song were released by the same artists, these are identified as version *one*, version *two*, and so forth. If the artist merely released an alternate live concert version of the song, this new version is simply identified as *live*.

Examples:

Across The Universe (two) 248, 347
indicates that this track is an alternate version recorded by the Beatles and appearing on two records, both listed as entries in *All Together Now*. Specific musician credits are listed in the *By The Beatles* section of the title index in *All Together Now*.

Venus And Mars — live (M) 538
indicates that this track is a live concert version by Paul McCartney of a song he also released as a studio track. It appears on one disc, listed as entry 538 in *The Beatles Again*. Details of the recording also appear there.

No Secrets (MFO) (LP) 335
indicates that this album contains a track with Paul McCartney associated as either producer, writer or backing musician. The album is listed as entry 335 in *All Together Now*. Specific musician credits are listed in the *McCartney For Others* section of the title index in *All Together Now*.

Roger Daltrey (M) 556
indicates that artist Roger Daltrey worked with Paul McCartney and that the song involved appears on one disc, listed as entry 556 in *The Beatles Again*. Details of the recording also appear there.

Not Guilty (Bot) **260, 263**
indicates that the track is a Beatle studio out-take, discussed twice in *All Together Now* (pages 260 and 263).

As Sweet As You Are (boot) (LP) **129, 248**
indicates that this is a bootleg album discussed in both *The Beatles Again* (page 129) and *All Together Now* (page 248).

LS Bumblebee (nyw) **93, 286**
indicates that this track is sometimes mistakenly attributed to the Beatles. Explanations can be found in both the *No, You're Wrong* section of *The Beatles Again* (page 93) and *All Together Now* (page 286).

Sundown Playboys (ap) **183**
indicates these performers have no direct Beatle association, but their work as Apple artists is covered in *The Beatles Again* (page 183).

Chipmunks (frs) **117**
indicates that these performers have no direct Beatle participation in the recording listed, but this material is obtusely connected with the Beatles' music. It appears in *The Beatles Again* (page 117).

For further ease of reference, we conclude with an alphabetical listing of the abbreviations used in this index, singly or in combination, with a restatement of their meanings:

ap = Apple Records section in *The Beatles Again*
B = By The Beatles
BFO = Beatles For Others
boot = Bootleg
dh = Dark Horse Records section in *The Beatles Again*
dj = Special disc jockey record
EP = Extended play recording
frs = *Friends, Relatives And Total Strangers* section of *Pandemonium Shadow Show* in *All Together Now* or of *Pandemonium Aerial Ballet* in *The Beatles Again*
H = By Harrison
HFO = Harrison For Others
L = By Lennon
LFO = Lennon For Others
LP = Long-playing record (album)
M = By McCartney
MFO = McCartney For Others
nyw = *No, You're Wrong* section of *All Together Now* or *The Beatles Again*
ot = Out-take
ro = Ring O' Records section in *The Beatles Again*
S = By Starr
SFO = Starr For Others

Abbey Road (LP) 223
Across The Universe (one) 231
Across The Universe (two) 248, 347
Across The Universe (LFO) 439
Act Naturally 122, 126, 143, 147
Ain't She Sweet (LP) 98
Ain't She Sweet 66, 74, 76, 98, 157, 247, 285, 419, 514
Ain't That A Shame (L) 432
Ain't That Cute (HFO) 238, 254
Air Male (Tone Deaf Jam) (LFO) 296
Air Talk (LFO) 342
Aisumasen (L) 367
Alan Freeman's History Of Pop Vol. 2 (BFO) (LP) 380
All By Myself (S) 415
All I've Got To Do 28, 34
All My Life (LFO) 395, 427
All My Loving (EP) 42
All My Loving 28, 34, 42, 44, 63, 346
All My Loving – live 553
All Right (Sot) 89, 128
All That I've Got (HFO) 234
All Things Must Pass (H) (LP) 265
All Things Must Pass (H) 265
All Things (Must) Pass (HFO) 255
All This And World War II (LFO) (LP) 529
All Together Now 193
All You Need Is Love 169, 174, 193, 347, 533a
Alpha Band (S) 569
Alright (SFO) 324
The Amazing Beatles (LP) 157
Ambush (SFO) 327
Amsterdam (L) 227
And I Love Her 75, 77, 83, 84, 103, 346, 573
And The Sun Will Shine (MFO) 178
And Your Bird Can Sing 147, 150
Angela (L) 325
Angel Baby (Lot) 270
An Jenem Tag (Those Were The Days) (MFO) 186c, xx
Anna (Go To Him) 9, 15, 23, 32, 36, 52, 97, 99, 115
Annie (Bot) 258
Another Beatles Christmas Record (1964) 112, 270
Another Day (M) 275
Another Girl 122, 123
Another Thought (SFO) 331
The Answer's At The End (H) 455
Anthology (MFO) (LP) 336
Anyone Who Had A Heart (BFO) (EP) 57
Anything (Bot) 258
Any Time At All 77, 84, 105, 515
AOS (LFO) 269
Applejacks (B) 70
Apple Scruffs (H) 265, 274
Appolonia (HFO) 468, 501
Approximately Infinite Universe (LFO) (LP) 342

Approximately Infinite Universe (LFO) 342
B.J. Arnau (M) 354, **282**
Art Of Dying (H) 265
Ashton, Gardner & Dyke (H) 258, 277
Ashton, Gardner & Dyke (HFO) (LP) 258
As I Come Of Age (SFO) 449a, xxiii, **125**
Ask Me Why 6, 9, 32, 36, 42, 45, 52, 97, 99, 115
Ask Me Why – live 551
As Sweet As You Are (boot) (LP) **129, 248**
Atlantis (MFO) 190a, 193a, 217a, 327a, 454a, xx, xxii, xxiii, **383, 384**
At My Front Door (SFO) 327, 381
Attica State (L) 325
Attitudes (dh/S) 554, 567, **201**
Au (L) 325
Autum Leaves (Sot) **264**
Awaiting On You All (H) 265
Awaiting On You All – live (H) 307
Awakening (HFO) 401

Baba Teaching (HFO) 304
Baby Face (Mot) **270**
Baby It's You 9, 15, 32, 36, 97, 99, 115
Baby Love (HFO) 572
Baby's Heartbeat (L) 203
Baby's In Black 108, 110, 118
Baby You're A Lover (HFO) 200, 207
Baby, You're A Rich Man 169, 174, 533a
Back In The U.S.S.R. 190, 347, 515, 516
Back Off Boogaloo (S) 318, 466
Back Seat Of My Car (M) 282, 293
Bad Boy 119, 160, 515
Baddest Of The Mean (LFO) 330
Badfinger (ap/M/H) 229, 233, 237, 302, 306, 309, 419, 461, **144**
Badge (HFO) 194, 198, 215, 228, 319, 333
Badge -- live (HFO) 358
Bad To Me (BFO) 16, 22, 37, 54, 71, 276a, 419, 528, 563, xxi
The Ballad Of Boy Dylan (LFO) 321
The Ballad Of John And Yoko 208, 239, 347
The Ballad Of New York City (LFO) 321
Ballad Of Sir Frankie Crisp (H) 265
Banana Anna (HFO) 348
Banaras Ghat (HFO) 304
Band Of Steel (SFO) 511
Band On The Run (M) (LP) 372
Band On The Run (M) 372, 382, 387
Band On The Run – live (M) 538
Bangla Desh (H) 290, 533, xviii
Bangla Desh – live (H) 307
Bangla Dhun (HFO) 307
Barabajagal (MFO) (LP) 217a, xx, **384**
Barabajagal/Hurdy Gurdy Man (MFO) (LP) 454a, xxiii, **384**

263

264

266

267

Grimms (frs) **103**
Carl Grossman (ro) **214**
Guru Vandana (H) 187
Gypsies In Flight (S) 570
Gypsy Wolf (LFO) 330

Hallelujah, I Love Her So 551, 559
Hamburg Star Club Tape (Bot) **71, 126, 249**
Hands Of Love (M) 349
Happiness Is A Warm Gun 190
Happiness Runs (Pebble And The Man) (MFO) 195, 197, 216
Happy Xmas (L) 303, 458
A Hard Day's Night (LP) 75, 77
A Hard Day's Night – Film (EP) 103
A Hard Day's Night -- Album (EP) 105
A Hard Day's Night 75, 77, 78, 80, 160, 346
A Hard Day's Night – live 553
Harder To Live (HFO) (LP) 457
Hard Goods (MFO) (LP) 382a, **xxiii**
A Hard Rain's Gonna Fall (HFO) 307
Hard Times (HFO) (LP) 456
Hare Krishna Mantra (HFO) 218, 283
Hari's On Tour (Express) (H) 422, 425, 436a, **xix**
Ray Harper (M) 541, 543
Bobby Hatfield (S) 315a, **xxi, 384**
Have I Told You Lately That I Love You (S) 245
Haven't Got Time (HFO) 400, 429, 437
Have You Got Problems (MFO) 406
Have You Heard The Word (nyw) **287**
Have You Seen A Horizon Lately (LFO) 342
Have You Seen My Baby (Hold On) (S) 366
Hear Me Lord (H) 265
Heartbeat (MFO) 552, 555
Hear The Beatles Tell All (dj) (LP) **222, 254**
Heart Of The Country (M) 282, 293
Heavy Cream (HFO) (LP) 333
Helen Wheels (M) 362, 372
Hello Goodbye 173, 174, 347, 533a
Hello Little Girl (Bot) **247**
Hello Little Girl (BFO) 19, 43, 276a, 537, **xxi**
Help! (LP) 122, 123
Help! 121, 122, 123, 160, 346
Help! -- live 553
Helter Skelter 190, 513, 515
David Hentschel (ro/S) 433, **214**
Here Comes The Sun 223, 347, 533
Here Comes The Sun (H) 307
Her Majesty 223
Here There And Everywhere 150, 154, 573
Here We Go Again (Lot) **128**
He's So Fine (frs) **116**

Hey Baby (S) 524, 536
Hey Bulldog 193, 515
Hey Diddle (Mot) **128**
Hey--Hey--Hey--Hey! 108, 119, 133, 515
Hey--Hey--Hey--Hey! – live 551, 559
Hey Jude (LP) (also called **The Beatles Again**) 239
Hey Jude 181, 239, 347
Hi Hi Hi (M) 340
Hi Hi Hi – live (M) 538
The Hip Generation (LFO) 321
The Hippie From New York (LFO) 321
Hippy Hippy Shake 551, 559
Hirake (also called *Open Your Box*) 278, 296
History Of British Rock (BFO/J+P+GFO) (LP) 378
History Of British Rock Vol. 2 (B/BFO/ MFO) (LP) 419
History Of British Rock Vol. 3 (B/BFO/ MFO/HFO) (LP) 461
History Of Eric Clapton (HFO) (LP) 319
History Of The Bonzos (MFO) (LP) 383
History Of The Mersey Era (BFO) (LP) 537
Hit '69 (HFO) (LP) 228
Hits Of The Mersey Era Vol. 1 (BFO) (LP) 565
Chris Hodge (ap) **154**
Hold Me Tight 28, 34
Hold Me Tight (M) 349
Hold On John (L) 268
The Holdup (one) (HFO) 312, 323, 545
The Holdup (two) (HFO) 373
Holly Days (MFO) (LP) 555
Home Is In My Head (nyw) (LP) **97**
Honey Don't 108, 110, 113
The Honeymoon Song (Bot) **248**
The Honeymoon Song (MFO) 195, 197
Honey Pie 190
Mary Hopkin (ap/M) 183, 186, 186a, 186b, 186c, 195, 197, 197a, 201, 216, 222, 233a 332, 461, **xix, xx, 155**
Nicky Hopkins (H) 348, 351
Larry Hosford (H) 518, 520
Hot As Sun (M) 246
Hot Chocolate (ap) **159**
Hot Legs (nyw) **288**
House In My Head (MFO) 180, **106**
How? (L) 295
How Can You Say Goodbye (HFO) 200
How Do You Do It (Bot) **94, 129, 248**
How Do You Sleep? (L) 295
How I Won The War (L) 171
How The Web Was Woven (HFO) 235, 242
Hunting Scene (S) 237
Husbands And Wives (S) 415

I Ain't Superstitious (SFO) 289

268

273

278

279

MORE ABOUT THE AUTHORS

Harry Castleman was born in Salem, Massachusetts in 1953 and is already losing his hair.

Wally Podrazik, born February 23, 1952 in Chicago, was once described as a dead ringer for Yves Saint Laurent. He isn't.